YOU
WILL
SEE
FIRE

ALSO BY CHRISTOPHER GOFFARD

Snitch Jacket (a novel)

YOU
WILL
SEE
FIRE

A Search for Justice in Kenya

Christopher Goffard

W. W. Norton & Company

New York . London

For information about permission to reproduce selections from this book,
write to Permissions, W. W. Norton & Company, Inc.,
500 Fifth Avenue, New York, NY 10110

For information about special discounts for bulk purchases, please contact
W. W. Norton Special Sales at specialsales@wwnorton.com or 800-233-4830

Manufacturing by RR Donnelley, Harrisonburg
Book design by Chris Welch
Production manager: Devon Zahn

Library of Congress Cataloging-in-Publication Data

Goffard, Christopher.
You will see fire : a search for justice in Kenya / Christopher Goffard. — 1st ed.
p. cm.
Includes bibliographical references and index.
ISBN 978-0-393-07742-1 (hardcover)
1. Kaiser, John Anthony, 1932-2000—Death and burial. 2. Murder—Investigation—Kenya.
3. Kenya—Politics and government—1978-2002. 4. Kenya—Politics and government—2002–
5. Political atrocities—Kenya. 6. Christianity and politics—Kenya.
I. Title.
HV6535.K4G63 2012
364.152'3092—dc23

2011029509

W. W. Norton & Company, Inc.
500 Fifth Avenue, New York, N.Y. 10110
www.wwnorton.com

W. W. Norton & Company Ltd.
Castle House, 75/76 Wells Street, London W1T 3QT

1 2 3 4 5 6 7 8 9 0

To Jennifer, Julia, Sophia, Olivia,

and my parents

A man who does next to nothing but hear men's real sins is not likely to
be wholly unaware of human evil.

—*G. K. Chesterton*

CONTENTS

YOU
WILL
SEE
FIRE

1

THE HOUSE AT THE EDGE OF THE DARK

WHEREVER HE WENT, the man of God carried his shotgun. Like its owner, the double-barrel twelve-gauge was old and broken in places, dusty from miles of hard African road. He kept the splintered stock bound together with a length of black rubber, and he believed it might be his only protection, save for the good Lord and his American name, in a country that had never felt more dangerous.

John Kaiser's redbrick parish house, without a gate or guard or phone, sat on a twenty-nine-acre plot at the edge of an immense valley rolling away toward the Serengeti Plain. It was the finest house in the township, with five bedrooms and small outdoor water tanks. He would be awake before dawn, lifting his head with difficulty from his narrow metal-frame bed, blinking into the darkness of a room as spartan as a cell. Shapes congealed around him: the crucifix on the wall, the cluttered desk, the shotgun.

He'd be walking the grounds before sunrise, clutching his rosary beads and praying in the dark, his arthritic neck already encased in a thick orthopedic brace. At first light, the rutted murram road running past the parish house acquired a pinkish hue. As the countryside awoke, birdsong filled the surrounding trees, and from the long, wet grass, insects thrummed at his passing heels.

A few yards from his front door stood the church he had built soon after his arrival, five years back, in this tiny township in the heart of Masailand. It was a rough and functional structure, like dozens he'd thrown up across the countryside: corrugated-iron roof, concrete floor, unburnished wood pews, and exposed crossbeams in the vault overhead. He had developed a reputation as a ferocious and tireless builder during his years in Africa; this alone made him an unusual figure among white missionaries. He'd gone up ladders with pockets stuffed with bricks and pulled long roof beams after him by rope. But scattered around the compound now were crude brick structures—the shells of a girls' dormitory and schoolhouse and dispensary—that he had not mustered the energy to finish in these last pain-racked years. He had begun to doubt he would.

The year was 2000. It was late summer. From his radio came the Voice of America, the cadences of home, where the news of late had been dominated by the presidential race to succeed Bill Clinton. He would sit down to breakfast in a dining room with lime green walls, adjoining a living room with a plain worn couch. His diet was as spartan as his room, and his breakfast, laid out by his housekeeper, Maria, would be quick and simple—some *mandazi*, a fried sweetbread, and *ugali*, the maize porridge that was the country's staple.

By midmorning, he would be steering his Toyota pickup over the gravel driveway onto the red-dirt ribbon that formed Lolgorien's one main road. As in many of Kenya's disease-blighted towns, there were only a few intact families. Flanking the main road on either side, for a few blocks at the center of town, were tumbledown clusters of one-story shops topped by rusty roofs of corrugated iron, *dukas*, wood-plank stands, dirt-floor hotels. Milling there were police, game wardens from the Masai Mara, government functionaries, and the pack of prostitutes that served them. Shoulder-to-shoulder on the porches lounged gaunt, long-limbed Masai men, sinewy, sandaled, with shaven scalps, the ropy skin of their stretched and punctured earlobes bright with beads, their bodies wrapped in crimson and vermilion *shukas*. Their staffs were slanted across their laps or angled over their shoulders; a Masai male who didn't carry one was considered a worthless guardian against the lions, and the tradition persisted even as the lions had begun to vanish. They were nomadic cattle herders who lived in *manyattas*—circular arrangements of loaf-shaped mud-and-dung huts, where they corraled their cattle at night, secure from predators behind lashed-together fences of thorned acacia branches. Cows supplied their diet: milk mixed with blood collected from a small arrow puncture in the animal's neck. White missionaries sometimes talked of feeling like strangers among Africans, even after decades of taking their confessions and serving them Mass and burying their dead. No group elicited this sense of exclusion as powerfully as the Masai. During the priest's years in Masailand, conversions had been slow, nothing like the success he'd had for decades among the Kisii. The priest knew he was a peculiarity to them, maybe the strangest *mzungu* they had known—an American, rich by definition, who insisted on a life of hard physical labor in the sun and had chosen to live without a woman or children. Inexplicable enough was a lifetime without physical love—only witch doctors live alone, people said—but a man who consciously forsook progeny meant an even deeper strangeness.

From his truck, as he rumbled through town with the shotgun and rosary beads resting beside him, he could see the Masai watching him from the porches, their gaze indifferent and unreadable in the baking sun. He had to assume that some of them were monitoring his movements, informing on him, reporting back to the man some called "the Butcher," Julius Sunkuli. Many—it was impossible to know how many—were linked to Sunkuli by family or clan or ties of financial loyalty or fear.

This was Sunkuli country. He held the local parliamentary seat. He was not just the area's political kingpin and its most prominent Masai but also one of the most powerful figures in the country. He had grown up on the grass plains, tending his family's goat herds. He had been an altar boy and a Christian youth leader, and remained a conspicuous member and benefactor of the Catholic Church. He had been plucked from the margins of power by His Excellency the President of Kenya, Daniel arap Moi, East Africa's longest-reigning gangster-statesman, who had given him a place in his inner circle. As minister of state in charge of internal security, Sunkuli commanded a vast police network, and was widely rumored as a possible successor to the president. When he

smiled, the gap in his lower jaw showed where his teeth had been chis-
eled out, evidence of his childhood initiation as a Masai warrior. Sunkuli
was different from some of Moi's other top men, with their charm and
European degrees. Sunkuli emitted a raw street fighter's intelligence, a
backcountry roughness that had persisted through his years as a lawyer,
magistrate, and political boss. "He is a baptized Catholic, also an inciter
to mass murder, a defrauder of poor people from their land and a serial
rapist," Kaiser wrote to his brother in Minnesota. "I think you would call
him a lapsed Catholic."

To Kaiser, Sunkuli seemed the crystallized embodiment of Moiism,
the perfect product of a culture of Big Man impunity—widely feared,
apparently untouchable by the law or the electorate. For years, the priest
had received reports that Sunkuli had been preying on schoolgirls; some
said the countryside was dotted with his unacknowledged children. Kaiser had helped push a legal case, now working its way through the courts,
in which a young Masai girl from his parish had accused Sunkuli of rape;
it had made headlines. The priest described him as his "biggest worry."
It will be one or the other of us, he told people. There was no way to know
how many spies he might have. Some people said that one of them was
living in the priest's own house.

Kaiser would pass on, into the countryside. His truck had a whimsical
name, "the Helicopter," because it frequently left the roads, heaving and
lurching over terrain that brought anguish to his neck. Throughout the
day, he would venture deep into the grasslands, through drenching rains
and sucking mud and hard sunlight, to reach the scattered outstations of
his vast parish. He had traversed this mapless landscape so many times
that the topography itself supplied his signposts: a fig tree, a ridge of rock,
a gulley. Certain arcane knowledge accrued to a man over a lifetime in
the bush. He had learned to start his truck with a coin when he lost the
key, and he understood the utility of a bar of brown soap to patch cracks
in a leaking gasket. He had learned to deflate the tires to surmount a bad
hill, and to sit on a crate when the front seat fell apart.

A fiercely doctrinaire Catholic who espoused obedience to the letter of Vatican law, he was nevertheless adept at bush-missionary improvisation. He found that a Coke bottle was a serviceable receptacle for holy water. When he'd traveled hours, only to discover he had forgotten the Communion wafers, he looked for the nearest kiosk that sold chapati—a doughy flat bread resembling a pancake—to transform into the Savior's body. A crack shot, he'd been vanishing for years into the elephant grass with his shotgun, stalking wildebeests and impalas, warthogs and zebras and buffalo. He would skin the carcasses—sometimes yanking the skin free with ropes attached to his truck—and carve up the meat and distribute it among the parish schools. He whittled the stocks of his guns and made his own bullets, shaving lead from an old battery and pounding the pieces into slugs. He shook in half rounds to conserve gunpowder and to mute the noise when he hunted, in case a game warden was within earshot. Poaching had been outlawed since the late 1970s, but that was one of man's laws and therefore negotiable.

Some regarded him as an unbreakable man, the "John Wayne of priests." They saw the six-foot-two former U.S. Army paratrooper who could creep close enough to a buffalo to kill it with a single half-powder round through the lungs or heart (to take a second shot gave wardens a bead on your location). They saw the hunter who refused to leave a wounded animal behind, despite the danger of pursuing an enraged, bleeding beast into the bush. He had promoted a fierce image, in part, as a form of protection. Even before he was an enemy of the state, he recognized the shotgun's value in deterring ordinary trouble. He hauled it outside now and then to shoot at birds; everyone knew the American priest was armed. He had performed prodigious physical feats well into middle age, hunting, hauling, digging, building. When he arrived in Masailand in his early sixties, he was still strong and fast enough to kill a rabbit with a hurled stone or a dik-dik with an ax, and he'd be on top of the animal before it even fell, hacking with a big overhand arc. He was still popping wheelies on his motorbike for the amusement of the Masai girls.

He'd come through the crucibles of any bush missionary—hepatitis, typhoid, malaria, amoebic dysentery. He'd broken bones in motorcycle spills and survived a roof beam crashing on his neck during a construction project.

But the last few years had been brutal even by his standards; his body had become a catalog of anguish. Though he hated seeing the doctor, he'd gone dozens of times. He'd endured prostate cancer, and multiple bouts of malaria that grew increasingly resistant to quinine and left him helpless, sweating through fevers and convulsions and hiding from harsh sunlight and the gouging of birdsong in the ears, the terrible cold seizing him, his body without bones or muscles or volition for weeks. At times, as the decades accreted in the bones, a man could feel like the sum of all the stumbles off his motorcycle and falls in the mud, a creature of collapsing cartilage and inflamed joints and ulcers. He was a former soldier, and a soldier did not complain, but on his best day now he couldn't move his neck without pain. He wore the cervical collar everywhere, except at Mass. There, facing his faithful, he refused any concession to his decaying sixty-seven-year-old body. His parishioners streamed down from the hills in their bright tribal wrappings to hear him speak in Swahili of the risen Savior, to stand in line at Mass as the enormous old white hands, aching now like the rest of him, leaking strength every day, cradled God Himself aloft.

Everybody in the area knew the American priest, and many depended on him for food and school fees; they would surround him as soon as he pulled up to a cluster of huts or to the little brick schools or churches. By the side of the road, in the shade of eucalyptus trees, he bowed his head and listened to their confessions. *I have stolen a cow, Father. I have slept with girls, Father. I have struck my wife, Father.* So much of his knowledge about the country had arrived in this fashion; the chronicle of sins formed an infinitely more accurate barometer of the country's soul than did the Nairobi newspapers.

With luck, he would be home before nightfall. The road bristled with bandits, or *shifta*, and the sun didn't linger on the horizon. It was nothing like the protracted twilights of his Minnesota childhood—that long dream hour of crying cicadas and droning mosquitoes. Here near the equator, night scythed down as swiftly as a panga knife; one writer compared the experience to having a sack pulled over your head.

The shotgun would stay with him as he walked the grounds at night, locking the church, shuttering the windows of his home, double-checking the locks; it stayed with him as he walked down the long, shadowed hallway to his room, the last on the left. Scattered before him at his desk, dimly illuminated by generator light, were dangerous documents. They told the story of the secret history of his adopted country, a subterranean narrative of land and blood. They chronicled the sins of Kenya's rulers— decades of land-stealing, ethnic carnage, rape. There were affidavits from peasant farmers, land deeds, newspaper clips, correspondence, accounts from local girls. He had been collecting them for years. He spent hours in his room, reading, poring over documents, making notes in his journal. For some time, he'd been anticipating his violent death, warning friends and family in the States to expect it.

For most of his career as a bush missionary, save for the church and the tribes he had lived among, few in Kenya had known his name. He had done a fair job of impersonating the other good, hardworking, politically impassive men of Christ. He had raised little noise outside the Church, with the rationalization that he had plenty of God's work to keep him busy. Then, no longer young or even middle-aged, he'd become chaplain at a hillside displacement camp called Maela, where he witnessed a scale of misery that nothing had prepared him for—ubiquitous choking dust, mud, disease, burned skin sloughing off children's hands like gloves, and then the government's nighttime raid on the camp. Good Lord, some of the refugees had even been singing as they were crammed onto trucks to be scattered across the countryside, singing because they'd actually believed the president's promise that he would find them land. That six-month experience—culminating in his own beating and banishment from the camp—had forced him to reexamine his silence. Some of the lightness went out of him; photos showed a depth of sadness shadowing his eyes after that.

It would have been possible, even then, for him to melt back into his missionary work. His bishop, whose mantra was "Don't provoke," had sent him to the house in Masailand at the country's southwest edge—about as far as he could go without spilling into Tanzania—with the hope that the remoteness would keep him out of trouble. The bishop had been mistaken. It had not deterred Kaiser from appearing at the Akiwumi Commission—a tribunal launched by President Moi, with the ostensible goal of probing the causes of the tribal clashes that had killed more than one thousand people in recent years. The real purpose, many suspected from the start, was to conceal the government's central role in the carnage. Kaiser had been warned against speaking. His bishop believed the tribunal a waste of time, and Kaiser's intention to name names a pointless provocation.

Some African churchmen considered it an embarrassment that a white man should presume to lecture them about their affairs. The missionary's role in Kenyan history had been a fraught one. Determined to bring pagans of the Dark Continent into the Christian fold, the early missionaries preached not just salvation but also the superiority of white civilization. Many of Africa's independence leaders, including Kenya's, had been products of missionary educations. But it was easy for Africans to view the missionary legions with ambivalence, if not outright hostility. They had built schools but taught Africans to hate themselves. The Church had been a spearpoint of the colonial land grab, legitimizing the conquest, and had sided with the British against the Mau Mau uprising of the 1950s, defining the struggle as one of light versus darkness, God versus Satan. Jomo Kenyatta, Kenya's first president, had put it this way: "When the missionaries arrived, the Africans had the land and the missionaries had the Bible. They taught us to pray with our eyes closed. When we opened them, they had the land and we had the Bible." Kaiser had inherited this uneasy legacy. For many of his colleagues, guilt fostered paralysis and passivity—a feeling that African politics was best left to Africans, lest the Church be accused of reproducing its past sins.

Yet Kaiser had gone to the tribunal, braving the bad roads, waiting in the makeshift courtroom in his ironed clerical blacks, with his neck brace and his Roman collar and a folder of documents. Up he walked, a broad-shouldered, long-limbed man with a loose, slightly bandy-legged gait and thinning white hair. He was not a churchman of rank, not a bishop or a nuncio, not even the priest of a politically important parish like Nairobi. He was, up until then, a man of small importance to history—just a bullheaded old *mazungu* from one of the country's poorer corners.

His voice was high and thin, almost feminine, incongruous with his cowboy gait, but it had not betrayed him that day. He had named names— a roster of the regime's untouchable potentates. Sunkuli was prominent among them. This was dangerous enough, but then he went on to do the unpardonable: He named Moi himself. People would remember his voice as steady and even and insistent. Listening to it, it had been impossible to tell that he'd been sleeping with his shotgun for weeks, afraid that he would never be allowed to speak, afraid that once he began, he'd never be allowed to finish. He testified for two days, sparring with government lawyers, trying to distill the dark knowledge he had absorbed. Long portions of his testimony ran verbatim in Kenya's daily newspapers, and in an instant the backwoods missionary had become a symbol of national conscience, a source of hope, a galvanizing force.

That was how it began: not just the fame but also the steady note of dread in his letters, the unbanishable sense that he would be called on to die violently in this green, malarial patch of East Africa. In the eighteen months since then, he had been upping the stakes, demanding not just that Moi be prosecuted at the Hague, where he vowed to serve as a witness, but pressing for criminal charges against Sunkuli, as well. The good, gentle men of his missionary order found it exasperating, his unwillingness to listen to reason, to moderate his tone, to demonstrate a normal man's respect for death. *You're going to get us killed, John.*

AGAINST HIS WINDOW pressed the cold deep-country dark, and from it rose the distant bedlam of hyena packs on the savanna. Cackles, whoops, rattles, gibbers—in the right state of mind, these sounds could be calming, melodic. Africa's nightsounds used to be music to him, and there were nights as a young missionary in the open Mara that he would recount as if he were the world's luckiest man. Picture him: the stars ablaze above, the breeze rippling quietly through the dry waist-high grass, the winged ants battering his lantern, the carcass of a wildebeest or zebra gutted in his truck and the aftertaste of its fried heart in his mouth, and all around the cacophony of animals in their night rituals. He had lived close to nature's beauty and cruelty since childhood. It had suited him, this life. Now, the veldt noises lashing against his room's little square of light seemed to remind him of the closeness of his own death. Again and again, the priest told people, *That is what they will do to me if they catch me. Leave me as carrion.* Human flesh was familiar to the scavengers, for the Masai still were known to leave their dead unburied, smeared with animal fat to hasten the bodies' disappearance. Nothing lasted long out there, among the immense spear-beaked marabou storks—bald, Boschian grotesques whose wrinkled heads seemed born in some stygian pit of blood and ash—and the hyenas, spotted, hulk-shouldered, level-eyed. These he seemed to fear most. They fed deep on the entrails of living, thrashing gazelles. They ate the viscera and the muscles and the skin, crunched through bone and swallowed the hair, whole corporeal forms vanishing in the space of hours. They were, to assassins, an ideal evidence-disposal system. Everyone knew the story of the young English traveler Julie Ward, who had been murdered not far from here, her body devoured by animals, and the truth about her death—like so many crimes in Kenya—gone with equal thoroughness.

As a paratrooper, he'd been taught that darkness can be a friend and ally; a trained man can turn it to his advantage. Here, however, the mind peopled that void with innumerable evils; he knew the advantage was theirs, not his. Every odd sound, every rustle and crunch, seized his attention, his body tensing. He knew they could be out there even now, crouched, smoking, silent, patient, catching a glimpse now and then of his tall silhouette passing by a window, waiting for him to be separated from his gun, for his vigilance to slip. *They'll say I killed myself. Don't believe it.* He clutched his rosary beads. He prayed for strength.

THROUGH THE SUMMER, his missionary bosses and fellow priests made the trip from Nairobi to plead with him: *Go back to Minnesota, John. Rest.*

They knew there was small chance of reasoning with a man of such preternatural stubbornness. If he went home now, he explained, Kenya's rulers would probably never allow him to return.

Any of his superiors could have ordered him out of Lolgorien, back to the States. He had taken a vow of obedience, and he very well might have complied; his last years would have been spent peacefully among his boyhood haunts in Otter Tail County, Minnesota, fishing quietly among the mayflies, visiting old friends and family, and browsing the cemetery slabs for childhood names. But his bosses gave no orders. Their preferred method was to offer suggestions, appeals to reason, pleas for prudence. These, he could ignore.

The summer was a dry one in Lolgorien, the green leaching from the hills until the grass was brown and short and brittle. His water tanks were depleted, and across the hills the skin tightened on the ribs of the cattle. The Masai watched the sky constantly, knowing that if it remained empty, their calves would begin to die first. Cows were not just their livelihood but God's special bequest to their tribe. Every few seasons, droughts stole them in large numbers, and it was a terrible thing to hear the weeping of a proud Masai. They prayed and made sacrifices, and still nothing brought the rain.

All that summer, for the priest, the warnings kept coming. One day, returning home, he found someone had hurled a large rock through a window of his house. Another day, a friendly Kenyan contact—a game warden or policeman—came surreptitiously to say, *A decision has been made to eliminate you.* Another day, he opened a letter that had arrived in his mailbox and found an unsigned threat in Swahili: *Utaona moto.* You will see fire.

Much later, Francis Kantai, one of his catechists—a young Masai he had enlisted as a helper and a cultural bridge to the local people—would describe the priest's sudden unease as he opened the letter. *What is it, Father? What does it say?*

As Kantai recalled, the priest gave a curt reply—*I don't give a damn*— and took the letter down the hall to his room and closed the door. The threat was apt. Fire had been the medium of terror in village after village, defenseless thatched-roof huts and wooden hovels transformed into the tinder of infernos across the countryside. Flames took them quickly and completely. Even in his house of brick, there was little protection against a torch in the night.

It's easy to imagine that the priest sat on his bed and prayed, clutching that note. It's possible that he brooded, too, on his young Masai catechist, who slept down the hall from him. To many of the priest's colleagues and acquaintances, why he permitted Kantai's presence was a mystery. He was widely believed to be a spy for Sunkuli, and he had confessed to burning houses for the police. The priest had repeatedly defended Kantai, had once even smashed a table in rage when his name was impugned.

By this point, however, there were signs that he had begun to distrust Kantai himself. His housekeeper, Maria, told him that Kantai had let Sunkuli's men into the parish house, into the priest's room—the place where he allowed no one, the place where he kept his papers.

The priest had asked a Kenyan friend, *Can Francis hurt me?*

The friend had responded with a Swahili proverb: *Kikulacho kimo nguoni mwako.*

It meant: The bug that bites one's back is carried in what one wears.

IN THE THIRD week of August, the rains came and the grass greened, and from his veranda he watched the cows dance.

One of his catechists, Lucas, handed him an envelope.

A letter for you, Father.

The priest opened it. It had been hand-delivered all the way from Nairobi, passed between church assistants. It was a summons from an authority he could not refuse—Giovanni Tonucci, the papal nuncio, the Pope's representative in Kenya. The priest was to report to him immediately. The matter was apparently urgent, though unspecified.

Kaiser was certain what the meeting would entail. He would be thanked for his years of service in Kenya, and told to return to the United States to take an extended rest. It would mean, he was sure, his departure from the country for good. He would have to obey. Thirty-six years, and now it was over.

What he did in the days that followed would invite the most exacting scrutiny, his actions weighed and analyzed and puzzled over, his phrases parsed, word by word, and subjected to dramatically different readings. After the summons, his mood changed. He wept at Mass. He asked for prayers. He grabbed his duffel bag, then climbed into his truck with his ax and his rosary beads and his Bible and his neck brace and his shotgun, disappearing down the red-dirt road on the half-day trip to Nairobi.

2

THE LAWYER

THE LAWYER'S PHONE started ringing early that morning. *They've killed Kaiser.* He was at home in Ngong, on the outskirts of Nairobi. He felt a chill spread between his shoulder blades. The first details to reach him were vague, secondhand, filtered through a network of informants whose voices were tight with panic. It was August 24, 2000, four days after Kaiser's departure from his parish house, and his body had been found in a weedy ditch that morning in Naivasha, about forty miles outside the capital. Nobody could determine what had brought him there. People were saying that his head had been blown apart, that his own shotgun lay nearby.

Charles Mbuthi Gathenji was fifty-one, a man of stocky build and medium height. He had a thin mustache, thinning gray-black hair, and sharp cheekbones. He possessed an air of wary circumspection informed by decades on the wrong side of a police state. His eyes were deep-set and heavy-lidded, and his thin, rimless glasses contributed an aura of scholarly gravity, an impression reinforced by his careful, formal English, his accent thickly Kenyan and punctuated with phrases like "It is quite in order."

He did not deviate from his daily routine on this day. He put on his suit, picked up his leather briefcase, and steered his Mitsubishi Pajero into the cacophony of the capital's morning gridlock. He had an appearance at the High Court and some appointments at his office. But the sense of prickly unease that had never entirely left him these past few years was very close now. *They've killed Kaiser.* In recent weeks, under the employ of the Catholic Church, the lawyer had been preoccupied by a case that felt eerily similar—the slaying of an Irish monk named Larry Timmons. The monk, not nearly as well known as Kaiser, had accused a Rift Valley policeman of demanding bribes, and one night the cop had shown up at the mission house—in response to a robbery—and shot him to death. A terrible accident, authorities said, but after all, it had been so dark. Now, three years after the shooting, Gathenji was arguing to bring murder charges against the cop; they were in the thick of a protracted inquest, and his witnesses were slowly dismantling the official narrative.

When Gathenji returned home that evening he turned on the television news and got a glimpse of the scene where Kaiser had been found. There was the priest's body, with its fringe of white hair, supine in the weeds, clad in light gray slacks, black leather shoes, and a leather jacket. There was his Toyota pickup aslant in a drainage culvert, with a twisted right front wheel. There was the interior of the dirty cab, with the priest's rosary beads hanging from the steering wheel and the sharp edge of his ax visible under some clutter. There were the dark-suited plainclothesmen and black-hatted officers milling around the truck in the sharp country sunshine. There was the shotgun—wrapped, ineptly and incompletely, in police plastic. There was the large crowd of onlookers massed on a nearby berm, mothers standing with arms crossed and children sitting at their feet in the brownish red dirt, all watching wordlessly and immobile as statuary. There was the sky as it had been that morning, pale blue and clear beyond the towering, slender-branched fever trees, and the road already alive with zooming buses as the body was wrapped and loaded into the back of an official Land Rover.

For the last five years, their lives had been closely linked, the lawyer's and the priest's. Kaiser would materialize at Gathenji's office unannounced, always on a crusade, always in dusty shoes. To call ahead of time would have increased the possibility of being followed. He'd bring in people from his parish who needed legal help. He'd scribble notes on newspapers or whatever was on hand. He'd seek advice on how to build cases against government men, and how to get supplies to refugees displaced by violence.

If the Church remained one of the few institutions in Kenya that had raised its voice against the government, it did so mostly in a carefully hedged and muted way. As a corporate body, it preached reconciliation but rarely went further. The American priest had been an exception: He'd named names, and looked for every opportunity to do it again.

As Gathenji saw it, over their years of working together, their bond had evolved into something more profound than mere friendship. They shared the understanding of two colleagues who knew for a certainty that their work could get them killed. They were brothers in a foxhole.

Temperamentally, they were poles apart. Kaiser had a hard-charging, elbows-out approach, always racing toward the cannon's mouth. Dogged but not personally flashy, Gathenji was quiet, methodical, and preferred to operate behind the scenes. He had a wife and two children. Despite his high-profile battles with the powerful, he tried to speak through his legal work. He saw no reason to draw more attention to himself than necessary.

Many of his peers had cultivated political connections and made themselves rich. He did not view the law as a stepping-stone for political power; to him, his country's politics had a rank taste. He wasn't an editorial writer or a maker of screeds and fiery speeches. He seemed to know everybody but made it a point to avoid social clubs. He would not be found mingling with the nation's legal stars on a Nairobi golf course. He couldn't be mistaken for a member of the *wabenzi* class—the Swahili term for those possessed of a Mercedes-Benz, the badge of arrival. He stayed away from bars and made it a habit to be home on his small farm, with his family, well before sunset.

Much of his work, championing the victims of political violence, carried small financial reward. And so despite being one of his country's best attorneys, he labored in what he characterized as the lower-middle class. He described himself as a simple man, a working lawyer with a Mitsubishi and, when he could afford it, a clerk. He thought of himself as a foot soldier, and had the instincts of a survivor.

For years, he had worked from a respectable fourth-floor office in a tower across the street from the Central Law Courts in downtown

Nairobi, but the place had stopped feeling safe a year back; one of Moi's ministers had moved into the floor below, and Gathenji nervously found himself passing the man's security detail in the stairway.

Now, in the summer of 2000, he was in semihiding in an old, peeling, out-of-the-way office bungalow on Chania Road in a compound of decrepit trees and flowers. The red-tiled roof leaked when it rained, and the cold days were bitterly uncomfortable. He had removed his name from the telephone book and changed his numbers. He was doing mostly low-level legal work to make a living—most clients had deserted him after his incarceration as an alleged enemy of the state a few years back— and quietly consulting human rights groups on strategies for bringing Moi to justice for his crimes.

To Gathenji, Kaiser's death had the feel of a classic state-sanctioned hit, carried out by a cadre of professional assassins. It was the work of what he called "Murder, Inc."—a vast apparatus of spies, security forces, and hit men with links to State House. He had not thought Moi would be brazen enough to kill the American priest. It meant anyone might be next; it suggested there might be a list the assassins were working from. His own name could plausibly be on it; many of the calls he would receive in coming days were from people concerned for his safety.

The country was two years away from the most important election in its postindependence history, a potential pivot point in East Africa's rueful political trajectory. There was hope that Kenya's fragmented ethnic groups might finally do what had seemed impossible before, coalescing long enough to defeat Moi's machine. The ruler was apparently growing desperate, his grip threatened as never before.

SIX DAYS AFTER Kaiser's death, as the priest lay in a glass-lidded brass-and-teak coffin under the vault of Nairobi's Holy Family Basilica, Gathenji sat in the crowded cathedral among Catholic bishops, human rights activists, diplomats, and the priest's friends and colleagues from across the country. The anger in the air was palpable. Gathenji listened as the papal nuncio—the man who'd issued Kaiser's final summons to Nairobi—stood before the crowd, extolling the American priest's crusade for justice and declaring him a martyr to the faith. In life, he'd been a troublemaker, an obstinate and single-minded man who'd railed against the Church's passivity and clashed with his bishops, his missionary bosses, his fellow priests. Now it was possible to ignore the rough edges and complicated history.

The transformation had been instantaneous: The priest had been rubbed as smooth and flawless as a Masai bead, delivered from his aching body and messy humanity to abstraction, a clear and perfect symbol. After twenty-two years of Moi's misrule, Kenyans were ready for such a symbol. The president's face stared from every shilling in their pockets and the wall of every shop they entered—his name was on schools, streets, stadiums—and they had no trouble envisioning his hand steering the American priest to his grave. On everyone's lips was a litany of political murders, unexplained car wrecks, implausible suicides. Outside the basilica, thousands crammed the streets in mourning and in rage. The American had already become a byword for Moi's ruthless determination to stamp out dissent, and a rallying cry for the forces gathering against the dictator. Gathenji noticed that the regime had sent no representative to the funeral ceremony.

After the Mass, the priest's body was loaded into a church van for transport to Kisiiland in the west, where Kaiser had spent decades, and then on to the gravesite in his last parish, in Lolgorien.

Gathenji did not follow the church caravan; there was no telling who might be waiting to ambush him on those long stretches of country road. His association with Kaiser was well known. He believed it best to lie low until facts could be gathered, the scope of the plot uncovered, the killers identified. On this score, there were grounds for hope far beyond what anyone could have expected. A team of FBI agents, summoned by the U.S. ambassador, Johnnie Carson, had crossed the Atlantic to begin investigating. Even now they were fanning out across the countryside, gathering evidence, digging up witnesses.

The ambassador had promised the Bureau's investigation would be an independent one. To Gathenji and to others, this was a crucial reassurance, since no rational person expected the slightest help from the Kenyan police themselves; it was widely rumored that they'd played some role in the death.

Gathenji was heartened by the FBI's reputation, by its awesome resources and name for professionalism; the agency had been instrumental in rounding up suspects in the terror bombing of the U.S. embassy in Nairobi two years earlier.

But even now, a piece of not-so-distant history supplied grounds for anxiety. A decade earlier, Moi had invited New Scotland Yard in to investigate the murder of his foreign minister, Robert Ouko, but had curtailed the probe when it pointed to members of his inner circle. The president had used the legendary British agency as an unwitting pawn in his cover-up. The investigation had supplied the illusion of the pursuit of justice while anger abated and memories faded and witness after witness died, some of them mysteriously.

No, Gathenji thought. This investigation was in good hands. The Kaiser case would not be like Ouko's. The Americans wouldn't permit themselves to be Moi's dupes, and they would raise hell if they were trifled with. So seriously was the case being treated in the United States that senators there were taking to the floor of Congress to demand justice for Kaiser.

Gathenji's day-to-day work representing victims of political violence was dangerous enough, and the Kaiser case promised even deeper hazards. He did not think it prudent to venture too soon to the crime scene in Naivasha, a closely surveilled area with a reputation as a regime stronghold, where the slightest political talk could easily be overheard.

In the weeks that followed Kaiser's death, he would make discreet inquiries, trying to retrace the priest's final steps. Mostly, though, he waited. It might not be necessary for him to get involved.

The case felt coldly familiar to Gathenji in a personal way. His father, a Presbyterian evangelist, had been the victim of a politically charged slaying in September 1969, dragged from his home by fellow Kikuyus for refusing to swear an oath of tribal loyalty.

Charles Mbuthi Gathenji. For the Kenyan attorney who lost his father as a young man, Kaiser's death had personal echoes. *Photograph by Carolyn Cole. Copyright 2009,* Los Angeles Times. *Reprinted with permission.*

Gathenji, a twenty-year-old student at the time, believed the attack was sanctioned by elements of the Kikuyu-dominated government of Kenya's first president, Jomo Kenyatta. No one had ever been punished for his death; there had been no trial, and nothing resembling a real investigation. The experience, more than any other factor, had pushed the young Gathenji into a career in the law, which he perceived as a process—at its best—of ferreting truth from darkness and lending strength to the helpless. He had developed an abiding wariness and a deep-seated distrust of institutions, including ecclesiastical ones.

Like Kaiser, Gathenji's father had been an inveterate builder and a tough former soldier who had ignored reported warnings to adopt a more compromising stance. He had suspected that his betrayer would likely be a friend, a church mate, someone scared enough to sell him out.

Kaiser had been aware of the story of Gathenji's father, of course. During one of their last meetings, the harried priest had invoked the lawyer's father as a reminder of what they were both fighting for.

Both deaths had had a feeling of inevitability. Both of the dead had seen it coming, clear-eyed, from a great distance.

3

THE COLLAR AND THE GUN

H E ARRIVED IN December 1964, stepping off a freighter into the harsh equatorial sunlight at Kenya's eastern port of Mombasa, into a country that had just reeled exuberantly through its first year of independence from the British. Across the continent, the apparatus of European domination was being shuffled off, with varying degrees of violence, and the sense of possibility was unbounded. Kaiser was thirty-two years old and just ordained, fair-skinned and squared-jawed, a big-framed man with an army duffel bag under a thick arm. He boarded a prop plane, which carried him over the vast bulge of land toward his first parish in western Kenya. It was his first sight of the country in which he would spend most of his life—the great forests and maize farms and tea plantations, the ice-capped towers of Mount Kenya, the staggering cleft of the Great Rift Valley.

Kaiser's early years in Kenya seem to have reflected the country's own mood of hope and possibility. He lived in a cool, high region of softly sloping green hills dotted with huts and little granaries and covered with groves of black wattle trees, eucalyptus, and cypress, grass pastures, and terraced fields. This was the land of the Kisii, or Abagusii, a place the British had declared off-limits to European settlers.

Crowds swarmed to meet the missionary as he settled into a parish with eighteen thousand baptized Catholics and eighteen Catholic schools. Winds from Lake Victoria rustled maize rows that soared above a tall man's head, and from the high hills of Kisiiland he could glimpse the great gulf. Families tended small farms called *shambas,* growing tea and coffee, as well as sweet potatoes, finger millet, and corn. Along the narrow dirt roads the women toted heavy kerosene tins of corn kernels to the power mills. Sclerotic little buses called *matatus* raced by helter-skelter; frequent rains stalled them in thick, impassable mud.

English and Swahili were of limited use here. The Kisii, isolated in the hills for two hundred years, were Bantu speakers whose language was grasped by few outsiders. There were no dictionaries or written grammatical rules. Kaiser set to work mastering the language, and after four months he was conversant enough to hear confessions.

The Kisii were fond of late-afternoon drinking parties, and men clustered together on stools, thrusting three-foot-long bamboo drinking tubes into pots of boiling, gruel-thick beer made of fermented millet and maize flour. The sociable Minnesota priest, invited to partake, confided to friends that he found it awful-tasting but learned how to fake a sip.

John Kaiser during his first years in Kenya, in the 1960s. He lived among the Kisii in the fertile highlands of western Kenya. A stout six foot two, he built churches across the countryside, quick, crude structures of red earth and river-bottom sand, and went up ladders with pockets stuffed with bricks. *Photograph courtesy of the Kaiser family.*

The huts were windowless, with walls of mud and wattle. All night during the cold months, upward through fissures in the tight grass thatching of the high-coned roofs, filigrees of smoke curled from hearth fires where families huddled, asleep on cowhides scattered across floors of dried mud and dung.

On some levels, the area was as foreign to Kaiser's native Midwest as it is possible to conceive. Despite the presence of Catholics and Seventh-Day Adventists, most Kisii remained animists steeped in traditional practices. Polygamy was ubiquitous. For a man, the highest ambitions were abundant offspring—the only insurance of personal immortality—and multiple wives, each with her own hut, between which he would rotate. Fecundity was celebrated, the ultimate badge of a woman's worth, and she was expected to give birth every two years while it was biologically possible. Giving birth to fifteen children was common. The Kisii birthrate, one of the world's highest, was to Kaiser "a great sign of Divine favour." Population control he regarded as evil. In Kisiiland, a pregnant woman did not speak of her pregnancy for fear she would appear boastful and invite malevolent envy. Any perceived advantage, in fact, invited envy and witchcraft.

"No one dies without carrying someone on his back," went one proverb. This reflected a dark vision of invisible forces harrying people to their graves. Everything required a cause, an explanation, especially major calamities. Rancor between co-wives was a given, and a woman who found herself infertile, or who lost a child during pregnancy, inevitably suspected some machination of the women who shared her husband. The wealthy lived in fear of the poor; the poor lived in fear of the very poor; the very poor lived in fear of the wretched. It was understood that for the powerless, the jealous, and the angry, there was no recourse except through magic, and so the community's most miserable and reviled members—childless, neglected old women, for instance—were often the most feared and vulnerable to murder. The killing of accused witches was common.

Once, Kaiser would recall, he installed a drain under an old woman's hut, but she remonstrated with him over the shallowness of the ten-foot hole he had excavated. No, she said—they might claw down into the earth and witch me with my used bathwater: the *omorogi*. These were malign grave-robbing entities in human form, witchdoctors capable of casting a hex on anyone whose clothing, hair, fingernails, or excrement they could lay hold of and boil into a lethal brew.

Against those forces stood friendly diviners who could diagnose frightful omens and determine whether they were a function of witch-craft or, perhaps, of ancestor spirits angry at some slight. Other divines prescribed the proper sacrifices to banish spells, indicating whether the occasion called for the slaughtering of a black hen or a white he-goat. Kaiser viewed these divines as "clever rogues and excellent students of human psychology." Professional witch-smellers were paid to scour one's hut and root out the charms hidden in the roof and the walls. Having surveyed the grounds ahead of time and planted the charms, they waited for a crowd to gather, removed the alleged artifacts with a flourish— animal tails, potions, little pots—and dramatically announced that they would identify the witches responsible unless the plots were ceased immediately. Even progressive-minded Christians, lectured at church not to believe in witchcraft, secretly kept potions as a hedge against it. Some converts to Christianity abandoned it to take multiple wives, and some abandoned it in the face of serious illness or death: Confronting such calamities, you took no chances with new and unproven gods like the Nazarene.

For the Kisii, the supernatural was everywhere, but they lacked what some anthropologists called "an organized cosmology." Their religion was essentially an ancestor cult. In a volcanic peak, shapeless as the wind that swirled around its high ridges, dwelled immortal ancestor spirits called "grandfathers"—a fickle, prickly, demanding pack that meted out rough justice in human affairs, punishing homicide and adultery and incest. They sent death and disease, killing bolts and madness, barren wombs and ruined crops. They were not deities, the object of daily prayer and ritual, but their hand was detected when misfortune struck; in this sense, they more closely resembled demons or furies. When angry, they placed omens in your path—an aardvark or copulating snakes—to signal their need for appeasement by funerary and animal sacrifices.

Kaiser perceived the Kisii outlook as one of profound "fear and fatalism," akin to the pagan Europe of his Irish and German forebears. This enlarged the exhilaration of his missionary work. He saw himself bringing the good news of Christ's victory over death and evil, liberating a superstition-enslaved people from their terrors. People sought his protection against the curse left by a lightning strike on a homestead; a sprinkling of his magic water could remove it. Once, he came upon the corpse of a young girl killed by a lightning bolt, and was warned not to touch her: It was certain to bring death, unless goats were sacrificed. Kaiser disregarded the warning, hammered together a wooden coffin, and lifted her into it for burial. If he didn't banish the belief in curses, he seemed at least to possess a special power to defeat them. His celibacy set him apart from the community's normal rhythms and aspirations, and that sense of apartness—coupled with his connection to the spirit world, his ability to influence hidden forces—made him a relation of traditional Kisii diviners.

In a study of the Kisii conducted a few years before Kaiser's arrival, ethnographers Robert and Barbara LeVine described them as a "distinctively paranoid" people who viewed families and neighbors as nests of potential enemies. They sued one another with astonishing frequency—over stolen cattle, boundary lines, beer-party brawls. Litigants were expected to fabricate elaborate stories to avoid admitting guilt, which is why, outside the courthouses, there stood small flowering *omotembe* trees—oath trees—on which they were made to swear; to lie was to invite supernatural disaster, and to refuse the oath was tantamount to confession. In matters of justice, families closed ranks, and many killers avoided trial for want of witnesses. Punishment by the human justice system was regarded as meaningless against the rage of the spirits.

Studying the Kisii, the ethnographers found a streak of sexual puritanism and sadomasochism. Women who initiated sex were seen as

prostitutes; faced with a male overture, they were expected to demonstrate serious reluctance, a practice that obscured distinctions between
consensual sex and rape. On her wedding night, the bride mounted a
show of resistance while the groom's clan mates tore off her clothes and
forced her onto the marriage bed. In a kind of ritualized contest, she
would have stashed a piece of knotted grass under the bed or a piece of
charcoal in her mouth, magic amulets meant to render the groom impo-
tent. Multiple sessions of intercourse were expected of him that night; it
was cause for pride if he injured the bride so badly that she couldn't walk.
There was also a form of ritualized rape (still enduring in the late 1950s,
though growing less frequent) called "taking by stealth": On the occasion
of annual initiation ceremonies, boys were permitted to sneak into girls'
huts, where "a few boys achieve a hurried and fearful act of coitus with
girls who pretend to be sleeping."

As in the midwestern farmland of Kaiser's youth, cows were ubiquitous in Kisii country. Along with the number of wives he managed
to collect, cattle was the mark of a man's wealth and status. They were
a dowry for a daughter and an insurance policy, convertible to cash in
emergencies that required payments to a witch-smeller or medicine man.
And as in the Midwest, the rhythms of life in Kisiiland were dominated
by the seasons, the rain and the crops, and survival depended on how
well you read the signs. The year began with groups of women entering
their little fields, their infants bound to their backs, their panga knives
slashing the underbrush, their hoes pulverizing clumps of dirt in preparation for the broadcasting of millet and corn. Then came the long rains
and the weeding and the waiting, and by August the granaries would
be depleted, and the families, when they ate, survived on sweet potatoes and bananas. In the months that followed came the harvesting, and
with it the initiation ceremonies, including mass clitoridectomies, the
culture's central ritual for girls. To an outsider, the rite involved bewildering dramas. Girls expressed great eagerness for the painful procedure
in the face of older women who mockingly discouraged them. By this
playacting, girls were signaling their mental readiness to enter the hut

of the surgeon, who waited with a harvesting knife or razor; to flee the ceremony, once it had begun, was a disgrace to the family and an affront to the spirits.

Despite the vast cultural differences, Kaiser felt a kinship with his parishioners. They reminded him of the Scandinavian farmers he'd known as a boy in Minnesota. They were "tenacious and stubborn, yet warmhearted and generous, tight-fisted and grasping, superstitious and religious—perceiving the influence of the spirit world in every occurrence," he wrote in a memoir late in life. Kaiser came to respect native medicine men who used herbs and leaves to rescue people from the throes of mental breakdowns after modern medicine had failed. A sick Kisii saw no contradiction in treating his affliction with both a pill and a sacrifice to an offended ancestor.

This, then, was the land that Kaiser entered in his early thirties, the place he would spend much of his life. He came to regard himself not just as an African generally but as a Kisii in particular.

THE COUNTRY, WITH its fierce light and impenetrable dark, its jumbo maize rows and seasons of starvation, was immense, large enough to contain his clashing selves: the priest and the paratrooper, the healer and the hunter, the collar and the gun, the man of obedience who chafed at authority. The duality of his character had been obvious since his childhood, and partly a function of it. He was born in November 1932, the second of four children in a devoutly Catholic family in Otter Tail County, a backwoods patch of wild Minnesota where the children worked the farm and wandered deep woods of ash and poplar and basswood, and where learning to shoot was both survival and a poor boy's central entertainment. The young John Kaiser, thin and sandy-haired, evinced a penchant for solitude, and he thought it would be a fine life to live as a trapper. He spent dark winter mornings roaming with his .22 rifle or single-barrel shotgun, hunting for muskrats and inspecting traps he had set. He became renowned for the speed with which he could detach a skin from the carcass. Animal fur earned the family a few dollars for a day's work.

Religion, like firearms, saturated the Kaiser farm's rhythms. Prayers began on awakening. Mom and Dad drilled their children in the proper responses to the Latin Mass. Their small, white, steepled church had frosted glass, plain wooden pews with uncushioned kneelers, and a wood furnace under the sanctuary. At the pulpit, a German-born priest named James Mohm upbraided parishioners by name for their sins and for their ignorance of the faith. He was opinionated, confrontational, deeply involved in the life of the congregation, and widely loved, a man Kaiser would later describe as a strong influence.

One Christmas at his one-room country school, Kaiser drew a nativity scene on the school chalkboard, carefully detailing the three kings, lovingly texturing the wool of the sheep, scrupulously shaping the halo around baby Jesus' crib. Nights at home, he sat with the family around the kerosene lamp, creating images that might have sprung from the covers of a boys' pulp magazine: horses, sheriffs, gunslingers, elaborate battle scenes. In one image of men at war, he lavished detail on the soldiers' uniforms, on the sights of their M1 rifles, on their anguished faces as bullets riddled their bodies.

His capacity for concentration was married to an impetuous streak. One winter morning as a high school freshman, he and his elder brother, Francis, were exploring the deep woods with their rifles in search of mallards. Coming upon an ice-sheathed pond, the boys approached on elbows and knees, waiting silently for ducks to cluster in the pond's melted center. They fired; the birds shuddered and lay floating. John Kaiser plunged into icy water above his waist to retrieve their prize. He emerged trembling uncontrollably and unable to speak. He ran home, a good mile's distance, to be wrapped in a quilt and warmed by the potbellied cast-iron stove.

Rheumatic fever came on quickly, confining him to his bed for months, the vibrant sandy-haired boy shrunk to the bones. From his bed, he tracked animals with his rifle through the open window. The seasons changed around him, sending their messages: howling blizzards, snowmelt trickling from the eaves, the scratching of june bugs against the screens.

He would never forget his body's capacity to betray him. During the slow recovery and afterward, he hardened it against another possible mutiny, steeling it with endless sit-ups and barbell curls, pushing it beyond endurance.

For years, people noticed his hand fluttering up to his heart involuntarily; in photographs of the period, people remarked that he stood like Napoléon. The habit lasted through his years at St. John's Preparatory School, where he grew tall and fast and strong, catching footballs one-handed and setting a class record in pole vaulting, and through his two years at St. Louis University, where he competed formidably on the wrestling team. It survived well into his army career.

Kaiser had enlisted, following the example of his brother Francis, who had fought in Korea. What survives in official army archives is scant. He served from April 29, 1954 to April 26, 1957, and was discharged as a corporal at Fort Bragg, North Carolina. He was part of the Eighty-second, also known as the "All-Americans," a celebrated elite airborne division that fought in some of World War II's decisive battles, including the Battle of the Bulge, and participated in the invasion of Normandy.

Kaiser joined during one of the hotter periods of the Cold War—the armistice that brought a cease-fire to the Korean conflict was just nine months old, and an uneasy peace prevailed. The Eighty-second had been kept in strategic reserve from the conflict, poised to repel Soviet invasions elsewhere. Ready to fly, ready to jump: That was the unit's raison d'être, its outsized pride, the justification for a training crucible that made the men swagger even in the company of marines. "We were much more disciplined than the Marine Corps because of our unique position," recalled William Meek, the son of a Kentucky coal miner, who roomed with Kaiser at Fort Bragg and trained with him in Company D, a heavy-mortar platoon in the Eighty-second. "We were to be prepared within a few hours' notice to go anywhere in the world where there was a

trouble spot. We were to stay in top physical shape. Even the mess stew-
ard, if we were overweight, would determine how big a portion of potatoes we could have." He would recall Kaiser as a loner who rarely left the
base on off days, venturing instead to the library, the swimming pool, or
the woods.

As a paratrooper and a noncommissioned officer, Kaiser earned $50 a
month on top of his $120 wages, and he sent as much home to his family
as he could. At the firing range, Kaiser proved an expert shot. He learned
to take apart his M1 rifle and reassemble it blindfolded, to disable an
enemy with a thrust of the butt plate to the jaw, and to kill with a lunge
of the bayonet. To strengthen their legs for parachute jumps, the soldiers
endured endless marching and running, the men in formation count-
ing cadence in eight-mile jogs around the base, sounding off, and in the
blazing summer heat stripping to the waist, so they ran only in boots
and khakis, the sweat from one man's swinging arm splattering the bare
back of the man ahead, and that man's sweat hitting the man ahead of
him, all the way through the ranks in the unremitting North Carolina
sun. Over and over, they practiced the paratroop roll, learning to let
their weight hit the ground in degrees, bodies folding up accordionlike
to lessen the shock of impact. Suited up, latched into the restraining rig,
they left the tarmac in C-119 Flying Boxcars and sat in two facing rows,
twenty men on each side, climbing above cotton and peanut country
dotted down below with the tiny shapes of farmers and mules. *Look
straight out, not down.* A layer of planes leveled out at eighteen hundred
feet, another at three thousand. Then came the interminable moment:
standing at the open bay door, waiting for the green light to trigger the
plunge. Then the air filled with falling soldiers, two thousand at once,
"like Cheerios in a bowl of milk," Meek recalled, jostling one another as
parachutes opened.

By now Kaiser could lift more than his two-hundred-pound weight
over his head. His hand still crept to his heart, a decade after his fever,
as if to suggest why he seemed to spend every free minute condition-
ing his body with push-ups and sit-ups and barbell curls, an exercise

regimen so intense that Meek thought it bordered on the neurotic. Once they were swimming in Chesapeake Bay, Kaiser and Meek and another soldier, diving, having a hell of a time, and found themselves about a mile offshore in the shipping lanes. They had brought an army air mattress in case someone cramped up, and an exhausted Meek wanted to ride it back to shore. Kaiser would not surrender it, announcing, "You're just now building muscle." When Meek insisted, Kaiser answered by letting the air out of the mattress. Meek cursed and started swimming, and succeeded in making it back under his own steam. How had Kaiser calibrated the risk? Perhaps he believed he'd be able to rescue his friend with little trouble should he flounder; nobody doubted that he would have risked his own life to do so. Still, Meek thought that the Minnesota soldier's behavior was foolish, stubborn.

By all accounts, Kaiser relished the physical life of a soldier and considered it, for a time, a vocation. It's possible that military existence, with its elaborate codes and structures, rituals and hierarchies, supplied a kind of peace to a man whose energies sometimes threatened to overtop their banks; an impetuous temperament can find psychic freedom in order, routine, and clear lines of authority. Still, he seemed to like skirting rules. He kept a .22-caliber pistol buried in a plastic bag at the base, Meek recalled, though he couldn't say what Kaiser intended it for. And Kaiser once staged the clandestine nighttime excavation of a buried crate of surplus ammo—he could not abide the waste of good bullets—and then smuggled it out of the base in his car trunk, with his mother smiling obliviously from the passenger seat.

Kaiser faithfully attended the Latin Mass on the base and wrestled with the possibility he might have to take a human life in war. The fearsome presence of the water-cooled, tripod-mounted .50-caliber machine gun that, as a squad leader, he carried—the weapon spewed six hundred rounds a minute, punctuated by phosphorescent tracers, and grew so hot that it boiled the water in the tanks—made it impossible to ignore the question. The army was shaping him with ruthless efficiency into a Red-killing machine. "We discussed that very thing," Meek said. "I had a lot of problems myself with it, if I could fire into human beings with that weapon or not." Still, he recalled Kaiser as "very much a patriot," a full-blooded soldier ready to follow orders. Ecclesiastes told him there was a time to kill, as did the Church doctrine of a just war. Deeply embedded in his ideological firmament was a sense of the malignancy of global communism and the "materialistic atheism" it represented; the struggle against the Soviet Union was nothing less than a fight against the principalities of darkness. It was one thing to pray for the conversion of Russia, as every good Catholic did, but only a fool forgot his gun.

NEAR THE END of Kaiser's three-year army stint, he was demoted from sergeant to corporal in an incident whose details remain obscure. Having lost certain archives in a warehouse fire, the army has no record of what cost Kaiser his rank. "Some of the black soldiers under his supervision refused to work and he confronted them," according to an FBI summary of his sister Carolita's account. "As a result of his intolerance of reverse discrimination and his actions at the time, he was demoted." Later, she said her brother's *solidarity* with the black soldiers got him in trouble—racist townsmen surrounding the Fort Bragg base were aghast at the presence of the black soldiers Kaiser had stationed to guard a barracks of white nurses. Refusing to remove the black soldiers, or to apologize to the townsmen, he accepted demotion rather than relent.

That account was echoed by Kaiser's brother Francis, who portrayed him as a victim of the army's racial backwardness and cowardice: "The townfolks didn't want 'niggers' guarding people. He said, 'I don't have niggers. I have soldiers.' "

It takes only a little imagination to reconcile the variations of the story. It's easy to picture Kaiser as a hard-driving, brook-no-nonsense commander who demanded the strictest discipline; he obeyed orders unstintingly and likely expected the same from his troops, who might have bristled at his harshness. It's possible that his black soldiers, sensing the danger, did not particularly relish the duty of guarding a barracks of white nurses in the Jim Crow South of 1957. It would have been consistent with Kaiser's character to insist: Right is right; wrong is wrong.

By the time he was demoted, his sister recalled, he had already made the decision to leave the army. He had grown tired, he would later tell people, of teaching recruits how to kill.

His time in uniform coincided with a tense but quiet period for America's fighting forces, and he left the service, unlike his brother, without having seen a battle zone. There is no record of a sudden mystical experience, an epiphany, a catalyzing moment that led to his enrollment, at age twenty-five, at the Mill Hill Missionaries' Jesuit school at St. Louis University, in Missouri. His decision to pursue the priesthood surprised no one, since he had spoken of its appeal for years. He told people that he considered it the world's most important job.

"He was sidestepping God until he couldn't do it anymore," as his sister put it, though he did not relish the prospect of urban priesthood and "having to go to ladies' circles, all the stuff you have to do." Missionary work seemed the logical fit for a midwestern farm boy still seeking adventure and a measure of freedom.

Mill Hill, a London-based missionary society, had a reputation as a strict and exacting order. Kaiser got a single bed in a little wood-frame house, and he became fast friends with his roommate, a former air force pilot named Tony Barnicle. Their long nighttime chats flouted the rule of *magnum silencium*, or "the great silence," which students were expected to observe through the night and morning rituals. The course load encompassed metaphysics, Latin, Plato, Aristotle, and massive doses of Thomas Aquinas.

In snatches of downtime, the seminarians watched films on a sixteen-millimeter projector and played fiercely competitive games of bridge and Monopoly in smoke-choked rooms. Everyone save Kaiser seemed to smoke. Even as they immersed themselves in doctrine, they wrestled with the prospect of giving up any semblance of a normal life. There was a sense of terror, of the massive weight they had agreed to shoulder, when strangers on campus noticed their cassocks and greeted them as "Father."

"Both of us had a lot of doubts," Barnicle said. "Every time I was ready to leave, John talked me out of it. Every time John was ready to leave, I talked him out of it. We had both had lives as adults in the military. We had no illusions about going into a life of celibacy." The ache was sharpened by the site of pretty coeds wandering the campus. Barnicle had had girlfriends; Kaiser acknowledged to his roommate that he was a virgin. "I'm sure he'd fallen in love a couple of times. Daily, you're faced with the sacrifice of a family," Barnicle recalled. "We talked about our vocations, and we talked about girls, but we mostly talked about Thomistic philosophy."

After two years in St. Louis, Kaiser accompanied Barnicle to the four-year course at St. Joseph's College in London, where they were among the few Americans. They received a red sash to drape over their cassocks, a sign they were willing to shed blood for the faith. Missionary work had its hazards, though it was less risky than it had been in the years before quinine, when an assignment to a place like Kenya, where Mill Hill had been sending men since 1904, often meant quick malarial death. The seminary was dominated by archaic rules, in the fashion of a Benedictine order. After night prayers, students were expected to observe the *magnum silencium* the instant they placed a foot on the first step leading to the dormitory area, and it reigned till morning Mass. The rooms were tiny, primitive, with a small bed, a cupboard, a desk, a lamp, a chair, a cross on the wall. To discourage "unhealthy friendships," a euphemism for homosexual trysts, there was a strict prohibition against visiting one another's rooms.

Harrie van Onna, a Dutch seminarian, would remember Kaiser as a quiet man of great warmth who possessed a naive idealism about the faith but sometimes clashed with the men who ran its institutions. The missionary order left little room for individual dissent on matters of doctrine—Kaiser expressed skepticism about the logic of celibacy but agreed to adhere to the vow—and the seminary structure was an infantilizing one. Like Kaiser, van Onna had commanded men in the military; now they were required to ask permission to take a trip into downtown London.

Having studied Spanish, Kaiser had anticipated a posting to South America after his ordination. But Mill Hill needed priests in Africa. He had no special knowledge of the continent and spoke none of its indigenous languages; he was not able to conceal a sense of disappointment at the assignment. Still, he was a man of obedience, and adaptable to any terrain. That had been the pride of the Eighty-second Airborne, after all: the ability to go anywhere in the world with little notice, mountain or desert, city or bush.

He would, at least, be spared the mundane duties and circumscribed routines of a big-city priest, for which he understood himself to be temperamentally unsuited. Plus, he relayed with delight to his brother Francis, he would be able to take his hunting rifle to Africa.

A YEAR AFTER his arrival in Kenya, he steered his motorcycle southward out of tightly packed Kisii country into what some people called "the other side"—the immense open plains of Masailand in the Transmara region. He stood on a hill overlooking the Migori River and beheld a vista alive with elephants, buffalo, topi, waterbuck, and impalas. He felt, he wrote, as if he had been admitted to the Garden of Eden, a hunter's paradise. Kaiser applied for a hunting license and, on free days, when other missionaries headed to the cities, he disappeared into the tall grass, at times in the company of traditional spear-bearing Kisii hunters. Traveling the region with his gun, he learned every square mile of it. He did not pursue trophies—seeking only the game meat he used to feed himself and his parishioners—but he was thrilled by the hunt. He elbow-crawled with his shotgun to within twenty yards of a warthog, which he considered the best meat in Kenya.

This was Kenyatta's country, still in the childhood of its independence, and Kaiser would write of its "easy peaceful aspect."

During his fourth year in Kenya, he boarded a night bus out of Kisii with a few belongings, heading to the Nairobi airport in October 1968. For reasons that are unclear, Mill Hill had reassigned him to the States.

He would be the rector of the missionary order's house in Albany, New York, the headquarters of its American operation. It's not certain whether Kaiser sought this assignment, but his writing suggests that he believed it only a temporary departure from East Africa.

The bus was traveling along a high, cold road, he recalled in a memoir years later, when it approached an intersection crammed with trucks. All along the roadside, under a chilly rain, crowded hundreds of Kisii peasant farmers with the sum of their possessions—chickens, goats, bedding, pots, pans. Some were huddled near piles of blazing firewood they had foraged. He climbed off the bus and began asking questions. The farmers, he learned, had pooled their savings and purchased a large estate— they displayed documents to prove it—only to discover, after making the journey to their new home, that someone else had bought the land and was occupying it. A fraudulent company had swindled them out of everything.

By Kaiser's account, the spectacle profoundly affected him. He decided that when he returned, he would have to immerse himself in the villagers' lives and familiarize himself with the nation's laws. He was so troubled by the farmers' plight that he stopped by the American embassy in Nairobi to find out whether he could become a Kenyan citizen. He thought it might somehow put him in a better position to help. But renouncing his United States citizenship would leave him at the mercy of the Kenyan authorities, who might deny him a visa if he wanted to visit the States, where his two brothers and sister and aging parents remained; he might find himself trapped in Africa if he needed to leave in a hurry. However much he thought himself a Kisii, American citizenship—and the measure of protection that implied—amounted to what he called a "great asset."

His stay in the States would last a year. He returned to Kenya in November 1969, bearing what he called "my luggage & idealism & my lousy novels." Entering the Mill Hill house in Nairobi to find other priests and a local bishop drinking tea, he braced himself for their reaction. Word had circulated among Africa's Mill Hill priests that something dreadful had happened during his time in New York. That he'd made accusations against the eccentric head of the society there. That he'd shown a streak of volatility some had already glimpsed in him. That he'd resisted police and been briefly institutionalized. "I had predetermined to be calm and serene & so I was extremely nervous, but everyone rushed to my aid and paid me much complimentary attention or else fled the room in cowardice," he wrote in a letter to Barnicle. "They don't so much think I am nuts as simply had a severe nervous breakdown—and no doubt they might be right." Kaiser acknowledged that "there is the possibility that I am subjectively dishonest—nuts," and he mocked his own imprudence during the New York episode: "Prudence, Tony, that's the governing virtue." Enthusiastic about returning to Kisiiland, he ended the letter on a note of optimism, but he hinted at the psychic toll the last year had taken: "The future looks good for me Tony—I have no place to go but up."

4

OATHS

IN SEPTEMBER OF that year, in a town called Kikuyu in the countryside about fifteen miles northwest of the capital, a twenty-year-old student named Charles Mbuthi Gathenji stood beside the hacked and beaten body of his dying father. Hours before, the young Gathenji had been pulled out of his Nairobi classroom by a summons to the headmaster's office. There was a phone call waiting for him—a nurse from Kikuyu Hospital saying, "Your father has been admitted." If he received further explanation in that conversation, he wouldn't remember it later. He didn't need much explanation anyway: The attack on his father was no surprise. He rushed from the school and found a bus. He climbed aboard, squeezing between a crush of bodies. He would remember standing for the interminable hour-long drive over the tarmac, jostled by bodies, thinking, *I hope I will meet him alive.* He would remember the kindness of the bus driver, a devout Quaker, who seemed to know exactly what had happened when he explained where he was going, and why. It was a terrible time for Christians.

THE ATTACK HAD its origins deep in Kenya's bloody preindependence history, in the green and war-racked countryside in which Gathenji had grown up. He was the second-oldest boy in a family of seven children. His immediate family, poor and landless Kikuyus, lived north of the capital in a mud-walled house roofed with corrugated iron in what the British euphemistically called a "protected village," a place he

38

later regarded as a modified concentration camp. Ostensibly, they were being protected from the Mau Mau, Kikuyu rebels whose mass peasant insurgency was then at its height. White settlers had confiscated tens of thousands of acres in the Kikuyu heartland, and the rebellion's rallying cry was *ithaka na wiyathi*, or "land and freedom." Its tactics—machete attacks, arson raids, assassinations, decapitations—inspired terror even among sympathizers.

Gathenji had been three years old, in October 1952, when the colonial government declared a state of emergency. The British had responded to the rebellion by forcing most of the Kikuyu population into barbwire-enclosed camps and villages like this one, with its encircling spike-filled moat, one entrance and one exit. A cadre of Home Guards—Africans loyal to the Crown who had been given rifles and uniforms—policed the premises, collected taxes, and inspected the despised dog tag–like identity cards, called *kipandes,* that all adults were made to wear around their necks. The guards, with their berets, long black trench coats, khaki shorts, and heavy black boots, were remote and fearsome figures with a reputation for casual cruelty, more loathed than the British soldiers themselves. Their whistles would pierce the air before dawn; Gathenji's parents and other adults would be herded off to perform compulsory "communal work," digging ditches and clearing brush on the surrounding European farms.

Gathenji watched them beat anyone suspected of Mau Mau sympathies, and he watched them whip old people who were not quick enough in answering the whistle. Once, he was whipped himself after attempting to walk to school during a siege. Around their homes, villagers were forbidden from erecting fences or growing thickets that might impede the guards' view as they patrolled the pathways between the long, straight rows of huts.

The village was structurally divided between the "Royals"—those seen as sympathetic to the government, like Gathenji's immediate family—and Kikuyus deemed sympathetic to the insurrection, a group that included Gathenji's paternal grandmother, a hard-eyed, slender woman clad in beaded necklaces and traditionalist wrappings and ornaments. Between the groups, there was always tension; their huts faced one another across a clear path. Now and then, boys from the other side pelted Gathenji's hut with stones and chanted songs depicting his family as traitors.

Sometimes, during insurgent raids on nearby villages, Gathenji could hear the screams and smell the smoke, and the gates of his village would close, the guards stationed in a protective ring. Sometimes the British troops, known as "Johnnies," poured into the village with their rifles, hunting for rebels. It was a childhood pervaded by fear.

If you were a Kikuyu boy growing up in a protected village in the 1950s, you knew certain things in the marrow.

You knew not to talk to the guards; if your people saw, you would be made to give explanations. You knew not to talk to the few white people you brushed past at the markets outside the village, or the ones you saw rumbling down the roads in their Land Rovers and Bedfords; they were armed, and any of them could do anything to you. You knew not to look in their eyes and draw attention to yourself. If possible, you disappeared.

If white people asked you a direct question, you knew to answer as briefly as possible and then shut up, to turn your face into a mask and your words into riddles, and never—never—to volunteer information. In many cases, your lingering distrust of white people would remain ineradicable even half a century later, and you would find yourself weighing your words carefully around them. You knew not to take shortcuts across the European farms, because you'd heard stories of other kids being shot as trespassers. You knew not to confide in the blacks who worked as field hands and domestic servants at those farms, because their allegiances were in doubt from every side: They might pass information about your family on to the whites, or they might be secret Mau Maus.

Above all, you were made to understand that talk was dangerous. You knew this at a cellular level, as law so universal and mundane that you couldn't even recall when you had first learned it, in the same way you had always known that the gigantic armor-plated ants known as *siafu* would draw blood if your bare feet landed in their nest for more than a few seconds.

AT THE CENTER of the insurgency was its loyalty oath, which drew on—and bastardized—a long Kikuyu tradition. In earlier times, oath takers held a Bible in one hand and a pile of earth in the other; now, as the fighting intensified, Scripture was scuttled in favor of goat meat. At secret ceremonies, initiates would pass under an arch of banana leaves and strip naked in a symbolic shuffling off of their old selves. The goat would be slaughtered, a piece of its flesh ingested, its hot blood smeared on the bodies of oath takers. A series of vows was affirmed: *Kill the enemies of Mau Mau. Never betray Mau Mau. Never reveal the oath to whites.*

To the British, the oathing represented the atavistic savagery of their enemy, "the most bestial, filthy and nauseating incantation which perverted minds can ever have brewed." To the Kikuyu, most of whom reportedly took it in some form, it was regarded as transformative, a rebirth, a thing of transcendent power: God, or Ngai, would visit death on those who broke it. In detention camps, the oathing flourished, sometimes accompanied by the promise that initiates would get a plot of land once the whites were banished. The oath was often coerced, and as the war dragged on, it came to involve the drinking of blood and the binding of initiates with goat intestines.

To reject the ritual meant one was too dangerous to live, a potential stooge. Kikuyu Christians, a minority, were especially vulnerable. Many refused the oath, not out of colonial sympathies necessarily, but because the Church portrayed the goat blood as a blasphemy, the satanic counterpart of Christ's blood. Militants strangled obstinate Christians with blankets, slashed their throats with jerry-rigged blades, and—if they were suspected informers—cut out their tongues.

On his mother's side, much of Gathenji's family sided with the rebellion, but his father, Samuel, an itinerant carpenter, occupied the gray and dangerous zone of staunch Christians.

After serving with the King's African Rifles in the battle against Mussolini in Ethiopia, where he had lost many of his front teeth, he had become a pacifist and an evangelist with the Presbyterian Church of East Africa. He preached at the pulpit and on the streets, anywhere he could find a crowd, and his themes were peace and reconciliation. He recited the story of the Good Samaritan and hummed "Nearer My God to Thee" when he walked.

He was a puzzle to his traditionalist, fervently Mau Mau in-laws. He had adopted the unswerving missionary stance against the genital mutilation of girls, which his in-laws clung to as an indispensable rite. He abjured old rituals, like spitting on your own chest as a blessing and offering goat sacrifices at the sacred *mugumo,* or fig tree. He rejected the notion that his wife, who had died as a young woman in childbirth in the late 1950s, had perished as a result of mistreating ancestor spirits, or, as her grieving mother insisted, by a curse placed upon her by a jealous neighbor.

He had a reputation as a consummately gentle man who avoided quarrels. When neighbors argued, they inevitably found themselves in Samuel Gathenji's hut, seeking a peacemaker's counsel. Still, he retained basic Kikuyu notions of child discipline and the importance of instilling obedience toward elders; he didn't hesitate to raise the cane when young Charles came home muddy from fishing for tadpoles at the lake or had strayed beyond the compound into areas where so many hazards waited—colonial soldiers, settlers, feral animals, and Mau Maus, who were rumored to anoint children into their cadres by smearing castor oil on their faces.

Though he had no interest in politics, some fellow Kikuyus perceived Samuel Gathenji as an ally of the Crown, so deeply was Christianity associated with the establishment. The churches had helped to provide the Manichaean language of the struggle, after all. Through the detention camp's loudspeakers, some missionaries railed against the evils of the rebellion, urging detainees to repent of their oaths and accept Christ's salvation.

In young Charles Gathenji's government-run elementary school, he and other children were tutored in the splendors of British civilization, made to memorize "God Save the Queen" and to recite the names of the royal family. They were taught the backwardness of Kikuyu traditions, from genital mutilation to the way one's grandparents dressed. To Gathenji, the intended message was unambiguous: African ways are evil.

In the ongoing Mau Mau war, he was taught, virtue resided solely on the colonial side. In civics class, teachers posed the question "Who are the enemies of your country?" The boy dutifully recited the required answers: rebel leader Dedan Kimathi and Jomo Kenyatta, the alleged mastermind of the revolution. Kenyatta was feared by settlers across the continent, and described by one governor of Kenya as "an African leader to darkness and death." In reality, he was a moderate with little sympathy for the Mau Maus. His imprisonment—on evidence now accepted as fabricated—did not have the intended effect of decapitating the movement. Instead, it transformed him into a living martyr and created a power vacuum into which militants swarmed.

The rebellion was crushed, but the nerve for continued occupation had raveled. In the summer of 1961, his cult having grown during his incarceration, Kenyatta was released. The man portrayed as the country's greatest enemy would soon be its first president. Gathenji stood with the masses when he came to Kikuyuland to speak. Thickset, with his gray beard and resonant voice, Kenyatta was the most eloquent man the boy had ever heard. Speaking in English and Gikuyu, defying calls for vengeance against those who had taken the colonial side, Kenyatta talked rousingly of *harambee*—transcending ethnic divisions and coming together as members of a single, self-governing nation. He urged the Mau Maus to come out of the forests. It was time to prepare for independence.

The protected villages were dismantled. Samuel Gathenji bought a small plot of land and built a three-room timber-walled home. In their new village there were no guards, no colonial chiefs and subchiefs to answer to, no forced labor, no curfew, no one telling them how to build. The sense of perpetual menace was gone.

Gathenji was fourteen years old on the night in December 1963 when he stood outside Kikuyu Station, the local government headquarters, to watch the Union Jack lowered for the last time; in its place rose the red-and-green-and-black flag of independent Kenya. It was the thirty-fourth African country to achieve independence. The cheering was ecstatic. The tribal songs and dances lasted through the night, and the free food seemed limitless, no small thrill for a scrawny boy who got a single full meal of *ugali*, a cornmeal porridge, on good days. It was an unalloyed joy to be young in a country that now belonged to its people, with a hero at the helm. It was the last nationalist celebration in which he would be able to lose himself.

Despite his talk of *harambee*, Kenyatta's policies would baldly favor his own ethnic base. On well-connected Kikuyus he would lavish prime land, jobs, generous funding, and contracts, with this explanation to those who remonstrated: "My people have the milk in the morning, your tribes the milk in the afternoon." As for the years of civil bloodshed, they were to be consigned to the past, banished to the sinkhole of national memory: "Mau Mau was a disease which had been eradicated, and must never be remembered again." Yet memory abided, and unhealed traumas lived close to the surface. Former guerillas and former royalists were now living side by side.

Young Gathenji understood there was a price to pay for the perception that his father had been on the wrong side during the independence struggle; he sensed it was the reason behind his eviction from one of the best local schools. Other factors militated against the likelihood that he'd complete his education. For years, he'd been shuttling between schools, forced to leave when money ran out. At night, he studied by the dim light of a paraffin-filled tin can.

He had been nine when his mother died during labor, and he still felt her loss sharply. He remembered her beautiful hair, her impressive height, her Somali profile, and how lovingly she had prepared him and his siblings for school every morning. During canings, she had told him she was beating the sin out of him. As her body was lowered into the grave pit, he felt a strangling in his throat and a numbness in his body. He could neither move nor cry. Staring hard at the sky, he heard one of his sisters wailing. It was his first real experience of loss and helplessness—a feeling that returned a few years later, when his older brother, Henry, was killed crashing his motorcycle. This left Gathenji to shoulder the burdens of the eldest boy. There was always water to be fetched or other chores around the house.

His father remarried and picked up steady work for the government and kept his home immaculate. On weekends, Charles accompanied him on long walks to construction sites, carrying the woven basket that contained the screwdriver and hammer and saw, the red dust rising at their feet as his father sang hymns.

Gathenji began attending an integrated government-run high school in Nairobi. Nobody thought he would go very far. His father disliked the idea of his being alone in the city: There were too many temptations and bad influences for a boy. You're wasting my money on that school, he told his son, urging him to drop out and train as a flight attendant. The son insisted on staying in school. In the capital, he'd found access to a good library, with shelves of American books. He absorbed tales of Abraham Lincoln and the war for the American West. He read *Tom Sawyer* and *Gone with the Wind*. He relished Erle Stanley Gardner's pulp novels about Perry Mason, the defense attorney who always managed to untangle the web of lies entrapping his clients, and to demonstrate—often by eliciting a courtroom confession—that the government's version of reality was illusory.

IN JULY 1969, assassins gunned down a young cabinet minister named Tom Mboya on a Nairobi street. He was a prominent member of the Luo, a populous ethnic group whose rivalry with the Kikuyu dominated the country's politics. Each group spoke a language incomprehensible to the other and looked askance at the other's rituals (the Kikuyu practiced circumcision, for instance, and the Luo did not). Stereotypes fueled mutual contempt: The Kikuyu were thrusting, greedy, and eager to emulate the West; the Luo were backward and in thrall to atavistic tribal beliefs. The Luo masses, who nursed a sense of bitter exclusion as their rivals came to dominate politics, business, and the civil service, perceived the hand of the Kikuyu elite in the assassination. Street riots and mob skirmishes erupted, crowds hurled stones at Kenyatta's motorcade, and there were reports that Kikuyus were being murdered.

Gathenji avoided the streets. As the sense of siege became widespread, and as Luo anger threatened to tilt upcoming elections, the Kikuyu resurrected a tactic from the years of insurrection: mass oathing ceremonies. Officially, nothing of the sort was taking place. When church leaders visited Kenyatta to express concern, he feigned ignorance.

But from cities and villages, on foot and by bus and hired truck, thousands made their way to secret ceremonies, some of them at Kenyatta's own compound, where they affirmed their loyalty to the House of Mumbi—the Kikuyu people—and to Kenyatta himself. It was the year of the American moon landing, and the pilgrimage was called "going to the moon."

Mercenary motives exacerbated the mania: Fees were demanded of the oath takers. To any number of teachers, government ministers, civil servants, professors, and other intellectuals, the ingestion of goat blood was a meaningless humiliation, the oath a coerced recitation of empty, superstitious words. As in the Mau Mau era, however, those who refused the oath—often on religious grounds—were considered dangerously unreliable, potential turncoats.

One day that September, Charles met his father during a lunch break in the capital's Uhuru Park, where the elder Gathenji was building the framework for a series of ponds. "People are looking for me," he told his son. The village headman and the regional parliamentarian had been organizing mass oathing trips; in some cases, gangs had been snatching people from their homes.

Samuel Gathenji, not content with quiet resistance, had been publicly denouncing the oath as divisive and un-Christian. When they found him—and sooner or later they would—they would give him a choice between the goat's blood and death. "This is the time for *shujaa*," he told his son. The word meant heroes in Swahili.

The younger Gathenji knew what could happen, but he respected his father's position. There would have been no point in challenging him, even if such a thing had been conceivable, which it was not: He was an obedient Kikuyu son.

Now, both of them understood, it was only a question of when it would happen and who would do it. The elder Gathenji guessed Christian friends with the Presbyterian Church of East Africa would betray him to the oath men. Some had initially joined him in defiance, only to acquiesce to the oath after beatings and threats. Some were hiring out their trucks to carry people to the ceremonies.

Gathenji watched his father's face. It had a faraway look. His father asked how he was doing in school. It was the kind of thing he never asked. Then he did something else that was out of character. He handed his son a few shillings to buy food, though he knew he would have been fed. Money had always been tight, and ordinarily he frowned on adults giving money to children, who were expected to spend it frivolously. But now he seemed to be reaching out. The abyss between them was imminent. The son sensed what was happening. He took the money, dread twisting in his stomach. For years, he'd comforted himself with the notion that God, having taken his mother and brother, would spare the rest of his family. His father, in particular, had seemed invulnerable. But now he told his roommate, "They will probably kill him."

WHEN THE BUS from Nairobi dropped him off at Kikuyu Station, he rushed to the hospital on foot. The first thing to strike him, when he found the room where his father was being kept, was the smell of blood. Samuel Gathenji lay on his back, breathing with difficulty. He asked his son to turn him over and said, "You see what they've done to me." His back had been skinned from the neck to the buttocks with a *simi,* a Kikuyu sword. During the accompanying beating, his internal organs had been crushed. He was barely alive, spasming when he tried to speak.

Gathenji read to him from Revelation, and they prayed. His father told him to take care of the family, to have courage, and to be careful whom he trusted. He said that he held no bitterness and that he forgave his attackers, and that he wished his son to do the same. Finally, he said, "I am cold." The son covered him with a blanket and walked out of the hospital room. Within minutes, his father was dead.

Later, a photograph of his father's hacked body—taken by a journalist who had found his way into the hospital room—was slipped to Gathenji. He would keep it in a file, along with newspaper clippings about the killing and accounts he'd taken from a handful of local women who had been snatched with his father that night. He'd tracked the women down and given assurance that he would not expose them: He just needed to know what had happened. From them, and from the account of his stepmother and younger brother Edwin, who had been at the house during the abduction, he pieced together the details.

He learned that about ten young men had converged on the house, and that some had worn the red shirts of the youth wing of the ruling party. Some were members of the campaign team of the local parliamentarian, Joseph Gatuguta, a longtime Kenyatta confidant who owed his power to the president. Some were unemployed young men to whom Samuel Gathenji had thrown construction jobs. Some were true believers, whipped into a frenzy by calls for tribal solidarity. Some just viewed the snatching as another job; incredibly, they would return to the Gathenji house afterward, having helped to kill their benefactor, looking for more construction work.

Gathenji was given further details: that his father had been packed into the back of a covered Peugeot pickup for a drive into the countryside to the oathing center. That he'd preached to the women who accompanied him in the truck. That they'd been singing. And that the attackers had had to force open his mouth to pour the goat blood down his throat.

THE STORY WAS carried in *Target*, a newspaper published by the National Council of Churches of Kenya. The accompanying photographs included one of the pastor's coffin as it was being carried to its grave, and a portrait of his bespectacled twenty-year-old son, Charles, his features rigid with fear and the weight of his new knowledge. Christian leaders mounted protests and visited Kenyatta, urging him to stop the oathing campaign. It ceased shortly afterward. The president had reportedly been unhappy with the evangelist's slaying. It hadn't been meant to happen, Gathenji thought. It had probably been intended as a beating—they'd inflict pain until he relented. They had misjudged their victim's nature.

Gathenji expected the Presbyterian Church of East Africa would honor his father with a memorial. Instead, local church leaders balked at the perceived danger; Kenyatta's security men were shadowing the family. Gathenji borrowed money for a tombstone. At the funeral, he found himself studying the faces of the mourners, wondering who had betrayed his father to the oath men. With his mother dead, his brother Henry dead, his father dead, and whatever trust he had in friends now an impossibility, he felt a deep and ineradicable sense of isolation.

He was not surprised that no inquest was conducted and no one was prosecuted. Everyone wanted the case forgotten. To dig too deeply into it would have implicated the nation's legendary founder and the men he kept closest.

Though he prayed for the strength to forgive, he wasn't sure he was capable of it. He was not his father, and the killers weren't coming forward to ask his forgiveness, in any case.

Replaying their last exchange, he came to think that his father had been trying to warn him away from the quicksand of bitterness. Telling him to find a way to move on, because there was no way to right this particular evil. Telling him not to let it become a devouring obsession. Telling him not to waste his life.

No, he thought, he couldn't forgive, but he couldn't realistically expect justice, either. He would have to accept that the situation was hopeless and make peace with it.

With help from his extended family he transferred to a government-run boarding school near Mount Kenya. He felt safer there; he wouldn't leave the compound for the whole term.

People still doubted he'd go far, as his education had been so erratic. No one in his immediate family had attended college. But the need to finish school had never felt more urgent. Quietly, he'd taken an oath of his own. Later, asked to explain his decision to pursue the law, he would never hesitate to point to his father's murder and the subsequent inability to bring anyone to book. Along with a deep wariness, he had developed a preoccupation with justice. He thought that the law, properly wielded, might be a searchlight, an antidote to historical amnesia, a counterweight to arbitrary state power and the madness of the mob. For all the ways it could be corrupted, the law lived on the ideals of order and reason and discipline; these would be his plank against the undertow of despair. "I want to be rational," he would say with characteristic terseness, trying to explain himself years later. "I think law assisted me."

Government scholarships paid his way through three years at the University of Dar es Salaam, across the border in Tanzania, then in the throes of socialist fervor. It was a scorching, mosquito-infested place, where, between law classes, he endured malaria and ideological instruction in the wisdom of Lenin and Mao. At times, he had an exhilarating sense of a broader philosophical world than his British-based schooling had exposed him to, though he regarded revolutionary ideology, like alcohol, as being best consumed in measured doses. His classmates nicknamed him the "Chief Justice," or "CJ," a nod to the air of gravity and conservatism with which he carried himself. After another year at the Kenya School of Law, where he was apprenticed to a criminal defense lawyer, he joined the attorney general's office as a prosecutor in 1975. It was a small office, and experience came fast.

The Kenyan courts were independent from the Crown but retained the trappings of Mother England. Lawyers appeared in black robes, and judges, called "Lords," most of them still English, wore powdered wigs. In one of his first High Court cases, he prosecuted a farmhand who had strangled a baby. He went at it with vigor, arguing that the man should be hanged. His anger and disgust were so obvious that the judge cautioned him to moderate his tone. A finding of insanity won the defendant a reprieve. Such outcomes rankled the zealous young prosecutor. So much seemed to ride on each case; he internalized the defeats. It was not long before he understood the importance of a more clinical approach. He would be seeing death every day, after all. Domestic homicides, bar-brawl homicides, slum homicides; greed-motivated murder, lust murder, stupid, logic-defying murder; bludgeonings, stabbings, shootings.

During those years, Gathenji haunted the Nairobi Law Courts. One of the fixtures there was Joseph Gatuguta, who had been a member of parliament at the time of Samuel Gathenji's death and was widely believed to have organized the oathing in the Kikuyu region. He had been voted out of office and was now a lawyer in private practice. Gathenji encountered him constantly in courtrooms and in corridors. It was unavoidable. Sometimes they'd be on opposite sides of the same case. Their exchanges were formal and tight. Gathenji had determined to bite back his bitterness and anger, knowing they might consume him. There was nothing to be gained by a confrontation. He was young and relatively powerless, recently married, with two young sons, plus five siblings who depended on him. He was just beginning to build a career and establish a foothold in the country's growing middle class. Gatuguta's manner seemed to suggest that he was punishing himself. In Gathenji's presence, he looked like a man in torment. Gatuguta knew who the young lawyer was, of course. As if to confirm their connection, he would address him as "*Kijana wa Gathenji*." Son of Gathenji.

. . .

THIS WAS STILL Kenyatta's country, a prosperous and relatively stable land whose capital, with its bright bougainvillea-lined corridors, was known as the "City in the Sun." The president had embraced capitalism-friendly policies and had enlisted the skills of Europeans and urged them to stay. For all that, his one-party state adumbrated horrors to come, from corruption to ethnic chauvinism to the assassination of political rivals. The so-called Kenyatta royal family grew wealthy smuggling coffee, jewels, and poached ivory (even as hunters eviscerated the nation's elephant population). The ruling family was untouchable, a fact Father John Kaiser witnessed firsthand one day when he came across a group of elephant poachers on the savanna and asked a game ranger if he planned to take action. The ranger explained that they were connected to *mzee* Kenyatta: certain people he could not arrest.

THE MAN KENYATTA appointed vice president in 1967, Daniel arap Moi, belonged to the small, pastoralist Kalenjin from the far hills of the Rift Valley, and was thus deemed peripheral to the Kikuyu-Luo rivalry. He was lanky and gravelly-voiced, a former herder and schoolteacher, a stolid, awkward teetotaler with a reputation for servility. He seemed little threat to the interests of the Kikuyu elite, who derided him as "the passing cloud," a marionette who could be counted on to serve their interests and then discarded. This was a miscalculation in the extreme. He assumed power on Kenyatta's death, in August 1978, outmaneuvering Kikuyu plots to thwart his ascent.

Moi made it a point to advertise his Sunday attendance at religious services. For a time, the country's churches embraced this pious mask at face value. "Indeed, we regarded him as a great Christian prince, 'Our Beloved President,'" John Kaiser would write in a memoir years later.

Moi liked to call himself the "Professor of Politics" and identified his philosophy as "Nyayo," or footsteps—suggesting he was following the path blazed by Kenyatta. Yet he lacked much of what had made Kenyatta effective: personal charisma and oratorical flourish, the mythic gravitas of an independence hero who'd endured exile and a nine-year prison term. Nor did he have the luck, as Kenyatta had had, of a good economy to help obscure his greed.

Crucially, Moi also lacked the backing of a powerful ethnic group. He would embody, and skillfully exploit, free-floating anxieties about the dominance of the populous, advanced, urbanized Kikuyu, anxieties that had been amplified by their rush into the Rift Valley under Kenyatta. Moi rewarded fellow Kalenjins with top posts in his cabinet, the military, the banks, and the civil service, while publicly condemning tribalism as the "cancer that threatens to eat out the very fabric of our nation." Despite his rhetoric of a unified Kenya, division was the spine of Moi's rule. The Kikuyu and the Luo together comprised more than a third of the nation's population; their numbers would overwhelm him should they ever unite in opposition. A fractious and tribally minded country was one he could rule indefinitely.

GATHENJI ENTERED PRIVATE practice in 1980. On his wall hung a photograph of Moi standing with Kenyatta. He represented clients who had been swept up in government raids in the northeast province bordering Somalia, which was under emergency rule amid threats of succession and widespread violence from militias and bandits, called *shifta*. Suspects were hauled in on gun-running charges on flimsy evidence. Residents were required to be in their homes between the curfew hours of 6:00 P.M. and 6:00 A.M.; someone caught outdoors fifteen minutes later would be charged. Gathenji argued for a broad interpretation of the definition of *home*: If you lived in a hut or a tent and stepped into the bush to relieve yourself, you were still on home ground. Few lawyers took these cases. He risked the perception that he was collaborating with the government's enemies.

The unhappiness with Moi already ran deep, and talk of coups was everywhere. Gathenji was not entirely surprised when, one morning in

August 1982, he turned on the radio and heard that the government had been overthrown. He was living with his wife and two young sons in a Nairobi suburb. Disgruntled junior officers of the Kenya Air Force—mostly Luos—had seized the airports, the post office, and the Voice of Kenya radio station. The country's new masters announced that existing codes of law had been suspended, effective immediately. Gathenji said to his wife, "Did you hear what happened? I no longer have a job." It was impossible to gauge the seriousness of the danger. The continent had become an ever-changing map of violent and quickly deposed strongmen.

In the pandemonium, rioters looted Nairobi, inflicting a disproportionate toll on businesses and homes owned by Asians, who occupied the merchant class and were widely resented as outsiders. Scores, perhaps hundreds, of Asian girls were raped. Moi's loyalists swarmed the city, fanned across the rooftops, and gunned down suspected insurgents and looters. The coup was crushed, and Moi was restored to power almost immediately.

Gathenji drove into town days later to inspect his office. He'd heard a rumor that the capital was safe, but it took only a cursory glance to sense it had been a false one. Bodies were still slumped inside bullet-riddled cars along the road. Televisions were lined up on the sidewalks, and broken glass glinted on the pavement. Every rooftop seemed to bristle with rifles. Soldiers were jittery. They ordered Gathenji to step out of his car and place his hands above his head and his ID card in his mouth. One soldier insisted that Gathenji had stolen his car, and he demanded that he prove otherwise by furnishing registration papers. Gathenji didn't have the papers on him. For a moment, he thought, *This is where I am shot.* On Uhuru Highway, heading back home, he drove frighteningly close to a camouflaged tank, planted in the road, before he realized what it was. He turned the wheel hard and found another way home.

Soon after the abortive takeover, when the courthouses reopened, Gathenji arrived in court and found the dock crowded with defendants, some of them wildlife rangers and civil service workers, who had been charged with celebrating the coup. He watched a few plead guilty and receive jail sentences; in an atmosphere still so highly charged, no judge would leave them unpunished. Gathenji gave the others some advice: Enter not-guilty pleas and wait until the temperature abates. It proved a solid hunch: The cases were soon dismissed. The president wanted to discourage the impression, it appeared, that any of his subjects had reason to celebrate his ouster.

Meanwhile, in Kisiiland, an obscure middle-aged missionary named John Kaiser was trying to assess the country's trajectory. "The coup attempt was a terrible shock to our Asian community & many of them are leaving the country," Kaiser wrote in a letter to Minnesota. "The result will be great harm to the economy of Kenya but you sure couldn't tell the average African that. On the day of the coup attempt I knew all policemen, G. wardens, etc would be in their barracks and huddled around radios so I took the opportunity to picky picky into Masailand a few miles and harvest a nice fat young w. hog." His humor veered into a rare, dark register. "We had to do without such delicacies for many months due to the pressure of the special anti-poaching unit in the Kilgoris area, so we were grateful to the coup leaders & look forward to many more." By the end of the month, Kaiser was sensing the atmosphere had changed permanently. "Things are quiet," he wrote, but added, "I'm afraid the country won't have the same easy peaceful aspect from now on."

5

THE DICTATOR

I T WAS A prescient assessment. The violence, and the fears it
unleashed, proved useful to Moi, who justified his tightening grip
as a safeguard against further anarchy. Paranoia became entrenched as
national policy. Because it was dependent on Western aid and tourism,
Kenya required the barest simulacrum of democracy and the rule of law.
This did not prevent him from outlawing opposition parties and expand-
ing the secret police. He eviscerated judicial independence at a stroke,
pushing through the parliament a law giving him the power to sack any
judge at his whim. The entire justice system fell into his grip; no one
would be prosecuted, or spared prosecution, if he decreed otherwise. The
courts, stacked thick with his stooges, were spiraling into a morass of
corruption so universal that there was little effort to hide it. Three out of
four judges, by Gathenji's estimate, expected bribes; clients expected to
buy their way out of trouble. More than once, he found himself preparing a case meticulously, building it airtight, only to lose on the flimsiest
pretext. Everyone knew: Somewhere, money had changed hands.

To Gathenji, a portal into Moi's nature—a suggestion of his tactics
and how he would employ them—came in 1983 when he destroyed his
ambitious attorney general, Charles Njonjo. Moi accused him of being a
traitor in thrall to a treacherous foreign power attempting to overthrow
the government of Kenya, stripped him of his power, and consigned him
to political limbo. He was allowed to live, technically a free man, but as a
nonentity. It was a lesson to potential rivals not to climb too high.

Gathenji could sense the president losing his mind. He watched as Moi systematically purged Kikuyus from positions of power. Journalists who asked questions found themselves in lockup. In one case that particularly infuriated Gathenji, he represented a woman who had been charged with possessing *Beyond,* an Anglican church magazine banned for its critical remarks about the regime. It had been found in her coffee table, and she was taken into custody with her newborn baby in her arms. He argued she hadn't known the magazine was there; people were known to work out grudges by planting a banned publication on an enemy's premises. The case was dismissed. Police had lost their interest in it anyway; it had been enough to scare the woman. That was the dynamic of dictatorship. To create an all-encompassing chill, you needed to lock up only a few.

"Foreign devils" and Marxists, said to be plotting constantly against the nation, became the convenient pretext Moi trundled out to crush enemies. "Bearded people"—intellectuals—were deemed suspect in their loyalties. Members of Amnesty International became "agents of imperialists" after they criticized his human rights record. He employed a colonial law called the Public Order Act, which forbade nine or more Kenyans from assembling without a government permit. As his search for enemies intensified, Moi dispatched people to "water rooms" under a Nairobi high rise called Nyayo House, where they were forced to stand in excrement-filled water for days. Moi expanded police detention powers so that those accused of capital crimes, such as sedition, could be held for two weeks without a hearing, ample time for torture squads to extract confessions. Scores of such prisoners were hauled before judges who accepted their guilty pleas and handed out four- or five-year sentences.

Moi carried a silver-inlaid ivory mace and wore a rosebud in the lapel of his Saville Row suits. With his claim on legitimate authority so flimsy, he mastered the tactics of large-scale bribery and intimidation. He made a practice of wholesale land stealing, using vast tracts of seized public land as payment to ministers and military officers; this was meant as a hedge against another attempted coup. He handed out stacks of cash to State House visitors and to the masses he met across the country during rounds in his blue open-topped Mercedes.

"I would like ministers, assistant ministers, and others to sing like a parrot after me," Moi said. "That is how we can progress." His subordinates vied to outdo one another in cringing sycophancy, their speeches hailing his mastery of foreign and domestic affairs, his deep compassion—yes, one declared, even the fish of the sea bowed before the Father of the Country. Parliament passed a law declaring that only Moi could possess the title of president, in any realm. Ordinary souls who ran charities and businesses would have to content themselves with the title of chairman. To his worshipers, he was "the Giraffe," an admiring nod both to his height and farsightedness, or "the Glorious."

"Kenya is a one-man state, and that man is the president," Smith Hempstone, the former U.S. ambassador to Kenya, wrote in his memoir, *Rogue Ambassador*.

Paranoid Moi was, but also skilled at shuffling and reshuffling his underlings to keep them forever off balance. "You know, a balloon is a very small thing. But I can pump it up to such an extent that it will be big and look very important," he said. "All you need to make it small again is to prick it with a needle." Under his command were more than one hundred state-owned companies, or parastatals, that did business only with "patriotic" firms; the slightest dissent meant one's contracts evaporated. The British system of pith-helmeted chiefs was gone, supplanted by a vast network of chiefs and subchiefs that provided Moi with intelligence and control all the way to the village level.

The Soviet foothold in Angola and Ethiopia seemed, to American eyes, a harbinger of continental Communist designs, and Moi reaped massive U.S. aid by positioning his country as "a pro-Western, free-market island of stability in the midst of a roiling sea of Marxist chaos," Hempstone would write. "Moi's one-party kleptocracy might not be a particularly pretty boat, but it was not to be rocked."

Here and there, Kenyan clergymen raised their voices, with harsh results. After a Presbyterian minister named Timothy Njoya called for "dissidents, malcontents, critics, fugitives and anyone with a grievance" to speak out, Moi swiftly summoned Protestant and Catholic leaders

Kenyan president Daniel arap Moi became one of Africa's longest-reigning dictators. Photograph by Francine Orr. *Copyright 2003*, Los Angeles Times. *Reprinted with permission.*

to State House to warn against such "subversive" sermons. Njoya was defrocked but won back his position. During marches for constitutional reform, he endured bayonet-wielding soldiers, beatings, tear gas, and jail. Once, attackers doused his parish house with gasoline and set it ablaze. He seemed to feel that it would have been worse if the president had not been a churchgoing man. "Moi's Christianity is our protection," he said. "That's our secret as pastors in Kenya."

Under Moi, brutality walked hand in hand with farce. When Ngugi wa Thiong'o published the novel *Matigari* in 1986, Moi ordered the arrest of its fictional hero after receiving reports that "peasants in Central Kenya were talking about a man called Matigari who was going round the country demanding truth and justice," Ngugi would write. The dictator was forced to settle for confiscating the books.

After the National Council of Churches, a mainstream Protestant body, objected to the abolition of secret balloting, Moi accused an Oregon-based missionary group, which had been digging water wells in northwestern Kenya, of plotting against the government. Police confiscated pellet guns the missionaries used to fend off snakes, a cache of uniforms sewn for local students, and shortwave radios used to communicate in a remote region without telephone service. These, by the state's account, were armaments, military uniforms, and sophisticated communications equipment, all intended to "cause chaos," Moi said, adding this complaint: "Why don't they use their resources to build churches and bring in related things—like Bibles?" He later deported seven American missionaries accused of "sabotage and destabilization." The evidence: a sloppily fabricated letter revealing their scheme to overthrow his government in collaboration with the Ku Klux Klan.

Once, during a spat with Hempstone, Moi sent police to seize a package of school textbooks—they included Booker T. Washington's *Up from Slavery* and Mark Twain's *Huckleberry Finn*—that the U.S. ambassador had donated to a poor rural school. Moi's men denounced the books as "sinister" and said they were designed to "pollute the minds of peace-loving wanachi [masses]."

The president's dour countenance glared from the walls of every shop on every block; his name was plastered on uncountable roads and bridges, stadiums, and schools. He put his profile on coins and a full-frontal close-up on bills. His prosaic daily pronouncements inaugurated the evening news on state-run television: "His Excellency the President Daniel arap Moi proclaimed . . . " He invented Moi Day, a holiday on which his people could express gratitude for his leadership. To celebrate his first decade in power, he commissioned an Italian marble statue in downtown Nairobi's Uhuru Park that depicted his enormous hand, clenched around his ivory mace, rising triumphantly out of Mount Kenya toward the sky. (Considering the mountain was both the nation's namesake and the Kikuyus' most sacred site, no less than the dwelling place of God, the monument carried a certain nasty symbolism.)

By the late 1980s, criticism was growing louder, even from within the superpower that was sponsoring him. Edward Kennedy publicly urged Moi to "pull back from the darkness of torture and repression and return to the bright sunlight of freedom, tolerance and the rule of law."

Faced with such talk, Moi had a typical response: Look at my neighbors. His record, he pointed out again and again, was much better than that of Ethiopia, Sudan, and Uganda. Why should Kenyans expect democracy? he asked, invoking the West's tormented history of race relations. The country had only gained independence in 1963. After breaking from the Crown, he argued, it had taken the United States two hundred years to achieve democracy.

Moi avoided interviews and wrapped himself in enigmatic silence. His authorized biography portrays him as a man who loved his Bible and simple country living, a ruler whose one-party state represented a bulwark against civil war in a cobbled-together nation of forty-two tribes and thirteen languages.

A more plausible glimpse of his psyche can be found in Ngugi wa Thiong'o's novel *Wizard of the Crow*, which proceeds from the moral premise that only fantasy can capture the absurd nightmare that is existence under a Moi-like dictatorship. It describes a megalomaniacal ruler who has been "on the throne so long that even he could not remember when his reign began," and who yearns to erect a tower that stretches to heaven, the better to call on God. At the core of this personality is a corrosive, all-consuming anger, an "insatiable desire for humiliating the already fallen." Having cringed beneath endless abuse during his rise to power, he now demands endless groveling from others. He foments pandemonium and then postures as "a Solomonic prince of peace."

• • •

JOHN KAISER WAS beginning to glimpe the scope of Moi's cruelty as early as 1986 and 1987. He was living in Nyangusu, on the border between the dense farming area of the Kisii and the sparsely populated vastness of Masailand. For years, he'd watched the groups skirmish over cattle and boundary lines, staging elaborate—and mostly harmless—face-offs that Kaiser viewed "more as recreation than a serious war." He'd watched as combatants assembled on either side of the mission football field, hurled menacing insults at one another through the night, and unleashed high arrow volleys that rarely proved fatal. If killing had truly been the aim, Kaiser reasoned, they would have charged with their spears.

But what he witnessed now, in the mid-1980s, had a different feel entirely. Thousands of Kisii peasant farmers were streaming through the countryside with their belongings. Political bosses had ferried in gangs of Masai warriors to burn their homes and destroy their schools. Informants told Kaiser the attackers belonged to the private mercenary army of William ole Ntimama, then the regime's most powerful Masai. Investigating the refugees' claims, Kaiser witnessed government paramilitaries and police evicting farmers from their land en masse as the police stood by passively, intervening only when the Kisii fought back.

In early 1988, Kaiser took the news to his bishop, Tiberius Mugendi, an aging Kenyan whom he regarded as a spiritual father. Mugendi had assumed the violence reflected "the usual fights over cattle rustling" and dismissed the possibility of government involvement: "Impossible!" That would mean the sanction of Moi, and Moi was the country's benevolent father.

Little would be written about the mid-1980s clashes, and Kaiser would later castigate himself for his passivity. Concerning the violence, he believed himself "the best informed Christian" and "the best placed to take effective action." He shared his findings with superiors, as well as with the Church's Justice and Peace branch, but regretted that he didn't go further. He could have contacted Western embassies, human-rights groups, or Bishop Raphael Ndingi of Nakuru, Kenya's most outspoken

Catholic human rights champion. "But I did none of these things. Like Pontius Pilate I washed my hands on the grounds that I had plenty of other work in a busy parish," Kaiser would write. "In so doing I stored up more fuel for a long hot purgatory."

Through the 1980s, his life remained a largely anonymous one of baptisms and herculean building projects, of confessions and sick calls, of rugged trips on his Honda motorcycle down crenellated laterite roads, across mapless valleys and hills. Fever and malaria, dysentery and pneumonia and rabies sent him again and again bearing bodies to ancestral burial plots deep in the bush, praying people into the earth as the clustered women sent up their stylized wailing and the men stood around the grave with spears and pangas, their faces blank and hard. He built tractors and oxcarts, planted crops, demonstrated Western methods of fertilizing. He bought second- and thirdhand trucks, not just to save money but because buying new ones would have enriched government men. He made a wooden wheelchair for a crippled boy and bought the family a donkey to pull it. He took confession in the shade of eucalyptus trees and threw up churches across the countryside, quick, crude structures of red earth and river-bottom sand. He earned a nickname, "Kifaru wa Maskini": Rhino for the Poor.

As often as possible, he vanished into the bush and returned with meat to distribute. The landscape of his missives teemed with animal carcasses, and he took a raconteur's pleasure in recounting close calls. One day near dark, walking along the edge of the woods, he heard "the grumbling of what I was sure were giant forest hogs in the bush," he wrote in one letter. "I loaded up with 00 Buckshot, put some dirt on my face (something it's not used to) & slipped into the bush as quietly as Hiawatha. I could hear the 'pigs' clearly & thought I would easily get one. But as I got deeper in the bush & closer to the grunting I detected a peculiar tone to their symphony & started getting apprehensive. When the grunting became growling the dirt on my face was being washed away by the sweat. I had come right into a pride of lions, at least 9 of them. One huge male stepped out from behind a bush about 15 yards away; he was very angry & nervous & his tail was whipping back & forth; by this time I was backing up full speed in reverse & they were all gentlemen enough to let me pass unmolested."

At one point Minnesota friends supplied him with jacketed bullets, a tin of rifle powder, and an H & R single-shot .30-30 rifle with a mounted Redfield scope. This allowed him to strike an animal from eighty yards. Now, entering the bush, he carried this "lovely little gun" slung on his back, along with his twelve-gauge double-bore shotgun with double-ought buckshot in his hands "in case of something unexpected like a lion or bad buffalo." Once, he tallied up a year's worth of rifle kills:

"12 impala—about 150 pounds. . . .
9 topi—350 lbs & over
8 oribi—40–50 lbs
6 grey duikers—30–40 lbs
2 Reedbucks—100 lbs
2 warthogs—120 lbs
1 waterbuck—300 lbs

That is 40 animals in a bit over a year which is not bad—about 3,560 pounds of meat after butchering."

Another letter from the mid-1980s described the abiding exhilaration of missionary work. "I have just come back from a sick-call which I was lucky to sneak in just before dark & not get rained on," he wrote. "The sick-call was for a young girl who is dying apparently having returned from hospital where the doctors have given her up. She is a very beautiful girl of 18 who received the Sacraments most beautifully and serenely. At such times I would not trade being a priest for any position."

THEN THE SOVIET empire collapsed, and with it the West's justification for reflexive support for Moi. In May 1990, soon after his arrival, Hempstone, the improbable U.S. ambassador—a blunt-spoken former editor of the conservative *Washington Times* who'd parlayed connections in the Bush administration into a diplomatic post—galvanized a weak and demoralized Kenyan opposition with a speech at the Rotary Club of Nairobi. From now on, he said, the United States would steer money to nations that "nourish democratic institutions, defend human rights, and practice multiparty politics." The regime's mouthpiece, the *Kenya Times*, answered his challenge with headlines like this: SHUT UP, MR. AMBASSADOR.

Dissidents took courage, even as the regime characterized the call for democratic pluralism as the latest thrust of white domination. The year was full of grim and portentous spectacles, including the murder of Robert Ouko, the country's urbane foreign minister, who had been compiling documents on high-level corruption. He was discovered on a hill, shot twice through the head, his body charred, a .38 revolver lying nearby. Suicide, announced police. The president promised that "no stone would be left unturned" in finding answers. To demonstrate his commitment to the truth, he called in New Scotland Yard, which took four hundred depositions over four months and discovered that Ouko had been at odds with Nicholas Biwott, Moi's widely feared right-hand man. The investigation also pointed to Hezekiah Oyugi, the secretary of internal security.

The head New Scotland Yard detective, John Troon, complained that he was not allowed to interview either of these two key suspects, who were briefly arrested and released for "lack of evidence." Moi closed the investigation and refused to accept New Scotland Yard's report unless Troon delivered it personally (a condition tough to meet, since Troon had already left the country). Moi appointed a commission of inquiry to take testimony, then dissolved it before it reached conclusions, sending the case back into the hands of the Kenyan police. By such methods, Moi could drag out an investigation forever. This would prove one of his signature moves. Memories would fade, and witnesses would vanish (within a few years after the killing, eleven people connected to the case, including Oyugi, would perish, some under strange circumstances).

The Ouko case would be etched in the national psyche as an illustration both of Moi's ruthlessness and his wiliness. He had used New Scotland Yard as an unwitting pawn in a cover-up. The U.S. ambassador, for his part, had no clear evidence of who had killed Ouko, or why, but "what did appear obvious was that the murderer was too highly placed and powerful to be apprehended," Hempstone wrote.

It was a season of smoke and truncheons and proliferating dissent. Activists and lawyers launched a group called the Forum for the Restoration of Democracy (FORD). Moi rounded up dozens of opposition figures; police fired on protesters and raided an Anglican cathedral where they sought sanctuary. The country's seventeen Roman Catholic bishops—representing Kenya's largest Christian group—issued a pastoral letter denouncing the ruling party's "unlimited authority," and complained that "the least sign of dissent" was deemed subversion. Mild as this seemed, it represented relatively bold language for the cautious bishops. In late summer, a milk truck plowed into a car carrying an Anglican bishop named Alexander Muge, who had denounced corruption and land grabbing by unnamed regime potentates; a parliamentary commission ruled it "death by misadventure," a verdict tough for many Kenyans to embrace. Moi's labor minister had recently warned that Muge would "see fire and may not leave alive" if he strayed into his district.

Though Kenya remained the largest recipient of U.S. assistance in sub-Saharan Africa—it had received $35 million the year before in economic aid and another $11 million in military aid—American congressional leaders now urged a freeze. With the Marxist menace dead, Moi's carte blanche had been yanked.

One day, the phone rang on Charles Mbuthi Gathenji's desk. The man on the other end was a reporter for the state-run television station. He wanted to know the lawyer's views on a recent controversy: The new chairman of the Kenyan Law Society, Paul Muite, was using his platform to denounce the president and call for reforms. Pro-government lawyers, for their part, had decried such "meddling" in politics.

Where did Mr. Gathenji stand?

He saw nothing wrong with Muite's remarks, he said; they reflected the sentiments of a good portion of Kenya's legal community, and nobody called it political meddling when lawyers *praised* Moi.

Gathenji hung up. Soon, he learned that his statement had made the nightly news. He realized that he'd been incautious. He knew this even before the letter came in the mail demanding payment for back taxes he supposedly owed, equivalent to more than six thousand U.S. dollars. He had ten days to pay, or his home would be seized. He knew other lawyers were getting similar letters. He called his accountant. Numbers were examined. He did owe money—about a fourth of the figure claimed. He paid up. He didn't want to give the government any excuse to harass him.

Now he understood the reason for the reporter's call. As dissent grew bolder, Moi wanted to know who was on his side.

MEANWHILE, IN KISIILAND, Kaiser, already in his late fifties, was feeling the effects of age. He described himself as "the chap who never got malaria for 20 years"—he'd been able to banish the early symptoms with a course of chloroquine—but in early 1990 the disease sent him to the hospital for a five-day course of quinine, incapacitated him completely for three days afterward, and stripped twenty pounds from his frame. "Malaria is no longer a minor nuisance & from now on wherever I go the net goes along," he wrote. Soon he was racing around on his Honda motorbike—a *piki-piki* in Swahili—joking, "I use a motorcycle every day but at a sedate & dignified pace such as befits my age & position." There had been some bad spills in recent years. Once, as he rode after dark, the blinding light from an oncoming bus sent him off the tarmac, and a sharp edge of asphalt opened a big gash in his shin. Another time, doing forty as he headed down a narrow gravel road to a sick call, he swerved to avoid a cow, breaking his collarbone and two ribs. Alone on the empty country road, he'd been forced to pull himself to his feet and find his way to the hospital without fainting from the pain.

The culture of corruption was making itself felt at every level. To repair his motorcycle meant paying a 200 percent bribe for the spare parts. The corrosion of the rule of law was increasingly painful and personal. That March, he learned that a friend named James Ongera had been working on his farm when three agents of the General Services Unit attacked him, for reasons that were unclear. His spine was broken, and his body was dragged to the Masai border and mutilated, apparently to convince the Kisii that the Masai had been responsible. The family brought suit against the three agents; the courts threw it out.

"There are almost daily murders in the Nyangusu area and the real culprits are the various government officials who use the army and police to drive out settlers in Masailand so that the land can then be grabbed and sold for huge profits," Kaiser wrote in the summer of 1991. He added that his bishop, Tiberius Mugendi, now in his early seventies, "looks old & worn out and I suppose it is no wonder considering the chaos of his ministry." Kaiser's own energy was ebbing. Even a proud man had to concede the toll. A year would pass without a hunting excursion, apparently a record hiatus. "I have quite a bit of building to do in finishing up the convent & it poops me out in a hurry; in a few years I'll have to find a rocking chair," he wrote. Reminders of his mortality sometimes seemed to ambush him. Looking at himself, he glimpsed a reflection of his father, Arnold, who had died five years back. "I got a haircut a week ago & the guy had a mirror in front & another one in back & so I could see him trimming the back of my neck & I said, 'Hey, that's not John that's Arnold Kaiser.' Look at that grey hair & the wrinkles in the neck; it was a shock."

An avid newspaper reader and BBC listener, he was closely following the unfolding political drama. International donors kept turning the screws on Moi's increasingly desperate and beleaguered regime. The United States slashed nearly a quarter of its assistance, including fifteen million dollars in military help. In November 1991, an array of Western benefactors voted to suspend World Bank aid until Moi embraced democracy and curbed corruption.

Considering foreign aid comprised 30 percent of the national budget, this was no small blow. Days later, Moi hastily assembled party delegates at a Nairobi sports stadium and stunned them with an announcement. He would rescind Section 2A of the constitution, which had made Kenya a de jure one-party state nine years earlier.

He made it clear that the West was forcing his hand. "Tribal roots go much deeper than the shallow flower of democracy," he would say. "That is something the West failed to understand. I'm not against multi-partyism but I am unsure about the maturity of the country's politics."

What followed fulfilled his warning—or, as many understood it, his threat—that in an ethnically fractured nation, democracy would lead to bloodshed.

Facing ruin, he sought insurance in the usual playbook: the exacerbation of ethnic antipathies. To ensure party supremacy, militias descended on opposition strongholds, purging rival voters from areas where they were registered.

Village after village erupted in flames; within several years, more than 1,000 people would be killed and 300,000 displaced. Moi banned public rallies and sent helmeted agents plowing into defiant crowds on horseback and on foot, firing tear gas, swinging truncheons and pickax handles. By early 1992, even Kenya's cautious Catholic bishops were uniting to accuse the government of complicity in the brutality. Regime hard-liners publicly urged the eviction of groups that had settled in the Rift Valley after independence. The Kikuyus were "foreigners" there, and the land they'd occupied for decades constituted *madoadoa,* or "black spots," on the map: they needed to be erased.

6

THE CLASHES

As violence roiled the countryside through the early 1990s, and as reports of the bloodletting reached Kaiser's parish in increasing numbers, his rift with his elderly bishop, Tiberius Mugendi, grew wider. The two had been close; Kaiser regarded him as a "Spiritual Father." Mugendi's autocratic streak was deep: He bristled when subordinates challenged him. He would travel to the various parishes of his diocese to interrogate young catechists on matters of doctrine. They were to recite correct answers about the mysteries of the Host and the rosary; a sloppy answer might provoke a slap.

At one church meeting, Tom Keane, an Irish priest from the Mill Hill order, suggested this approach showed a lack of faith in the priests' ability to teach the children. Other priests echoed the sentiment. Days later, Mugendi summoned Keane to his house, accused him of leading a rebellion against him, and ordered him out of his diocese immediately. Mugendi's back was turned as he spoke, and Keane would remember, years later, the sight of the veins bulging on the enraged bishop's neck.

Keane grasped the subtext: To criticize your bishop in public was to cause him to lose face. It was a display of Western effrontery. It was not to be done.

Kaiser, for his part, never absorbed the lesson. He criticized not only the bishop's method of grilling confirmation candidates, but of promulgating doctrines, such as a three-part liturgy, that preceded Vatican II reforms. Kaiser also attacked the bishop's judgment in appointing a headmistress to the local girls school whom Kaiser considered dishonest. As

John Kaiser's passport photo. One of the few American members of the London-based Mill Hill Missionaries society, he inveighed against what he saw as his order's feckless response to state violence in Kenya. He would be past middle age himself by the time he began waging a public campaign against the Moi regime. *Photograph courtesy of Francis Kaiser.*

was his habit, he carefully and bluntly enumerated his reasons in a letter, with numbered points and subpoints. The headmistress was often absent from the school, he explained, had collected money without reporting it, and lingered provocatively around married men. "Let me ask you in all respect, my Father-in-Christ," Kaiser wrote. "What qualities did you see in this woman or in her past record that you would recommend her as the H/M of a Christian School?"

The dispute with his bishop ran deeper still. With villages erupting in a pandemonium of flame, arrows, and machetes, Kaiser questioned Mugendi's refusal to take a forceful stand against what seemed clearer by the day: that the regime was exciting the Masai and Kisii to war. It was Kaiser's insistence on doing so in public, before other churchmen— including young African priests—that Mugendi found intolerable. The American priest was breaching the deep-dyed cultural prohibition: An

African bishop, like a president, was a paternal personage not to be challenged. "Here in Africa you never discuss the Father, much less criticize him in public," Kaiser wrote.

Other priests warned Kaiser that his style was too confrontational. Ignoring pleas to back down, Kaiser wrote a letter, detailing his objections to Mugendi's leadership and pointing out "the Catholic failure as regards Human Rights."

Mugendi had had enough. He sent word to Kaiser's superiors: Remove this priest from my diocese. Maurice McGill, the London-based superior general of the Mill Hill order, informed Kaiser that he should leave immediately, and invited him to spend some time at Mill Hill headquarters in London.

"I can hardly be appointed away from this place without an appointment to someplace else," Kaiser wrote back. "Your invitation to visit Mill Hill is kind, but at this point I need clear orders and not an invitation. I will make no preparations for leaving here until I have heard from you and I would consider at least two weeks, but preferably four weeks, to be a reasonable time to finish up here and say goodbye to those I have lived with for nearly thirty years." He said Mugendi had refused to speak to him that morning.

"I confess, Maurice, that I am deeply hurt by your action or rather lack of action as well as those Mill Hill superiors who have assisted you in withdrawing me. I would have thought that a minimum response from a superior would have been to ask the Bishop to put into writing the reasons for expelling me," he continued. "I would not for any reason in the world contradict Bishop Mugendi except that I should think that not to do so would be disobedient to the clear teaching of the church. I will make a report of this affair for the priests here, the Kenya Hierarchy & the papal representative & also send you a copy."

He distributed his letter widely within the Mill Hill organization and the African Church. He also reportedly sent a copy to the Vatican, a further humiliation for Mugendi. "I told him not to write the letter," Keane recalled. "If he had something to say and do, he had to do it, regardless of whether it destroyed you or not. John would reprimand you and he wouldn't care if you were hurt or not. He had also that cruel side in him, that justice was everything." Keane said that Mugendi wept when he read the letter, and that it caused "tremendous hurt" between the mostly European Mill Hill members and the African Church. "They didn't like the white man attacking the black bishop," Keane said. "It wasn't in John's vocabulary to express regret." It seemed no coincidence that people called him the "rhino priest." This was the same John Kaiser, Keane recalled, whose answers to a psychological test administered by Mill Hill earned him a comparison to the animal said to charge friend and foe alike.

"My conscience is clear and I will not apologize for any of my statements or opinions," Kaiser wrote to a friend that June. "I can always admit & lament the fact I am an undiplomatic clod, but for me that is not the point."

Kaiser remained in Kisii as the elections approached. There was little doubt about the outcome. Violence was not Moi's only tactic. The registration forms of illiterate voters could be invalidated by purposely misspelling their names; by these and other means, an estimated one million Kenyans were prevented from voting. The American ambassador was troubled by his nation's decision not to boycott the election. Hempstone reasoned that such a boycott might have led to civil war, and yet "having put our imprimatur on a flawed electoral process, we seemed to be certifying that second-rate democracy was good enough for black people."

In one sense, Moi had read his country accurately: The vote fractured along ethnic lines. By and large, political loyalties were not animated by ideology, not defined by particular stances on foreign and domestic issues, but by the understanding that whoever controlled State House would lavish the national resources—jobs, schools, roads—on their own. When the results were counted, Moi had won 1.9 million votes, 36.5 percent of the total. His three opponents divided the rest. He solemnly lifted the Bible and took the oath of office for a five-year term. After riots and protests, after tear gas and truncheons, after a crush of domestic and international pressure, after the long-awaited introduction of multiparty politics, the dictator had wrested from his ordeal a new prize: the veneer of democratic legitimacy.

KAISER CLUNG STUBBORNLY to his job in the Kisii Diocese, until finally, in the summer of 1993, his superior general sent him what he called "a letter firm in tone," ordering him to leave immediately. He said one final Sunday Mass, packed his few belongings, and departed for the missionary house in Sotik, a few hours east. He was sixty years old, and devastated. "Exile," he called it. He had given three decades to the Kisii people; he knew their language and customs; he had baptized thousands and heard countless confessions; he considered himself one of them. And he had loved Bishop Mugendi.

Kaiser was frustrated by the superior general's failure to give clear orders regarding his next assignment. "These days it's mighty hard to get a superior to say 'I appoint you to Timbuktoo, period,' " he wrote.

Kaiser would not be nudged out noiselessly; he was unwilling to establish roots elsewhere without having had a face-to-face meeting with Mugendi. He wanted an official release from his duties in the diocese. It's possible that Kaiser realized he'd gone too far and wanted forgiveness.

Kaiser drove to the bishop's house in Kisii and insisted on seeing him. Mugendi declined. Kaiser waited. Hours passed. Finally Mugendi emerged, walked past Kaiser, and climbed into his car. He refused to acknowledge the priest.

"I want your blessing," Kaiser said. The man who would hurl his body before the bloody juggernaut of Kenyan history, daring it to change course or crush him, lowered himself to his knees before the bishop's car. The bishop must have known that his most obstinate priest was prepared to wait forever. He relented, dismissing him with a quick and perfunctory wave, his hand tracing a cross in the air. It was enough. Kaiser climbed to his feet.

• • •

SINCE LATE 1992, Gathenji had been receiving ominous reports about the storm brewing in Enoosupukia, a high, fertile plateau of terraced hills in the Rift Valley. Once the grazing area of Masai pastoralists, the land was now tended by Kikuyu farmers who grew maize, beans, and potatoes. The Catholic Church had asked Gathenji to investigate claims that Kikuyu landowners were being threatened with eviction by the fiery William Ntimama, Moi's minister for local government and the nation's most powerful Masai. He was the most flamboyant advocate of *Majimboism,* which called for a constitutional reform that would turn the clock back a century. Groups lacking ancestral roots in a particular region would be forced to abandon their lands without compensation.

"Lie low like envelopes or be cut down to size," he reportedly told the Kikuyu, warning them that their fate would match that of the Ibo, a reference to the Nigerian ethnic group slaughtered en masse in Biafra. It didn't matter that the Kikuyu had been settling in this area of the Rift Valley for decades, and that he'd sanctioned the influx himself. Nor did it matter that the Kikuyu possessed deeds to land they'd legitimately purchased; he declared them "mere pieces of paper."

Ntimama portrayed himself as a man betrayed: The Kikuyu had backed his rival in the recent election. "People say I hate the Kikuyu," he was quoted as saying. "But it is they who have driven me to that extremism. Because they were never grateful for what we had done for them." He ordered their eviction. His pretext: to preserve the land as a water-catchment area for the Masai, whose traditional grazing grounds were supposedly parched by the misuse of the Kikuyu interlopers. In his rhetoric, the Kikuyu were an extension of the colonial yoke. "The British suppressed us, and we cannot have the Kikuyu suppressing us again!"

In October 1993, five hundred Masai warriors dressed in crimson wrappings swarmed over the surrounding hills and descended on Enoosupukia. They overran the village with bows and arrows, spears, clubs, and machetes, lancing people and hacking them down in their gardens. "They slashed people like caught antelope," one witness reported.

Among the attackers were game rangers, police, and members of the army disguised in *shukas*. In some cases, they killed with silencer-equipped guns and then slashed their victims to conceal the bullet wounds, the better to perpetrate the myth that the attack was a "spontaneous" uprising of local Masai. Police watched passively, intervening only when the Kikuyu mounted resistance. In some cases, the faces and names of the attackers were familiar to the victims as those of their long-time neighbors. Some thirty thousand Kikuyus were chased from their homes, and several days of fighting left at least twenty people dead. The victims were men; the Masai had allowed women and children to escape.

Ntimama announced that the Kikuyu would not be allowed to return to their land. "No way," the *Washington Post* quoted him as saying. "They entered there illegally. They might as well go back where they came from. . . . It's survival, okay?"

The legal system's response to Enoosupukia and other ethnic massacres was indifference. Attorney General Amos Wako admitted that only seventeen murder charges had been brought in connection with the clashes—representing perhaps 1 percent of the murders—with just eight convictions. Asked why he didn't prosecute Ntimama for incitement, Kenya's top lawman replied that such a move would cause riots. Ntimama himself was personally amiable and totally without remorse. Regarding the Rift Valley violence, Ntimama laughed and said, "We never really cleansed anywhere other than Enoosupukia." Then he laughed again and said, "I deny ethnic cleansing." He shrugged at the thought of what had happened to the Enoosupukia refugees. Who cared?

By the thousands, those refugees had endured a five-mile trudge down the mountain, saddled with their belongings, driving mules weighted with huge bags, to a squalid hillside tent city called Maela.

There they would meet an American priest who was in exile himself, and change him.

7

THE TERRIBLE PLACE

OF MAELA, PEOPLE remembered the dust. They tasted it in their teeth and coughed it into their hands and slept with it in their blankets. It covered the ground, pale and powder-fine, inches thick, and was lofted by the breeze and the bare feet of children. It enveloped the polyethelene hovels and one-room clapboard shacks where families of six or eight huddled against the nighttime cold and sweated in the daytime heat, so close to the sky, seven thousand feet high. It turned hair white and made it stand straight up. It coated the wattle-and-dab shack where Kaiser lived without water or electricity, where at night he ate by the light of a paraffin lamp and lay uneasily on his cot, unable to sleep amid the wailing of children. Under the chilly rain, the dust turned into an expanse of thick mud, and people sank into it with their blankets to sleep.

"This terrible place," Kaiser called it. He arrived in July 1994, sixty-one years old, having been appointed chaplain by his new superior, Colin Davies, the bishop of Ngong. Nearly a year had passed since his eviction from Kisii. He'd been to a theological retreat in Ireland, had taken a Swahili course in Tanzania, and had received medical treatment for pinched nerves in Kenya. He'd waited anxiously for a new appointment. He arrived in Maela at the coldest time of the year. He did not speak Gikuyu, the tongue of the refugees, who comprised the eight thousand poorest of the thirty thousand Kikuyus forced from their farms during the Enoosu-pukia raids. Most were children. The day he arrived, Kaiser encountered a two-year-old girl sitting in the dust. He lifted her; she clung to him desperately. It was a startling reaction in a land where small children, usually carried everywhere by mothers or siblings, were hesitant among strangers. In their torpor and despair, the priest learned, many parents were letting their children wander the camp alone.

Some mothers boiled cardboard in the water and told their children they were drinking tea. Dozens had already died from disease, hunger, malnutrition, and ghastly accidents. Kids were scalded as they reached for saucepans and were brought to him with blistered, peeling skin; infants asphyxiated on the fumes from cooking fires.

Kaiser met an emaciated sixty-year-old man named Julius Chege, who had wounds from the raid and had starved himself to feed his wife and five children. His was a typical Maela story. For fifteen years, his family had grown maize and beans on a small plot in Enoosupukia. Masai raiders had burned their home and claimed the land as theirs. Chege asked Kaiser to look after his family. Days after rushing him to the hospital, Kaiser was returning his body to his widow for burial.

At one point, Kaiser visited Nairobi archbishop Maurice Otunga and asked him to visit Maela to witness the conditions, "but he refused without giving a reason," Kaiser wrote. He suspected the archbishop feared his visit would provoke the government. The bishops had denounced government failures, "but we haven't done much to confront such evil with action," Kaiser wrote.

He pleaded with friends in the States to send donations. He prayed over the dead. He organized a group of men to dig a latrine trench. He said Mass every day for a group of about forty of the faithful; on Sundays, there were hundreds. "I pray that those who are responsible for their great sin may repent and return the farmers to their lands," he wrote in a letter, "or they will surely burn in hell because their days are numbered on this earth."

The United Nations Development Programme had assumed control of humanitarian relief at the camp, but Kaiser regarded them as "a bunch of bureaucrats with high-sounding titles" who were effectively useless, and possibly corrupt. Kaiser attributed the UN's passivity to its dependence on the Kenyan government; it needed access to the airports and

Mombasa Harbor to supply larger refugee camps in northern Kenya, Somalia, Ethiopia, and Sudan. "Compared with these big camps poor little Maela is (in U.N. judgment) expendable," Kaiser wrote.

Through the window of his shack, Kaiser watched the lines forming, hundreds of women and children waiting with plastic containers for meager rations of corn, beans, and cooking oil. When charcoal stopped coming, people chewed corn kernels raw.

When Kaiser ventured up to Enoosupukia, he found it desolated by fire and looting. Abandoned dogs wandered deserted dirt roads and farms. The Masai had moved their herds of goat and cattle onto the fields, and the crops were rotting. It reminded Kaiser of Longfellow's *Evangeline,* a poem he'd memorized as a boy, with its depiction of a ravaged village returned to "the forest primeval." This was Masai land now, Ntimama warned: It would be a "declaration of war" for the Kikuyu to attempt to return. Nevertheless, some Masai elders visited the camp to plead with the Kikuyu to come back. They were going hungry without farmers to grow the crops. This undermined the regime's characterization of the violence as a spontaneous uprising by Masai looking to reclaim traditional grazing lands.

At the camp, amid constant fear of further Masai raids, children were grappling with the horrors they had witnessed. Many had lost parents and brothers and sisters. Nuns gave them crayons and paper and asked them to record what they had experienced. The images they produced were startling: red-cloaked warriors surging through the village like a wall of fire, slaughtering fleeing residents and stealing cattle, while government men stood watching passively with their guns.

ONE DAY, THE presidential motorcade came up the road toward Maela, lifting crimson dust. Tall and striking in his elegant custom-tailored suit, carrying his ubiquitous mace, His Excellency stepped out of his gleaming car. Moi did not venture into the thick of the misery, standing instead on a nearby football field as refugees swarmed around him. He told them he loved them, as he did all the people of Kenya, and that they had suffered enough. It was the president's wish for all Kenyans to live in harmony. It was multiparty politics, he explained, that had fractured the country along tribal lines. He denounced his political rivals as opportunists who sought to profit from the people's misfortune. He went on, in effect, to blame the refugees for their plight. He told the Kikuyu to respect the way of life of their Rift Valley "hosts" (meaning the Masai and Kalenjin), to cultivate mutual understanding with them, and to join them in supporting the ruling party, KANU. Only with unity would there be progress. He promised they would be resettled before Christmas.

It was a measure of Moi's success at illusion, and of the refugees' desperation, that his speech was greeted with elation, and that party operatives were soon busy signing up new members. Now, at last, the president himself knew of their plight. The party was their salvation.

Shortly afterward, the government established a handpicked "registration committee," intended, ostensibly, to separate legitimate Enoosupukia landowners—who were supposed to receive compensation—from alleged squatters, described by one government official as "joyriders" looking for free land.

Kaiser believed the process was fraudulent, another bit of cruel play-acting, and the evidence for this was soon unassailable: Everywhere he looked, he could find refugees in possession of landownership documents who were not permitted to register. Kaiser decided to compile a list of all eight thousand refugees himself. He wouldn't have time to complete it.

MAELA NEEDED TO be erased. Word of the hideous conditions had reached the international press. Human rights groups were raising a clamor. The camp had become an embarrassment.

Kaiser sensed its imminent destruction on December 22, 1994, when a policeman ordered him to travel to Nairobi to surrender his shotgun. There was no explanation. A raid was being planned, he surmised, and they wanted him in the capital when it happened; they did not need an old priest with a weapon in the way.

The next morning, rather than travel several hours to Nairobi, Kaiser went to the local station and turned in the gun. Around noon, soon after his return to Maela, the road to the camp was closed, and by early evening a convoy of government trucks had assembled on the outskirts. They swept in—police and soldiers and members of the party youth wing—as refugees were cooking dinner over their charcoal fires.

The district officer, Hassan Mohammed, gave his order over a loudspeaker: They had twenty minutes to evacuate. They would be liberated from the horrors of Maela, taken to the "Promised Land," a place called Moi Ndabi, which the president had named after himself. Nobody knew what was going to happen. There was singing among the refugees, a sense of hope and promise mingled with a prickling of dread. Kaiser confronted Mohammed: Why was this happening at night? Why had nobody been informed? Why hadn't the press been notified, or the relief agencies, or the Church?

Kaiser was arrested and confined to his shack, where he was kept under police watch. All night from his veranda, he watched government men yank plastic sheeting off the tents, burn the frames, herd refugees onto trucks, and beat those who scrambled back for forgotten belongings. The trucks dumped more than one thousand refugees on a small patch of arid farmland forty miles away. Another seven hundred were dumped in an open stadium forty miles from Nairobi, which was soon sealed by police. Many others were scattered across the countryside on what the government called their "ancestral lands," the province that matched the birthplace listed on their identification cards.

By the regime's Orwellian account to the press, the refugees had themselves requested removal from Maela, fearing violence from local farmers. Turned into the regime's shill, the United Nations Development Programme's coordinator, Kilian Kleinschmit, denied that Maela residents had been forcibly evicted—they had wanted to leave Maela anyway and had boarded the trucks voluntarily. He could not approve of dumping people in the open stadium, however. This was a "bone of contention," he said. "We are investigating the matter."

Back at Maela, Kaiser remained among several thousand still huddled in the cold and rain. Police sealed the road, preventing doctors and other relief workers from entering. No food and water could get in. The plan was apparently to force the refugees' flight.

A few hundred were sheltered in a church, under Kaiser's watch, when police appeared on the morning of December 27 to demand their removal. He told police they had no authority there and demanded to see their chief, who said he was only following orders. By Kaiser's account, he replied that his authority derived from the bishops and from God, "and they by far outranked his authority."

About ten o'clock that night, the police materialized at his door. They were polite. They explained that they had orders to evict him. Kaiser replied that the refugees were under his protection; he had promised not to leave them.

We have orders, Father.

He announced that he would not go peacefully, and that he was obligated to resist them.

There were six or seven of them, and they converged on him. Even in his early sixties, he was tall and strong, with big hands, and a wrestler's training lived in his muscles. He pushed them off. Again and again, as they tried to force him through the doorway, he twisted out of their grasp. Soon they had overpowered him, knocked him down, cuffed his wrists behind his back, and carried him outside.

Shoot me and my troubles are over, Kaiser said, *but yours are just beginning.*

Another priest, Francis Mwangi, watched them carry Kaiser to the back of their Land Rover and toss him to the floor "like luggage."

They sat on him, boots crushing Kaiser's limbs and head against the metal floor, his head twisted to the side. As the truck lurched away, Kaiser could hear the screaming as police stormed the church. Despite Kaiser's vehement insistence that he stay to watch over the people, Mwangi insisted on accompanying him. He knew how easy it would be for Kaiser to disappear into Lake Naivasha. It would be harder with a witness. The truck heaved for an hour and a half through the night. In pain, Kaiser pleaded with them to loosen his handcuffs.

They dumped the two priests on the road outside the Naivasha Catholic church, giving them blunt orders: They were never to return to Maela. To sneak back would mean another beating, another eviction.

Kaiser called his removal from Maela "a great grief," even as he began recounting, with a touch of boastfulness, how it had taken six or seven men to subdue him. Paul Muite, a lawyer and leading dissident politician, summoned reporters from the *Daily Nation* and the *Standard,* seeking to make news of the event. The newspapers reported Kaiser's arrest briefly and perfunctorily. He had become a spectacle, albeit still a minor one.

THE VICTIMS OF the Masai raids refused to disappear from the news. The five-man executive committee of the Kenyan Roman Catholic bishops issued a statement, denouncing the "heartless treatment" of refugees. "Maela is only an example of widespread inhuman policy of attacking all those seen to be in some way anti-KANU," read the statement, the most forcefully worded the Church had made. But the bishops did not blame the misery on President Moi. Instead, they announced, "It is obvious that the president has been deceived by his administrators." The dictator, in short, was in the dark. This explanation would parrot Moi's own defense; the Church might have been acting as his public-relations wing.

In remarks to the international press, Kaiser showed signs that he was willing to push a little further. "The main engine behind the clashes is the government, not tribal animosity," Kaiser said, naming Ntimama as a force behind the land grabbing. He also accused the UN of corruption and excessive credulity toward regime propaganda.

Kaiser was soon packing for his new assignment: the far-flung parish of Lolgorien, in the heart of Masailand, at the western edge of the Masai Mara game park, not far from the Tanzania border. It was about as far as his bishop could send him without removing him from the country altogether. "No doubt to protect me," Kaiser wrote.

Yet Maela had changed him, and when he met with his bishop and other priests to discuss church business, his criticism was unrelenting: They were doing too little. "Some people aren't talking who are supposed to be talking," he would say. "We are the church! We should not keep quiet when people are suffering!" He was also critical of church leaders who took donations from politicians to build churches, a common practice. "We were cautioning him—'In Kenya, you have to shut up,'" Mwangi later said. "We were telling Kaiser, 'Let's move slowly.' He didn't want to compromise with anybody."

Every sensible churchman knew how easily accidents could be arranged for people. How a car might materialize on a dark road and drive you into a tree. How an assassination could be made to look like a highway robbery. The list of mysteriously slain priests went back generations. Months earlier, another had been murdered on a highway near the capital. It looked like a holdup, but in the absence of trustworthy investigations and a credible court system, who could ever be sure? The ambiguities extended the aura of menace. Everyone knew how vulnerable a man with a Bible was out in the bush.

8

THE RAID

CHARLES MBUTHI GATHENJI was asleep beside his wife, Hannah, in their Ngong home in the small hours of October 19, 1995, when they were awakened by insistent pounding on the door. Moments earlier, the elderly man hired to guard the house had looked up and seen a pack of heavily armed men converging on the front gate, at which point he'd decided it was prudent to disappear into the surrounding cornfields. Even before he reached the front door, Gathenji could hear the men moving around the outside of the house, encircling it. At the door, he found a wall of plainclothes policemen from the Criminal Investigation Department. Leading them was an assistant police commissioner, immaculately tailored in a sharp gray suit, a handkerchief flowering from his breast pocket. He was businesslike. His men were here to search the house.

"There's something you have that we need," he said.

Gathenji stood watching in his pajamas as they poured into his living room, study, bathrooms, and bedrooms, yanking open drawers, riffling through magazines, pulling books off the shelves, plowing through boxes and suitcases. It was a modest stone-walled home with three bedrooms, a red-tile roof, servant quarters, and a cattle shed.

At first, Gathenji didn't grasp what they were after. Only after police mentioned their interest in certain "statements" from military men did the truth dawn on him. Of late, he had been trying to bring a case against Minister William Ntimama for inciting the Enoosupukia massacre. The attorney general had ignored his pleas to prosecute. Gathenji had then taken another route available through the Kenyan justice system, bringing a private prosecution against the Masai demagogue on behalf of an aggrieved Enoosupukia farmer whose property had been destroyed by Masai raiders. The case had bordered on the carnivalesque. During one court date, several thousand Masai, bused into town, crammed the courtroom and thronged the streets outside in a show of intimidation, forcing Gathenji to elbow his way through a mob of people, who, luckily, did not recognize him. This time, the attorney general simply stepped in and threw out the case.

Not long afterward, as Gathenji plotted strategies to appeal, a slim young Kalenjin quietly appeared at his office, claiming to be an army officer. He said that his conscience was troubling him, that he and other officers had been taken to State House, where cabinet members had promised bounties for carrying out murders and arson attacks against the regime's enemies in the Rift Valley. Gathenji had asked the man to bring him signed written statements attesting to these claims. Soon he had collected twenty-four of them. He studied them carefully, trying to gauge their authenticity. He looked for excessive duplication, for hints that the accounts were derivatives of a master template. Were the statements part of some kind of setup? No, he reasoned, that made little sense. If Moi's police wanted to frame him, it would have been far easier merely to plant drugs on him. The statements ultimately struck him as genuine. He knew they were potentially explosive; he planned to use them to revive the case against Ntimama.

Now, as the plainclothesmen ransacked his house, he realized that the intelligence services had somehow discovered what he possessed. Perhaps someone had betrayed his army source.

It was past 1:00 A.M. Gathenji's teenage sons had been asleep in an outer house. The elder one, Leroy, was now awake and watching in a mounting panic.

Searching the shelves, one policeman found a piece of dissident literature and sneered at Gathenji, asking, "What are you doing with this?" It was a copy of Koigi wa Wamwere's *Conscience on Trial: Why I Was Detained: Notes of a Political Prisoner in Kenya*. Yet after three hours of searching the house and the cattle barn, the plainclothesmen had not found what they were seeking.

The assistant commissioner in his fine dark suit stood before Gathenji. He was not about to leave without the papers.

"Give me the statements or I will be forced to take you to Nakuru," Gathenji would later recall him saying, "and I can't guarantee that you will come back."

Gathenji did not consider this an empty threat. He had heard the stories about Nakuru National Park. It was one of the places they took people who required torturing. They strung you from a tree branch until gangrene overtook your limbs.

Gathenji explained that he didn't keep work documents at home. The assistant commissioner said, "Let's go to your office."

Gathenji was allowed to put on a shirt, pants, and a jacket. At one point, he went to pick up his telephone, which had been knocked off its cradle in the commotion. He put it to his ear and heard a dial tone. The existence of the dial tone appeared to anger one of the policemen, and as they led Gathenji outside, he understood why. His phone was not supposed to be functioning; one of the telephone wires strung along the house had been severed. It was, however, the wrong telephone wire. They had approached this raid like a military operation, taking pains to prevent the possibility that he might summon help from an activist, a journalist, or another lawyer.

He said good-bye to his children and was led into the back of a Peugeot. His wife insisted on following him in a separate car. He was squeezed between two plainclothesmen as the Peugeot purred toward Nairobi. He heard someone mention "sedition," a chilling word, a capital offense. His office was on the fourth floor of a seven-story building across from the stately Central Law Courts, which were presided over by an enormous statue of Jomo Kenyatta seated with his fly whisk. Across the capital, he knew, preparations would be under way that day for the celebration of Kenyatta Day.

The pack of plainclothesmen fanned into the building. The watchman was knocked to the ground . He scrambled to his feet and fled. The plain-clothesmen pressed into the elevator with Gathenji. In his office, they demanded that he open his cabinet safe. He replied that he was obligated to protest. This was a counselor's office, he explained, and the safe contained clients' documents. Their demand violated the law and attorney-client privilege. They could make him open the safe only with a court order.

"Open it," said the assistant commissioner. He evinced the seriousness of a man whose orders had come from very high. Perhaps, Gathenji thought, they had come from the president himself. That suggested no margin for failure. The assistant commissioner would not leave empty-handed.

Gathenji opened the safe. Inside were the statements they wanted.

After they had the papers, they pushed him back into the Peugeot. He wondered if they were going to take him to Nakuru after all. The car started. Soon he realized, to his relief, that they were headed to the Criminal Investigation Department's Nairobi headquarters. This meant he would live, at least for now. He would be criminally charged, and he could fight the case in court. Flawed as he knew Kenya's legal system to be, it was still the system to which he'd devoted his life; he retained enough faith in its workings to believe he would not be totally helpless there.

At headquarters, he was fingerprinted, and then he sat waiting for what seemed forever as the CID men prepared charges. The assistant commissioner had vanished with his team, and now Gathenji was in the hands of men who didn't seem to know exactly what his crime had been. Outside, it was now daylight. Finally, he saw the charges: twenty-four counts of publishing statements "likely to cause fear and alarm or disturb the public peace." This was an obvious absurdity—the documents had been in his safe, after all—and yet it brought further relief. It was not sedition. It occurred to Gathenji that the assistant commissioner had never cared much whether he was charged or not; he had just wanted to know what the documents contained.

It was late afternoon by the time they packed an exhausted Gathenji into the car again for a short drive to the Kileleshwa Police Station. He was led toward his jail cell. He had visited a hundred cells as a prosecutor and defense attorney but had never been locked inside one. The faces of the other inmates turned to watch as he entered. There were about fifteen of them, street toughs, slum kids, petty thieves, car boosters, pickpockets, one or two ragged old men. There was muttering as he moved between the tightly packed bodies.

Suddenly, one of the inmates was hooting enthusiastically and pumping his hand. Gathenji recognized him as a client he'd once defended, a gabby con man and incorrigible car thief. He was short and stocky, not the largest of the cell mates, but the most menacing, a man in possession of that intangible aura of violence on tap. He seemed to run the cell. He shouted at the others to shut up. "Listen! This is a very important *mzee*. No one will harass him. He's our lawyer."

And so Gathenji became the unofficial legal representative to a cellful of penniless pickpockets and petty crooks. At night, they honored him with a special position on the cell floor. The others slept belly-to-back, tightly squeezed across the cell's length, while he was allowed to lie down in the extra space between their feet and the wall. There were no pillows in the stuffy cell. He slept under a thin blanket, the hard ground pressing against his cranium and ribs. His back and legs ached. By day, he examined his cell mates' charges and gave them advice on what to say when they were brought before the chief magistrate. Some of them were sent home; the cell began emptying while he sat there, waiting.

There were small windows way at the top of the cell. As the hours wore on, he found himself sinking into a depression. His family brought him bread and fruit and chicken, which he distributed to his cell mates. A friend brought him a coat, and it became both his blanket and his storage locker, the pockets stuffed with his toothbrush and Bible. He read Proverbs. A full day passed, and then another, and then a third and a fourth. Colleagues at the Law Society had filed a writ of habeas corpus and started a publicity campaign, and his arrest had made the news wires. Friends visited steadily. Those who came provided a good index of whom he could count on. Some people he had considered friends merely passed their sympathies on through his wife. He was now an official enemy of the state; the danger of associating with him had suddenly been ratcheted up.

He had spent five days behind bars before two plainclothesmen led him into the High Court and placed him in the dock. He denied the charges of Publishing Alarming Statements. Muite led his defense team, arguing that the statements had been in his office safe. He asked for bail, noting that Gathenji was a long-standing officer of the court and a former prosecutor for the attorney general. The magistrate let him out on bail.

Shortly afterward, Gathenji appeared at the Intercontinental Hotel in Nairobi to discuss his experiences before a gathering of the Kenyan Law Society and to thank the league of lawyers who had backed him. He spotted a tall, aging, unkempt white man in a Roman collar in the crowd. He wondered if it was the American priest he'd been hearing about for months, the one who had been beaten at Maela. He was not surprised when, after his speech, the priest approached to extend his hand. The hand was enormous and carried a hint of crushing strength, but his voice was soft, incongruously reedy. He introduced himself as John Kaiser. He had been following the lawyer's story. Perhaps they could help each other?

They found a quiet corner but did not speak for long. Special Branch agents or their informants were almost certainly watching. Gathenji wrote down the address of his Nairobi law office and handed it to the priest. They agreed to talk further there. Soon the priest was paying regular visits. Gathenji would look up and see the disheveled American priest strolling bandy-legged into his waiting room, having made the hard overland journey from his parish in Lolgorien. He'd greet him as "Mr. Gathenji" in a voice that somehow remained remarkably cheerful, despite what he'd witnessed and endured. But the priest was a different man after Maela. His focus had sharpened. He was preoccupied with the scattered refugees, many of whom were still starving. Gathenji made calls. He facilitated food deliveries.

When Kaiser visited, he inevitably began by reciting what he'd been seeing and hearing in the countryside—a litany of outrages—and then by remarking that other churchmen were afraid and willing to just let it happen. Inevitably, too, Kaiser came equipped with papers to pass to the lawyer, documents he had collected and drawn up—in one case, a list of General Services Unit agents who had allegedly taken part in murders and evictions.

Against all this, he always asked, might there be any recourse in the law? If he could gather enough witnesses, could a case be built against Moi and his killers?

Kaiser was aware, of course, that Gathenji had tried painstakingly to build such a case against Ntimama, and that a stroke of the attorney general's pen had destroyed it. Doomed to failure in the Kenyan courts, perhaps from the start, the case had made a statement nonetheless, casting light on the regime's heavy-handedness.

Did another case stand any chance of more than a symbolic victory? Might the Hague take it up? Kaiser and Gathenji discussed the possibility. It seemed remote, although not unthinkable. The smartest course— the one Gathenji advised—was for Kaiser to continue gathering evidence, quietly, in case opportunities arose.

Gathenji was still facing hard prison time on the twenty-four counts of Publishing Alarming Statements. Prosecutors let the charges hang over him for months before dropping them. He filed suit for false arrest and malicious prosecution against the attorney general and the assistant commissioner and won a settlement of 300,000 Kenyan shillings (the equivalent of a few thousand U.S. dollars). It was small compensation for what he now confronted: a crippled law practice. Many of his steady clients, including a bank for which he'd done debt-collection work, had no work for an enemy of the state. A good 60 percent of his business would vanish. He had two teenage boys to send to school, and it was not cheap. He scraped by with low-level work, defending insurance cases, doing consultancies. It dawned on him that the brief jail stint had not been the real punishment. There were other ways of destroying you. He would be allowed to function in a maimed state, an ambulatory advertisement of the danger of getting a little too brave.

He knew he was being watched. It was difficult to see a white car without thinking, *There they are.* People said the security services used white cars to follow you, because they were supposedly the least conspicuous. It became a reflex to watch for them in his rearview mirror. He believed his phone was tapped. It was not just the occasional odd noise he heard on the line, the subtle shifts in volume, the inexplicable clicks. He began to notice that his phone bill was not arriving in the mail. Months would pass with no bill, and when he called to inquire, he learned the bill had been paid in full. He surmised that whoever was listening didn't want to risk the possibility that he would miss payments and allow his phone to be disconnected. He thought, *They want me to keep talking. They're listening, and they don't want me to stop.* Had their sloppiness allowed him to perceive their game? Or did they actually want him to know they were listening?

On the streets, in shops and restaurants, and in the Italian hotel near his office where he met people for tea, he kept glimpsing vaguely familiar faces. They'd dwell on the periphery of his vision, not quite placeable, blending into the background, watching. He was not sure whether he was meant to notice this, either. Sometimes complete strangers approached him like old friends, his name on their lips. Sometimes people wandered into his office, saying they were lost, looking for some other office. Sometimes people came in posing as clients, and he knew they were studying him. Sometimes he'd arrive and find that his office door had been jimmied open.

He continued getting unannounced visits from Kaiser. One day, the priest came to say that a nun would soon bring him a manuscript he had written.

Would he make corrections, and keep it in a safe place? In case they kill me, he said.

The manuscript was about a hundred typewritten pages, detailing Kaiser's experiences at the Maela camp. He had been circulating it among church leaders, his missionary society, embassies, human rights activists, and lawyers he trusted; he was insistent on somehow getting it published. The manuscript was making everyone nervous, not least the Catholic Church.

Gathenji read it. There was little to correct, and small likelihood anyone would dare publish it. He put it in his safe.

9

LOLGORIEN

ON THE SURFACE, there was little to suggest that Kaiser's new home wouldn't be a tranquil one. From the back veranda of the dark-brick house in Lolgorien, he could look out past a sausage tree pendent with its strange, heavy pods and on to the grassy plains rolling down in a series of gentle pale green bulges toward the Serengeti, and on them were buffalo, zebra, wildebeest, cows, and the darker green of trees. A pepper tree grew beside the house, and children played on its low branches. The front of the house faced a cratered red-dirt road massed on the edges with tall cypress and yellow-flowered senna. Just across the road rose a modest green hill people called the Hill of Golgotha where, with the day's pastoral duties behind him, he carried his shotgun in the late afternoon, hunting rabbits for the evening meal. Sometimes he would sneak up to a rabbit and kill it with a stone; sometimes he would hurl his ax at a dik-dik and pounce upon the stunned and struggling animal before it had hit the ground. He considered his new parish, wide-open and remote and shockingly green, "the most beautiful in the world."

He was approaching his mid-sixties. There was plenty to keep him as busy as he wished to be; it would have been a good place to fade into obscurity. But Lolgorien itself had been a site of contention, and its scars were nearby. Six years earlier, in 1989, Provincial Commissioner Moham-med Yusuf Haji had ordered the eviction of non-Masai from the area—later boasting that he needed no court order to do so—and non-Masai houses were soon burning. When an Irish nun named Nuala Brangan visited Kaiser at his new parish, the charred remains of these houses were the first thing he took her to see. To her displeasure, he gunned down an animal—probably an antelope—from the window of his truck during her visit. They ate it "for breakfast, lunch, and tea for a week," she said.

The pain in his neck, which had been worsening since the roof beam fell on him in the 1980s, was now sharp and persistent; he wore a neck collar to relieve the agony of crushed vertebrae and bone spurs. Against an osteopath's advice, he roamed the hills on his motorbike to reach the Masai. He spent nights in their dung-and-ash huts, and returned home crawling with lice and fleas. Kaiser had quickly come to love the Masai. They punctured their cows' necks and mixed the blood with milk. Given a straw, he smiled sociably, as he had with the Kisii, and pretended to sip.

Apart from his refusal to wear the cervical collar at Mass, he was indifferent to his appearance; he would wear a pair of pants for weeks, dust-covered, mud-splattered, bundle them into a pile, then put them on again a few days later. He told the housekeeper he had inherited, Maria Mokona, not to trouble herself with a thing as small as washing his clothes; he did it himself in the Migore River. He told her to save the money he gave her, and after a while he'd add to it and she could buy a house. He promised to take care of her son, Francis. "Your son will not even buy a pair of socks," he said. Sometimes he took her family on picnics to the river. He encouraged her to attend classes in written Swahili and Kuria, her native tongue. She was illiterate. Kaiser told her this did not bother him, but that whoever succeeded him might need her to make lists; he wouldn't be around forever.

ON HIS ARRIVAL, the compound had been overgrown with grass and lacked even an on-site church, so that he said Mass on the house veranda. His bishop thought the place well suited to a missionary like Kaiser, at ease in the wilderness, zealous to hew a church from the bush. Kaiser took to the building with his usual eagerness but with failing strength. He gathered the local Christian women and gave them the task of clearing the grass, and he brought them tea as they slashed with their pangas. He showed them how to shape bricks from the earth and cement and river-bottom sand. He began erecting the church a few yards from the house, parallel to the road, measuring the length by foot strides and using the crook of his hand to shape the corners. He argued with the local mason, who tried to give him advice; he didn't need anyone telling him how to build. He would be up at 5:30 A.M., with the radio tuned to the BBC, then would walk the compound with his rosary beads as the world woke up, cocks crowing, insects thrumming, trees singing with weaverbirds and starlings. "I should be studying Masai but I am not good enough in Swahili yet to jump into another language," he wrote in June 1995, not long after his arrival. "So I can greet people in Masai & that's about all. The men know some Swahili but not many women or little kids. So I carry some rock candy & the little ones seem to understand that at least."

He contemplated other plans for the church grounds, including the building of a dormitory and school for local girls, who otherwise had to walk long distances to school and faced the threat of rape or animal attack. In some cases, the danger was from their own parents. Once, a twelve-year-old Kuria girl was brought to him. Her parents were about to marry her off to a much older man, and she was scared. He told her she could stay with Maria in her little house on the grounds indefinitely. The girl's mother came in a fury, demanding of the priest, "Is she your child or mine?"

The town center was just one main road flanked by tumbledown stores and hotels with rusty roofs of corrugated iron. Masai men strolled with their long, skinny sticks. The surrounding countryside was dotted with their *manyattas*, branch-encircled villages of loaf-shaped mud-and-dung huts.

"Lolgorien is quite a town," Kaiser wrote in a letter.

It has about three or four solid stable families of one husband & one wife plus children. Then there are about one hundred policemen, gamewardens & government officers who serve the larger area of the Trans-mara. Then there are about thirty unmarried prostitutes who serve the police & game wardens and government officials and even a few of the surrounding Masai. These generally have two or three kids each & most of them also have the AIDS virus but are not yet sick with it. And so there are that large bunch of kids with no fathers who in a few years will also have no mothers. They tend to be friendly and uninhibited and very loveable.

NOT LONG AFTER his arrival, he began work on the manuscript that detailed his experience at Maela. He described the ghastly camp conditions, the fraudulence of the registration process, the brutality of the evictions. He assailed "major falsehoods promulgated by the Kenya government": that a popular Masai uprising had led to the crisis, that refugees had no legal claim to their land, and that many had found homes after asking to be removed from the camp. Many of the displaced, he noted, now populated the country's slums, and the few who had been resettled were on small plots of poor land. The solution was to return them to Enoosupukia. He invoked a Latin saying, *Res clamat domino*: a stolen thing cries out till it is returned.

The little book represented the culmination of much of his thought and experience. He cited an editorial in the *Daily Nation* that argued the president should not be discussed in the parliament on the grounds that he was the father of the country, and fathers were not discussed. Kaiser described this as "a serious mistake," asking, "Why is the President never directly blamed?" He described fatherhood as "the most transcendent of relationships," and argued that he did not want or expect fatherhood from an earthly president, certainly not from his native country's current president, Bill Clinton. He suggested that deference to Moi had become fear-saturated idolatry, a violation of the commandment against worshiping strange gods. "Is the exaggerated adulation given to President Moi by so many leaders—religious leaders too—given out of respect or fear?"

The Church had good reason to avoid provocations. Rational clergy-men knew that speaking up too loudly endangered not just themselves but their parishioners and the duty of administering the sacraments. To do the work of tending to people's souls, the thinking went, the Church depended on the government's goodwill. Kaiser's logic was different. Hadn't Pope John Paul II said the Church's role was to alleviate suffering? Hadn't he visited Kenya just that year, 1995, and urged priests to confront injustice? And wasn't the country's "paramount evil," its fratri-cidal violence, clearly the handiwork of the regime? "Why then do we so easily accept the admonition of government ministers that we who are religious should 'keep off politics'?" Kaiser wrote. Didn't the failure to address the problem head-on amount to a "terrible indictment of us all"?

In addition, Kaiser denounced Masai leaders for cheating their people on the pretext of defending their rights, and of attempting to keep them uneducated and easy to exploit, consigned to the role of majestic-looking postcard props.

On the manuscript's final page, he wrote, "I have no intention of leav-ing this parish voluntarily or going underground. Since I have been threatened before by the Rift Valley Provincial Commissioner, I want all to know that if I disappear from the scene, because the bush is vast and hyenas many, that I am not planning any accident, nor, God forbid, any self destruction."

It was a dangerous book. He sent it to everyone he could think of. People warned him it could get him deported or killed. He suspected that his bishop, Colin Davies, would advise against its publication but would not forbid it. "There is nothing in it against faith or morals. The only grounds he would have to forbid it would be prudence," he wrote to his sister. "I have asked Bishop Raphael Ndingi of Nakuru diocese to read it and give me his opinion & if possible write a preface. He is our best champion of human rights. I haven't attacked any Bishop in this book but it does make them all look a bit bad because I clearly expose the extent of the horror of the 'ethnic cleansing' here in Kenya and the Bish-ops have really failed to provide effective leadership in attacking the evil.

It is possible that Bishop Ndingi might warn me not to have it published on the grounds that the Bishops are succeeding behind the scenes and then I would have a bit of a dilemma."

To judge from Kaiser's subsequent letters, Ndingi did not oppose publication, but refused to collaborate or lend the weight of his name to the introduction. Kaiser could not find a publisher.

Increasingly frustrated both with church leaders' passivity and the fecklessness of his missionary society, he addressed a letter to his Mill Hill brothers, describing his chagrin with their recent gathering in Nairobi. He had mentioned "the need for our society to do something in a unified and organized way" to help the displaced reclaim their Rift Valley homes. In response, a member had cited "the interplay of huge international factors which made it practically impossible to even analyze much less overcome the problems." To Kaiser, placing blame did not seem terribly complicated. Though the roots of the trouble lay in "unjust colonial laws," the government was now grabbing land and exploiting tribal animosities. With the world struggling that year to assimilate the news of the Rwandan genocide, he was not alone in glimpsing the abyss into which Kenya seemed to be hurtling.

"And all we, one of the oldest missionary societies, can do is express our skepticism at determining the cause and our powerlessness at overcoming the enemy. How did we as a Society come to such a sorry state?" Kaiser wrote. He viewed the struggle in the broadest metaphysical terms, as "a war against the principalities and the powers of darkness."

Among the excuses for Mill Hill's inaction was the belief "that we cannot do much because we are not Bishops or because we are foreign," Kaiser wrote. Further, there was a sense of futility, a feeling that Moi would not heed protests from some white missionaries. What good was speaking out if you couldn't win? To Kaiser, success or failure in the current historical moment was not the point. "When our Lord stood before Caiphas and Pilate he knew very well that he would not overcome the Roman Empire in his own lifetime but he would overcome it," he wrote. "What Christ did was to witness to the simple truth, although he knew it would mean his life, and he calls us all to do the same." He wrote that "every baptized person is called to recapitulate the Paschal Mystery," a reference to Christ's suffering, death, and Resurrection; *paschal* is a Hebrew word meaning "the passing over" to eternal life.

"Bishops are rightly concerned that having a high profile, media-covered role in the fight for Justice is indeed a dangerous role for priests, especially young priests," Kaiser continued, then proceeded to deliver a few memorable lines that seemed both a gallows-humored taunt to his society brothers and—in light of later events—an eerily self-fulfilling prophecy. "Many Mill Hill missionaries are now aging, and once past 65 years what really is there to look forward to in this world, as far as honor and glory are concerned, except the funeral? Therefore, elderly missionaries who are ready for retirement could be sent to the Rift Valley as a final mission. Their grey hairs and bald heads would be respected by all as they challenged the lies of the D.Os [district officers] and D.Cs [district commissioners] with the simple truth. They might even end their careers with a bang rather than a whimper."

INTO HIS LIFE around this time came Francis Kantai, a gaunt, thin-voiced young Masai who had grown up in a nearby *manyatta* and described himself as the first person in his family to convert to Christianity. At some point, he unburdened himself of a grim tale that may or may not have been calculated to engage Kaiser's attention. It's possible that he sensed a singular opportunity in the person of the American priest.

By Kantai's account, he'd been visiting relatives in Lolgorien in 1989, when he was in his late teens. A Land Rover approached, crowded with half a dozen paramilitary and administrative police. They were friendly to him. They told him to come along. They took him to a Kisii town and asked if he knew what he was supposed to do. He said no. They handed him a matchbox and told him to set a house ablaze. He resisted. Their faces changed. Their friendliness vanished. He was afraid. He took the matchbox and lit the house afire. After that, he traveled with the police.

The police would chase people away, and he would close in with his matches. At one small hut, a man was trying to reattach a thatched-grass roof that police had ripped off. After watching them beat the man severely and chase him away, Kantai set his dwelling alight. He went with police from house to house, burning them in the daylight.

It's not clear how Kaiser reacted to the story or made his first assessment of its teller. The priest would not have been surprised to learn that police had orchestrated arsons; it was a common account, consistent with everything he'd been told for decades. Nor would it have been a difficult story for Kantai to fabricate and make believable. Possibly he sensed a way to make himself of special interest to Kaiser, telling him what he wanted to hear, expressing penitence and asking forgiveness—playing off the priest's belief in personal redemption—and offering to be a witness.

That Kantai materialized in Kaiser's life in the aftermath of Maela, just as the priest's crusade against the regime was acquiring momentum—and just when the Special Branch would have had good reason to start watching him—seemed to some more than mere coincidence.

Kaiser gave him a job and a room in his house.

EVEN WITHOUT POLITICAL entanglements, Kaiser seemed to be courting enough danger just by living in the remote, disease-ravaged countryside. People told him he was too old for his motorcycle, but in an area of few roads, he needed it "to reach these backward Masai herdspeople," he wrote. "My trouble is I don't act my age and sometimes have to pay for it." Once, after Sunday Mass, he spotted "a group of pretty young Masai girls looking at me so I roared off with my front wheel in the air, just like Evil Knivel [sic]." His rear wheel hit a stone hidden in the grass and sent him sprawling. "The ground was soft & I didn't break anything but it felt like my ribs were at right angles—and the girls came over to help me up. As the song says, when will we ever learn?"

His first years in Lolgorien coincided with a malaria epidemic; one of his catechists, a Kisii, lost three of his four children. Kaiser came down with another severe case himself in early 1996, his fourth bout in the last year. This time, it left him terribly weak for nearly two months. After quinine proved useless, he traveled to Nairobi for a course of Halfan. As he recovered, he was diagnosed with amoebic dysentery, which required more drugs. He endured a prolonged period of feeling "run down," and if his strength didn't come back, he believed he might be forced to return to Minnesota that summer, a prospect he clearly wished to avoid. Inactivity was anathema to his temperament.

In an April 1996 letter to his sister, apparently responding to her despair at the moral state of America, he wrote, "We should not go mad because that is an easy temptation and I have often come up against it." The antidote to the temptation was embracing God's mission. "The devil knows how to discourage us and he does that by convincing us that we cannot do it because of our sins of weakness. These weaknesses can be the source of our strength. . . . " By now, he was feeling well enough to abandon the trip to the States. "I begin to get strength again also some optimism for the future," he wrote. As the years gathered in his bones, he had the urge to put his life down on paper. He contemplated a book about his experiences in Minnesota, the seminary, the army, and Africa, and about all the people who had helped him to "see God's great plan—at least in a dark manner—and to love it all."

In late 1996, his strength having largely returned, he drove to Moi Ndabi—the arid settlement in which the president had dumped many Maela refugees—to do what he had been planning to do for more than a year: build a house for the widow and children of Julius Chege, the refugee who had elicited Kaiser's promise to help his family. They were still living in a plastic hut Kaiser described as a "rat hole." Using offcuts of slab lumber and an iron-sheet roof, Kaiser spent the better part of a week in "unbearably hot and dusty" conditions to construct the eighteen-by-thirteen-foot structure, which would at least serve to keep out the wind and the dust. The effort would have been little trouble before; now it left him exhausted.

As the new year began, his life seemed to be returning to its normal rhythms—building projects, pastoral work, hunting. His temper flared quickly and disappeared just as quickly. He was impatient with men who neglected their work. "He could easily slap you. But then it would go away," said Melchizedek Ondieki, a friend and carpenter. Then Kaiser would say, "*Pole sana*. Very sorry. But you have to work."

The Lolgorien church rose, yard by yard, built with whatever materials he could buy or scavenge. The structure was long and narrow, with a high angled roof covered with sheets of corrugated tin, a concrete floor, and a broad aisle separating two rows of plain wooden benches with bare kneelers. Wire-screened windows on each side admitted daylight. Above was an exposed lattice of crossbeams that he'd hauled in from the woods. Behind the altar he hung a heavy wooden crucifix, and on the crucifix he mounted a figure he had molded himself of gray concrete. It was a Y-shaped figure, vaguely human, emaciated, with smears of red paint for the wounds and a head encircled by a crown of bristling six-inch acacia thorns. It had little more than the rudiments of a face, with spots of dark paint for pupils, which seemed to bulge outward and downward from circles of surrounding white. In its quality of crude terror, it bore a resemblance to some species of cave art. Outside, white lines of mortar showed around each of the big handmade red-brown bricks, and the bricks near the base were stained with the darker red of the surrounding earth. Near the church doorway, he hung a big chunk of metal with a length of barbed wire; this he struck with a metal rod to summon villagers to Mass. Sunday mornings even before daybreak worshipers were kneeling in the wood pews in the darkened church.

Once, he took three Kisii nuns on a picnic and crept away to find a warthog; instead, he found himself ten yards from a large sleeping leopard. He fixed his shotgun on the animal's head and whistled. "The cat woke up & looked at me in great surprise & disappeared in a flash," he wrote. "I could have had his hide but it's illegal & no one here eats the meat."

Beyond these routines, though, there was a new intensity to his focus on justice. Crisscrossing the countryside, he was assembling the elements of an indictment. He gathered land deeds from dispossessed farmers. He documented calls for ethnic purges. "I'm perfectly safe," Kaiser told his sister. "I'm an American citizen. They're never gonna touch me."

IN JANUARY 1997, in what Charles Mbuthi Gathenji would later regard as a precursor to Kaiser's death, a Catholic monk named Larry Timmons was slain by a government rifle in circumstances of extreme and ineradicable vagueness. He was a Franciscan brother from Ireland who worked on the arid periphery of the turbulent Rift Valley. At least three other Catholic missions had been violently robbed that month, and nuns had been reported raped. Nobody could exactly prove it— there were abundant freelance cutthroats to go around, of course—but many saw the attacks as part of a pattern of harassment and intimidation meant to cow the Church as fresh elections approached that year. The president was requiring would-be voters to obtain national identity cards by the end of January; Kikuyus found administrative bosses tightfisted with them.

Timmons was in his forties, and, like Kaiser, he was an energetic builder accustomed to a climate of violence; years earlier he'd escaped a carjacking. In the days before his death, the monk had confronted local political bosses and policemen, accusing them of extorting bribes from students in exchange for the ID cards. He promised to take the matter to Catholic authorities and government higher-ups. He expressed confidence that his diocese would protect him. One of the men he accused, a policeman, materialized at the mission house one night—supposedly in response to a robbery—reeking of alcohol and with a blazing rifle. A bullet sliced through Timmons. Explanations were fatuous on their face. The policeman claimed he was firing skyward as a warning to the fleeing robbers; it had been an unfortunate accident. The district commissioner said the monk had been hit in the "crossfire" with robbers. It was very regrettable, everyone agreed, but it had been dark.

To preserve appearances and quell the clamor from the Church, the policeman was to face a murder charge, but Gathenji—enlisted by Catholic leaders to advise on the case—believed his acquittal a fait accompli in a trial where the Church had no standing to call witnesses. He urged another strategy: Let them drop charges, thereby clearing the way for an inquest, a proceeding in open court, where he could question witnesses liberally.

Gathenji concluded what many had believed obvious from the start: The robbery had been mere camouflage for murder. The inquest would drag on, year after year, but it would establish that the monk had been lying on the ground when shot, that the supposed robbers had carried no guns, that the bright moon would have allowed the policeman to distinguish between a white monk and black robbers, and that Criminal Investigation Department detectives had botched the case egregiously—crime-scene photos were lost, forensic reports went unwritten, eyewitnesses were ignored, and fingerprints were never taken. At trial, assessors found the policeman guilty not of murder but of manslaughter. A judge called it "recklessness" and imposed a ten-year prison term.

It was, Gathenji thought, as close to justice as they could have realistically expected. What never emerged were clear explanations about the whys of it. Had the drunken cop acted alone and opportunistically, or had he figured in a larger plot? Had the robbery itself been staged, timed to unfold as the cop sat drinking at a local bar, mustering his courage, waiting for his cue? Low in the hierarchies of power, a figure the system could afford to sacrifice, the cop was locked away, and not talking.

A SENSE OF fatalism pervaded the country as the 1997 elections approached. In cleaving to power for nearly two decades, the president had turned a prosperous nation into the world's twenty-second poorest. The education system was decrepit, and hospitals lacked basic medicines. The lights were forever going out. Foreign investment had withered; instability had decimated tourism; government coffers were depleted by corruption and mismanagement.

For regular Kenyans, bribery seemed to infect every other daily interaction. Cops, wildlife rangers, postal workers, and all manner of petty bureaucrats demanded "a little tea." The cities teemed with buckled roads and slums, sewage-redolent shantytowns constructed of tire hubs and rubber, where latrine trenches overflowed in the rains. Meanwhile, the *wabenzis* continued in their high style, and regime-friendly ethnic enclaves reaped jobs, roads, and other largesse.

At seventy-three years old, Moi was seeking his fifth five-year term. For an ossified Cold War–era dictator, the year held ill omens. A guerrilla army had forcibly ended the twenty-two-year kleptocracy of Moi's old ally, Zaire's Mobutu Sese Seko, sending him into exile in Morocco. Emboldened Kenyan protesters were shouting, "Moi-butu must go!" Also that year came the death of Hastings Banda, Malawi's former dictator, who had lived long enough to stand trial for murder.

As was his wont, Moi fended off criticism by invoking the wretchedness of his African neighbors. The Horn of Africa was desolated by starvation; there was war in Sudan, Rwanda, Mozambique, Angola, Nigeria, Liberia, and Ethiopia. He portrayed himself as a victim of hypocritical Western powers who had buttressed his rule and were now ready to sacrifice their longtime ally at the altar of liberalization. "Here in Africa Kenya has always been called a stooge," he told a reporter. "An American stooge, British stooge. All of a sudden they abandon Kenya with all this talk of democracy and human rights."

That summer, as a drought hit Lolgorien, Kaiser left for a trip to the United States. Diagnosed with prostate cancer, he underwent an operation and faced a slow recovery. Meanwhile, Kenya was roiling. Protesters demanded an end to the Public Order Act, which required a permit for nine or more Kenyans to gather, and church leaders called for constitutional reforms to curb presidential power.

The Indian Ocean city of Mombasa, with its palm-lined beaches, was savaged by violence. In recent years, Kenyans had converged from across the country to fill jobs created by the area's robust tourist trade. Now, party stalwarts were urging locals to oust the so-called outsiders, the same demagogic cry that had proven so calamitous in the Rift Valley.

Julius Sunkuli. One of Kenya's most powerful politicians, he became part of the inner circle of President Daniel arap Moi and a target of John Kaiser. *Copyright Nation Media Group Limited. Reprinted with permission.*

Targeting areas where the opposition had prevailed in the last election, the regime found gangs of unemployed young men, promised them land, and trained them to fight. Hundreds strong, they rampaged in packs through town, brandishing guns, panga knives, and clubs. Houses burned, merchants fled, and families hastily piled their belongings into trucks to escape.

Having recovered from his surgery, Kaiser returned to his corner of Kenya in mid-November, to find the people emaciated from drought and the atmosphere saturated with dread. Elections were a month away, and he predicted "a lot of chaos." Government-affiliated heavies were evicting Kisii and Luo settlers who opposed ruling-party candidates, and others took flight in fear.

A key culprit in the exodus, Kaiser came to believe, was the local member of parliament, Julius Sunkuli. Like the president, he had mastered the mask of public piety; he was a baptized and churchgoing Catholic, and a conspicuous contributor to church projects. He had grown up herding Masai cattle on the Kilgoris plains, and had been known as an altar boy and scout leader before making his name as a lawyer and magistrate.

Now an assistant minister in the president's office, he controlled the area's provincial administration and police forces.

He was the local Big Man, and a useful one to Moi. Like Ntimama, one of his chief rivals for the president's attention, Sunkuli could be relied on to summon the might of thousands of young Masai warriors. "Moi needed and wanted Masai political support," an American diplomat once explained. "It's not just the ballot box, but the ability to draw on them strategically to intimidate other communities. You can turn the heat up or down if you can draw on these armed groups."

Kaiser described Sunkuli as a "bully-boy" who was "for the most part despised by the Masai." Facing Masai candidates from other clans as rivals for the KANU nomination, he terrorized their supporters and managed to secure the nomination despite slim popular support, Kaiser wrote. "Nobody here wants him but Moi does because he is a loyal sycophant. His nickname here is the 'Butcher.'"

In the Kilgoris borderlands between the Masai and the Kisii, where the two tribes had been skirmishing for years over cattle and land, the sizable Kisii population had given the opposition a strong foothold. At a primary school in Lolgorien, Sunkuli allegedly urged the Masai to chase away non-Masai from the area. At one point, it was further alleged, he sent his government-issued Peugeot 504 to the Kisii police station to rescue a man being held on suspicion of murder in the clashes. As elections loomed, many who could afford to leave Kenya climbed on planes.

It was the season of El Niño, and hammering rains crashed on Kaiser's corrugated-metal roof and turned the roads into rivers of mud. He was cut off from half his parish, as well as from what he called his "escape route" south to Tanzania. The bridge south was submerged under two feet of rushing water, and trees were lodged in the torrent. In the other direction, the bridge to Kilgoris was on the verge of going under, the little stream it crossed having become a flood. "But everything is beautifully green and the animals seem to have reproduced well during my absence," Kaiser wrote.

He broke two ribs when his motorcycle took a spill on a muddy road.

Immobilized again, he watched his weight creep up to 211 pounds, eleven more than what he considered to be his ideal weight. This brought a sense of guilt as he considered the drought-induced gauntness of the people around him.

"Because of the murder & mayhem police are all over and so he [Moi] hopes to intimidate church monitors on the election day," he wrote. He drafted letters to the *Daily Nation,* blaming Sunkuli for the Kilgoris violence, and took a group of Masai to the newspaper's Kisii bureau to make a statement. Neither the letters nor the statement were printed.

Violence and the fear of violence had left his parish in a state of ghostly desertion. At Mass, the crowds were thin. He expected that a Moi-Sunkuli victory was preordained, and believed the Church should boycott the election; at least this would help undermine the patina of legitimacy Moi seemed to crave. To Kaiser's frustration, the bishops had no appetite for a boycott.

He retained hope, however, that church monitors might be able to gather evidence of election-day rigging. On the day of the vote, Kaiser oversaw fifty election monitors. An estimated fourth of the nation's districts were racked with logistical troubles. Ballot boxes disappeared or wound up hundreds of miles from where they should have been; some polling stations never opened; voters found themselves confronted by roads made impassable by mud and rain. Party supporters had an easier time, managing an impressive 105 percent turnout in some districts.

Moi's rivals again split the vote along ethnic lines. In a nation of nearly thirty million people, where most subsisted on less than a dollar a day, tribal logic—the iron understanding that whoever controlled the presidency controlled the allocation of resources—still predominated. In interviews, voters often said they thought first of a candidate's tribe. Explaining their support for Moi, members of minority tribes cited fear of domination by larger ones.

In Lolgorien, Kaiser watched "almost no one" line up to vote for Sunkuli, who nonetheless was declared the winner. "He is my biggest worry," he wrote.

Moi won reelection with 2.4 million votes, 41 percent. In a fair election, Kaiser estimated, that percentage would have been halved. "The Catholic Bishops know all this but they still accepted the result and did not protest on the grounds that the civil disturbance would be worse if they had protested," he wrote. The bishops had pinned their hopes of change on constitutional reform, but Kaiser was skeptical Moi would give ground on that front. "I doubt he will allow any constitution which would eat away at his Divine status."

At his swearing-in ceremony, Moi advanced a hard rhetorical line against graft. Skittish international donors and investors were meant to take reassurance. "We are determined to eliminate corruption," he announced. "I warn anyone who might have corrupt tendencies to beware. It doesn't matter how smart you may be. You will be caught one day."

EVEN FOR A man with an uncommonly high pain threshold, Kaiser's physical afflictions were increasingly harsh. Over the last four years, he had visited a Nairobi clinic twenty-eight times. He complained of stress, anxiety, a stomach ulcer, and neck pain so intense that he believed he might have to return to the States for surgery.

"I'm wearing down, no doubt," he wrote to his sister from outside Nairobi, where he spent a month in treatment. He remained dismayed about Mill Hill's weak leadership. "I judge that half of our European members just want a comfortable middle-class life and let the society quietly die off."

He was staying with his bishop, Colin Davies, an Englishman who was approaching his mid-seventies. In the face of state criminality, Davies tried to proceed with caution. "We must be as wise as serpents and as peaceful as doves," he liked to say. He disliked Kaiser's confrontational methods; this little book of his about Maela was hardly prudent. He particularly disliked Kaiser's suggestion that church leaders who favored a quieter approach were cowards. He believed Africans should take the lead in spurring reforms; he was conscious of the African Church's discomfiture at the prospect of white missionaries taking center stage. It's possible he felt this even more keenly as an Englishman who could remember the empire's awesome reach. He articulated his philosophy this way: "Africans have their own way. They go by and large slowly, but they go surely." He insisted that nothing he or the other bishops said would compel Moi to change his policies. Hadn't they been expressing their disapproval for years? In a memoir he wrote years later, Davies emitted an air of resignation: "Was my voice going to make a difference? I did not think so."

At church meetings, Davies became one of Kaiser's perpetual targets as he railed against church inaction. One of Kaiser's letters reflects a sense of isolation: "Most of our priests are now African and they will not argue with him nor support me when I try to argue with him about the scandal of our lack of leadership in the area of Justice & Peace."

One day, a man arrived from one of Lolgorien's distant outstations with word that he was needed. A widow with five children was desperate for the sacraments. Her husband had given her AIDS before it killed him, and now she was near death herself. With the rivers swollen and the bridges impassable, it had been difficult to reach the area for months. "I went & hid my motorcycle in the bush & waded the river & walked 4 more miles & said mass in her home," Kaiser wrote. "She was about 38, very thin & very grateful for mass in her home; confession, anointing of sick & H. communion. I told her I would make sure her kids finished school & kept the faith." It was the kind of errand that made Kaiser feel most alive. "A beautiful day," he called it.

His assistance was sought in other ways. Over the summer, some Masai warriors paid him a visit. A pride of "bad lions" was terrorizing their herds. Would he shoot some and drive the others to the Mara? He chided them, telling them that conquering lions was their job. They replied that lions were few now and they were out of practice in killing them. "Double 0 buckshot should work," he wrote. He accompanied them into the bush several times. The lions had vanished. He declared it a sign from God. It brought some of them into his church.

• • •

ON THE MORNING of August 7, 1998, Gathenji, his law practice still hobbled, was sitting in his fourth-floor Nairobi office, talking to his accountant, when Osama bin Laden made his ferocious entrance into global consciousness two blocks away. A terrorist attack was not in the Kenyan frame of reference, so Gathenji, like everyone else, had no way to interpret the booming sound he heard from the direction of the U.S. embassy building. From his window, he could see a sliver of the embassy on the other side of the Cooperative Bank House. He thought fleetingly that a tire had burst. Then came a terrible ripping, cleaving sound—something like the sound of lightning splitting the sky—which made no sense at all. His window was rattling, and the ground beneath his feet rumbled; the whole building felt as if it were rolling. Some of the windows in his building were shattered. Then came a moment of what seemed like absolute silence, followed by a cacophony of car alarms, horns, and screaming. Dazed, looking out the window, he saw the whirl of papers, dust, and debris billowing to impossible heights into the sky over the embassy. Then he was heading through the hallway and down the stairs. People were saying, "It's the teachers!" Nairobi's schoolteachers were about to strike; perhaps they were causing some kind of trouble. By the time he reached the street, everyone was yelling, "Bomb, bomb, bomb." In the pandemonium, some were running toward the smoke; others, drenched in blood, faces embedded with glass, were racing away from it.

Al Qaeda operatives had driven a bomb-laden Toyota truck into the rear parking lot of the U.S. embassy compound, which stood nakedly amid the downtown high rises at a busy intersection in the capital's business district. One terrorist had hurled a stun grenade at the guards. Hearing the noise, the curious and the startled had run instinctively to the windows of their offices, and those in passing buses pressed their faces against the glass to see. This compounded the horror of the bomb itself, as glass exploded from innumerable windows and from the glass "curtain wall" fronting the twenty-three-story Bank House, two doors away. Blizzards of shattered glass sleeted into people's eyes, blinding more than one hundred instantly. Big shards scythed horizontally through jugulars. People were hurled through high windows. Bus riders were incinerated where they sat. Passersby were maimed, their jawbones ripped off, their teeth blown from their mouths. Others were dead or dying under tons of debris, broken concrete, and steel. Next to the embassy, a secretarial college collapsed, and in a nearby building, the U.S. ambassador, Prudence Bushnell—who had warned the State Department repeatedly about the embassy's vulnerability—was knocked unconscious. The attack killed 213 people, including 12 Americans, and injured 4,500. (Minutes later, a second bomb went off outside the embassy in Dar es Salaam, in Tanzania, killing eleven more.)

On the street, Gathenji tried to steer the wounded to taxis that would speed them to hospitals. The dazed and the bloody screamed at his approach. In some cases, he had to wrap his arms around them and force them into the cabs. As the day wore on, he grew worried about his wife, who was teaching at nearby Kenyatta University, and he knew she'd be worried for him. He found a friend to drive him there. The car had a smashed window, and shards of glass were scattered across the seats. Only after he and his wife were back at home did he realize he was bleeding, and discover the thumbnail-size piece of glass embedded in his right thigh.

His involvement with the bombing victims would be intimate. After more than a decade of work with the Kenya Society for the Blind, he had recently been appointed its chair, and the cause had a ghastly new relevance. As rescue workers attacked the rubble with pickaxes and searched for the source of fading screams, and as surgeons busily removed hundreds of shredded eyeballs, Gathenji sent his staff to the hospitals to take names.

Kaiser, for his part, was nowhere near the blast, but soon traveled to Nairobi and observed the destruction firsthand. "That bombing had nothing to do with Kenya, I believe, being most likely done by an external Moslem fundamentalist group," he wrote. His preoccupation with what he saw as the evil of Western population-control policies informed his view of what had animated the terrorists. "Of course they have good reason to hate America because of our anti-population measures, but bombs aren't the way."

In assessing the attack's political fallout, however, Kaiser was clear-eyed, guessing that it would "play into the hands of our Dictator, Moi who will use it as an excuse to get American funds to beef up Security all of which will be primarily trained and paid to keep him in Power."

No longer needed as a bulwark against the Soviet Union, Moi could now position himself as a shield against global terrorism. His usefulness was instantly evident as FBI agents—converging on East Africa in awesome numbers—worked closely with Kenyan police to track the bombing suspects. At a Nairobi hospital, a patient was discovered trying to throw away a pair of keys that fit a padlock in the wreckage of the bomb-laden truck. Kenyan authorities surrendered him to the FBI within days, and acquiesced to American requests to extradite him and other suspects to the U.S. for trial.

Kaiser's hunch had not been far off. Al Qaeda had given Moi the gift of fresh relevance. Later, as theories circulated about Kaiser's death, some would point to this moment as the one that determined the American response to it.

10

THE TRIBUNAL

WHEN MOI NEEDED a delaying tactic, a distraction, a smoke screen, he convened a commission. The stated aim of the Akiwumi Commission, launched in July 1998, was to probe the tribal clashes that had claimed more than one thousand lives in the preceding seven years, and to recommend the investigation and prosecution of culprits. Three judges, handpicked by Moi, and subject to dismissal at his whim, would preside.

To skeptics, the inquiry was designed to buy time until anger dissipated and memories faded. It would serve as a pressure-release valve, supply the illusion of a search for the truth, and conceal Moi's central role in the clashes—built into its charter was the edict that the president himself was not to be critically invoked. A columnist wondered whether the panel would prove "the charade of the decade."

Kaiser understood the nature of the game, yet he saw an opportunity, a public platform, the megaphone for which he'd been waiting. He planned to name names. He knew the church leadership regarded his zeal to speak as pointless, foolhardy, or both. Bishop Davies would not stand in Kaiser's way, but his feelings about the tribunal were no secret: He considered it "a waste of time." Did Kaiser actually expect to change Moi's mind? Further, it was an embarrassment to African bishops for a white man to give evidence, and one visited him personally with this message: "John, we have to sort this out in our own African way." Yet for all their uneasiness, church leaders would not force his silence.

As he prepared to testify, his anxiety was increasingly obvious to his church mates, and there was fear that the isolation of Lolgorien left him vulnerable. To keep Kaiser company and to allay his fear, the bishop assigned another Mill Hill priest, Tom Keane, a stout, companionable Irishman, to live with him. They were good friends; Keane, like Kaiser, had lived for years with the Kisii. There was more than enough work in the parish for two priests, and they divided the duties. Together, they studied Maa, the Masai tongue.

Keane quickly sensed the depth of Kaiser's fear. From the next bedroom, he heard him wake, screaming from nightmares. Kaiser slept by day and was awake all night. Sometimes, Kaiser slept beside his shotgun on his mattress, Keane would explain, "like having a woman."

When Kaiser traveled by motorbike, he dismantled the shotgun and carried it in a basket. When they traveled together in the truck, Keane became accustomed to carrying the shotgun on his lap in the passenger seat. Keane watched Kaiser swing from heights of energy, aflame with purpose, to depths of despondency. Kaiser holed up in his spartan room for hours, playing solitaire on his bed, refusing to come out.

He read the Bible at night by solar lamp, returning again and again to chapter 2 of the Book of Sirach (Ecclesiasticus) in the Catholic Bible: *"My child, if you aspire to serve the Lord, prepare yourself for an ordeal. Be sincere of heart, be steadfast, and do not be alarmed when disaster comes. . . . "*

He made bullets, shaving off pieces from a block of lead. He took ginkgo biloba for his memory. He worried that his cancer would return. He wore his neck brace constantly. *". . . Since gold is tested in the fire, and the chosen in the furnace of humiliation. . . . Woe to faint hearts and listless hands, and to the sinner who treads two paths. Woe to the listless heart that has no faith, for such will have no protection. . . . "*

At night, with the day's pastoral duties behind him, Keane liked to relax with a Tusker lager on the south veranda of the parish house and listen to the hyenas for an hour or two; they were reliable entertainment. Keane would invite Kaiser to join him for a beer, saying, "It's a beautiful evening, John."

Kaiser refused to join him. Depending on one's mood, Africa's nightsounds were music or a reminder of the softness of human flesh and bone, the pulse of a great mindless drama of stalking and killing and feeding, rolling across the plains. The darkness ran deep and unbroken. He would not make himself a target for enemies who might be hiding in it.

AS KAISER MONITORED the tribunal's progress in the press, the Church's presence proved timorous and disappointing. On the third day of testimony came Nairobi's then archbishop, Raphael Ndingi, long regarded as the bravest and most outspoken leader of the Kenyan Catholic Church. But his testimony was cloaked in generalities. He had seen the carnage of the clashes firsthand and believed that the police had refused to stop it, on orders "from above." But he refused to give names; at one point, he even refused to identify the ruling party as a force behind the violence. He gave the reason for his silence: fear. Six years earlier, he explained, attackers had broken into his house and threatened his life. They had left a drawer of cash untouched; their goal had not been money, but to send a message. Around the same time, an anonymous caller had made it more explicit still: "Bishop Ndingi must be killed."

On the fourth day of testimony came a man who spoke as if he had nothing to lose, a former state lawyer named David Maari. During the 1992 violence, he explained, he had traveled to his brother's Rift Valley farm and found a decapitated head being eaten by dogs. "I identified it as my brother's head and we put it in a sack," he said. Swarming the area were raiders, armed with knives and bows and arrows, who were collecting five hundred Kenyan shillings—the equivalent of a few American dollars—for the delivery of enemy heads. They admitted to killing his brother because they saw him as an enemy of President Moi: "Those who do not vote for the old man will become manure," they said. The lawyer called Moi "my principal suspect" and demanded to know why Attorney General Amos Wako hadn't been summoned to explain his failure to bring the killers to justice. It was a rare instance of candor in a forum that seemed designed to chill it.

For the guilty and the complicit, the tribunal supplied an opportunity to exculpate themselves publicly. On day sixty-six, John Keen, Moi's former assistant minister in charge of internal security, parroted the party line by blaming the clashes on tensions raised by political pluralism. Asked why security forces had not stopped the lawlessness, he said they were hampered by bad equipment and transportation troubles, and had proven "inefficient and partisan." Drawing a moral equivalence, he explained, "Kikuyu police officers supported their kinsmen, while their Kalenjin counterparts supported their tribesmen."

But wasn't he in charge of the police that might have halted the carnage? "Do not forget I was a small man in that office and I was not taken seriously sometimes." Had the police been incited to take sides? "The whole system was riddled with failure. But definitely some officers were acting on orders from elsewhere." He portrayed the Enoosupukia violence as the righteous rage of Masai whose land had been stolen, and said it had "created some awareness" of their plight.

Was Ntimama behind the Rift Valley clashes? "I must admit there must have been some backing somewhere but I do not know where." Asked how politics had contributed to the clashes, Keen magnified his vagueness with metaphor: "When a senior wife knows that her husband is planning to marry another wife there is bound to be some problem. That is what happened. Those who were in power and were eating wanted to hold to their positions while those who had eaten earlier wanted to come back and eat."

Other officials blamed the lackluster police response on a shortage of manpower, fuel, vehicles, and police radios; one said an investigation into the slayings of thirteen Kikuyus at Enoosupukia had been dropped because witnesses could not be found.

When Ntimama appeared before the commission, he unapologetically reiterated his support for *Majimboism*—widely regarded as a code for ethnic cleansing—and said his 1991 rallies weren't to incite violence, but to educate the Masai that multiparty politics would mean Kikuyu dominance, and therefore the theft of Masai land. "There was the fear of the unknown," Ntimama said.

He denied having told the Kikuyu to lie low like an envelope, as the *Daily Nation* had reported. It had been a mistranslation from the Masai tongue, he explained; he had really referred to lying low like an *antelope*, to avoid being spotted by a leopard. This was hardly a less menacing image. He admitted to standing up in parliament and denouncing the Kikuyu as "a filthy community with protruding stomachs, red teeth, and jigger-infested feet."

"I told them that because of their arrogance, they will be cut down to size as it happened to the Ibos of Nigeria," Ntimama said.

"I KNOW FAR too much and will not be able to avoid naming names as Archbishop Ndingi of Nairobi did, to our great disappointment," Kaiser wrote to his sister in Minnesota as he prepared to testify. "I have been threatened by 3 different government officers during the past 3 years and I suppose I could be deported or worse. That does not bother me much, but what does bother me is to what degree I should implicate and accuse President Moi." He feared that Moi would call off the inquiry before he appeared. "He must know my guns are loaded."

At least theoretically, he had the protection of the Church and the U.S. government. He could afford to risk more than others, he told people. He was already older than most Kenyans, and felt that he had aged a full decade in the last year and a half. He told his friend Melchizedek Ondieki, "I am old, and it doesn't matter what they do."

Around this time, Kaiser performed an unusual errand, one that was in keeping with his character. It seemed to reflect a sense of heartland fair play, of something gentlemanly, almost anachronistic. In the company of another priest, he paid a surprise visit to Julius Sunkuli's home in Kilgoris.

Sunkuli greeted them civilly, and tea was served. The gist of the conversation would not be in dispute. He told Sunkuli that it was his Christian duty to return the dispossessed to their land. He wanted to inform him face-to-face of what he would say, should he get an audience before

the tribunal. He would blame him for the exodus of farmers from Kilgoris before the 1997 election.

Later, recalling the visit, Sunkuli would describe Kaiser as shabbily
dressed and unshowered. He asked the priest if he had witnesses to prove
his claims, and Kaiser kept silent. Sunkuli told him he would not let his
accusations stand unchallenged. The Masai and the Kisii had been fighting in the borderlands forever, he said. Why blame him?

IN EARLY DECEMBER, Kaiser climbed into his truck and endured
a half-day trip over red pitted dirt roads to Nakuru, the dusty farming
town where the tribunal was currently holding its sessions. With the
backing of the Law Society of Kenya, which had a seat before the commission, he had finally been given permission to appear.

He walked up to Nakuru County Hall with his brace on his neck
and a folderful of documents containing land contracts and affidavits
of evicted farmers. The setting had the look of a simple country schoolhouse. He waited through the day's proceedings and was finally turned
away. They told him to come another day.

His sense of isolation seemed to deepen as the year approached its end.
He felt "very out on a limb," he wrote to a friend in December 1998. "If
the Bishops have a plan of action they have not communicated it to me or
to others. If their great respect for the President is because of respect for
the Father figure in spite of his crimes I can respect that, but I don't want
to lie, so I need prayers for light." Twice more he made the long drive,
with the same result.

On February 2, 1999, he left before dawn on his fourth trip. He had
asked his housekeeper to clean and iron his best clerical blacks.

It was day 112 of the tribunal. Finally, he was called as witness 203.
He walked to the scuffed wooden table and swore on the Bible before
the three bewigged judges. A team of government lawyers prepared to
eviscerate him. Kaiser believed they saw a white foreigner's testimony as
"easy to break."

Underscoring the absurdity of the proceedings was the presence of Bernard Chunga, the tribunal's assisting counsel. Chunga had been the chief prosecutor of the infamous sedition cases of the mid-1980s, in which scores of suspects were confined by police for weeks, tortured, and then marched into court to offer confessions. More recently, as Kenya's director of public prosecutions, Chunga had failed to pursue perpetrators of the clashes. He was, in short, a key part of the machinery that made them possible. Now, at the Akiwumi Commission, he was empowered to lead the questioning and determine which witnesses to call; he served as a gatekeeper against inconvenient testimony.

Kaiser faced the room crowded with spectators, reporters, and church friends who had come to lend moral support. "I have been working in this country for 35 years as a missionary but I should feel like a guest," Kaiser began. "There are things which a guest does not normally do when he is in his host's house or country. One of those things . . . is to criticize the government of that country. So I would like to make it very clear that I am only here at the direct request of the Diocese of Ngong and the Diocese of Nakuru."

The words conveyed the impression that Kaiser had been called by the leaders of his church as a designated spokesman, and that his appearance was their doing, not his. This was not the case, but his motive in saying so seems clear: There was both security and moral authority in speaking not just for himself but for the Church. However much he might have felt it, he wanted to avoid the perception that he was there all alone.

After announcing that a guest should not criticize his hosts, he made clear that that was what he planned to do. Under questioning from Chunga and other attorneys, Kaiser told a sweeping story that detailed years of government-licensed violence and indifference to the human toll. The bloodshed did not arise spontaneously from tribal animosities over scarce land, as the regime liked to portray it. "It does not have anything to do with tribes," Kaiser said. "It is simply the big people eating the small people."

Detailing the horrors of Maela, he described "the fraudulency of the registration exercise" ostensibly intended to resettle the dispossessed. He had witnessed at least four hundred document-bearing landowners being turned away. He detailed the nighttime raid of the camp, its burning, his confrontation with police. At one point, he directly addressed Hassan Mohammed, who had supervised the camp's destruction and ordered Kaiser's arrest, and who happened to be in the courtroom. "I think you obey orders. You are a good soldier," Kaiser said. "I certainly do not blame you for either my arrest, or for any cruelty to the people. I blame your superiors."

As early as 1989, he continued, a Rift Valley political chief, Yusuf Haji, had urged the Masai to evict "outsiders" from the Transmara district. He watched farmers flee police violence by the thousand. "Some people were killed and a lot of property was stolen and I believe I can produce hundreds of witnesses to that effect," Kaiser testified. When he confronted a district commissioner about the eviction of settlers from Lolgorien, he continued, he was warned: "If you try to interfere, the same thing will happen to you as happened in Maela."

Aiming his attack at Sunkuli, he accused the minister of winning his seat by expelling settlers and outright rigging. "I believe Mr. Sunkuli is part of the same government apparatus who is responsible for driving out thousands of Kisii and Kuria people from the Transmara," Kaiser testified.

He named more names. He declared it "general knowledge" that cabinet ministers William Ntimama and Nicholas Biwott had organized the training of thugs to terrorize farmers.

Biwott's lawyer, Rajni Sheth, rose to denounce him as paranoid. "I put it to you that your evidence as it is contained, particularly the allegation against Honorable Biwott, is absolutely worthless!"

Kaiser was undeterred. To reimburse the dispossessed, he continued, government officials should sell their own property. There should be prayers, he said, "for their confession, conviction, repentance, and for the restitution of the landless people."

The priest's attack went further, encompassing the court system and the integrity of the present hearing. He told the story of how his school-teacher friend James Ongera had been murdered by the Kenyan para-military police, and how the courts had refused to pursue a case against the killers. "We cannot get any justice from the judiciary," Kaiser said.

Justice Samuel Bosire, the panel's vice chair, was moved to ask, "Do you expect that we will do a fair job in this commission?"

"That is a very difficult question," Kaiser replied.

"Do you expect that we will do a good job?"

"The courts in our area are generally very corrupt."

Justice Sarah Ondeyo: "That is a very wild statement."

Bosire: "And coming from a priest."

For hours, he sat in the witness box as lawyers and commissioners grilled him. It was early evening when the day's proceedings concluded. The chairman, Justice Akilano Akiwumi, asked Kaiser to return on February 11, 1999, nine days hence. He would have to face the lawyers of the men he had accused.

The country's big dailies, the *Daily Nation* and the *East African Standard,* ran lengthy accounts of his testimony the next day. Sunkuli responded with fury. He appeared that Sunday at a fund-raiser for a Catholic church in Kilgoris, where he made a generous contribution to the building's upkeep and piously announced that he would not allow the House of God to fall into disrepair. He used the occasion to denounce "a white Catholic priest" for fueling tribal animosity, and demanded his removal to another diocese; otherwise, the minister said, he would be forced to call for his deportation.

"The mere fact that a man is wearing a collar does not make him holier than other people, and Christianity will be better off without him in this district," Sunkuli was quoted as saying. "We'll not be intimidated to leave the church because of one man."

The next day, Kaiser wrote to his sister and brother-in-law, warning them that his mail, which he collected at his Kilgoris PO box, was being opened and resealed with DAMAGED IN TRANSIT stickers.

"I think they are really playing with me," he wrote. He told them to address letters to him under a cousin's surname, McAllister. He described his appearance at the tribunal as "eight straight hours grilled by lawyers representing the biggest crooks in our government," and explained that he would soon return.

"I have to admit that I am not as young or as tough as I used to be and the whole business gives me some anxiety," he wrote, in a decidedly soft-focus depiction of the mental terror he had been experiencing. "I can expect any kind of fabricated slander to try and discredit me, and I sleep with my shotgun near at hand."

He had a couple thousand dollars left in his Minnesota account, and his sister could use it to fly herself and their brother Fran over for his funeral "if I would die here in Kenya," he wrote. "I hope your passport is up to date."

THURSDAY, FEBRUARY 11, 1999, day 119 of the tribunal.

"Are you a Kenyan?" demanded Sheth, Biwott's lawyer.

"No, my Lords."

"So, you are a foreigner?"

"Yes, my Lords."

"Of course you are."

Sheth reminded Kaiser that he had sworn on the Bible to tell the truth, and accused him of "misleading the Commission" about the eviction of non-Masais from Lolgorien.

"My Lords, I put to you that that is the truth I had sworn to uphold before the Almighty God," the priest insisted.

Lawyers took turns badgering him. Sunkuli's lawyer called him a liar.

It went on for hours. Then Kaiser said something that electrified the room. It stunned even those in attendance, like Sister Nuala Brangan, who were aware of the priest's occasional inability—or refusal—to reckon extreme danger before he spoke.

His exact words, stricken from the official account, appear unrecoverable. But witnesses agree that Kaiser named Moi himself as the man responsible for so much of the country's pain, the man who had the power to stop the tribal clashes but had not.

It was a shocking breach of decorum. Moi was the father of the country. The father is not criticized.

The proceedings were halted. There was a flurry of lawyerly activity. Sheth suddenly announced that he had instructions to represent His Excellency the President. He argued that Kaiser's remark should be excised from the record.

Justice Akiwumi needed no persuading. The commission's rules forbade any adverse mention of the head of state. He purged the record of the Moi remark and ordered the press not to publish it.

At a lunch break, Kaiser was anxious and alert, his eyes darting. "We could be killed," he told Brangan. They traveled down a side street for a nervous lunch at a crowded African-style restaurant.

Back on the stand that afternoon, Kaiser circled back to the theme of the broken justice system, testifying that a subsistence farmer he knew well, Stephen Mwita, had been to court forty times, seeking recompense from the men who'd stolen his cattle. Kaiser had accompanied him to court repeatedly, and watched the case delayed on myriad feeble pretexts. "This case goes on and on, interminably, and the person in question here has lost all his wealth," Kaiser said. Kaiser had brought Mwita to the tribunal to tell his own story, if the panel wished to hear it.

Akiwumi: "You are giving the impression that the judiciary fully collaborates with the thieves in cattle rustling, simply because one man, a friend of yours, has been in court 40 times."

Kaiser: "Your Lordships, I have very many other people who have come to me and made similar statements."

Akiwumi: "What is your business?"

Kaiser: "I am a parish priest in Lolgorien."

Akiwumi: "Well, you seem to be very interested in other things than spiritual matters."

Kaiser: "With due respect, your Lordships, justice and peace for the people is a very important part of a priest's life."

Akiwumi: "Alright."

The justices demanded that Kaiser give them the names of the cattle thieves. He refused, on the grounds that the courts had them already.

"You seem to be involved in all kinds of things," Akiwumi said, and called him a "busybody."

Sunkuli's lawyer decided the priest's foreignness needed further emphasis. He asked, "What is your country of birth?"

"The USA, your Lordships."

Well, the lawyer asked, wouldn't judicial complicity in cattle rustling be considered serious in America? "If you have that kind of information," he said, "would it not be a proper step to take, to report to the authorities and see what they can do about it?"

"It depends on how far you think the authorities are implicated in the deception, your Lordships," Kaiser said.

Finally, Akiwumi said, "Very well. We have finished with you, God willing or not."

Kaiser's testimony dominated press accounts of the tribunal the next day, though with his reference to Moi dutifully erased. As he returned to Lolgorien, newly green and rainy after a severe drought, he believed his new profile would provide a measure of safety. They might be less likely to kill him. Of his appearance at the tribunal, he wrote, "It was exhausting but worth it to see the fear on the faces of those lawyers and it has greatly helped me with the Masai who do not want a religion which is subservient to government."

Sister Brangan had warned him it was not safe to return to Lolgorien.

"Don't worry, I'm a good shot," the priest replied. "I'll shoot a few bullets in the air, and they'll go running."

A question went unspoken: What if firing into the air didn't stop his attackers? What if they called his bluff? The former soldier was more than a match for any single attacker; from the window of his rolling truck, he could put a slug through an animal's lungs in the distant bush. And in a

John Kaiser testifying at the Akiwumi Commission at Nakuru County Hall in February 1999. For the priest, it was a time of terror and all-night vigils with his shotgun. Photograph by Joseph Kiheri. *Copyright Nation Media Group Limited. Reprinted with permission.*

showdown, he could rely on church doctrine that homicide was permitted in self-defense. But could he reconcile killing another human being with his conception of himself? Did he know the answer to the question himself? At Maela, his resistance had been mostly passive; he had fought back, wrestling police, but had stopped short of hurting anyone. Once, in the army, he'd prevented the beating of a friend by wrapping his arms around the attacker, a fellow soldier; in an effort not to hurt him, Kaiser had allowed the man to blacken his eyes. Another time, in the 1970s, he'd grabbed a lug wrench and charged a pair of paramilitary policemen he found sexually assaulting a Masai girl. It had been enough to scare them off, but what if it hadn't?

Who could predict how he'd react if he was cornered, a man expert in killing whose vocation was peace? It was easy to image the scenario. There he would be, confronted on a dark road, with no time to deliberate. Who could say which instincts would prevail, the priest's or the paratrooper's, in a climax that he seemed increasingly bent on forcing?

• • •

GATHENJI HAD BEEN watching the tribunal closely. From the outset, he had exerted a largely unseen influence on it. He was, in fact, indirectly responsible for Kaiser's testimony as a witness for the Law Society. As one of its supervising lawyers, Gathenji had applied for permission for the society to call witnesses. He also argued to admit evidence from the Catholic Diocese of Nakuru that implicated Ntimama for inciting violence. They had a witness who represented a group of displaced farmers, and who had sworn a thirty-point affidavit about the violence. Under pressure from government lawyers, the venerable judges refused to hear more than a paragraph of it.

During the hearings, Gathenji's name had surfaced in connection with his well-publicized arrest for Publishing Alarming Statements four years earlier. Akiwumi himself seemed indignant that a fellow officer of the court had been subject to such humiliation. In the box sat Noah arap Too, who had been chief of the Criminal Investigation Department at the time.

Akiwumi: "Do you agree it was not in order to arrest Gathenji?"

Too: "Yes, I agree it was not, my Lords."

"Is this how you conduct things in Kenya?"

"No, my Lords."

"Is this Russia, where you just storm into people's houses at the middle of the night to conduct investigations?"

By midsummer, as the hearings approached their close after more than three hundred witnesses, Gathenji and a colleague argued for an extension on behalf of the Catholic diocese: The church still had witnesses who not been allowed to testify. No, Akiwumi ruled. They were out of time.

When the Akiwumi Commission handed a detailed report of its findings to Moi, the president was surely not surprised to read that he bore no blame for his nation's sorrow. He could read, however, that his ministers had run amuck. The report found the clashes stemmed from systemic government neglect and incitement, and recommended the investigation of Sunkuli, Ntimama, Biwott, and dozens of other powerful figures.

The report described the raid on Gathenji's home as "sinister," a "shameful" act that was "reminiscent of the inhuman practices of the notorious KGB of the Soviet Union." The commission noted that its own assisting counsel, Bernard Chunga, had been director of public prosecutions at the time and had blessed Gathenji's arrest "even though there was not an iota of evidence" against him. As for the alleged Alarming Statements themselves—the soldiers' accounts that they had been recruited to foment violence—the commission concluded that although certain of their details "may well not be genuine," police had failed to question key persons mentioned in the statements.

The Akiwumi Commission had managed the tightrope feat of leaving Moi untouched while exposing the massive cruelty, criminality, and incompetence of the machine he controlled. For all its faults, the commission's report would prove a valuable historical record. Yet for any who doubted Moi's sham intentions, he now supplied final proof: He refused to release the report. It would take more than three years, and a vastly changed political climate, before the public could see it.

Meanwhile, Sunkuli's ascent had not been thwarted by the American priest's testimony. Moi elevated him from assistant minister to full minister. He would take control of the country's internal-security forces. The country's police would be answerable to him.

Kaiser believed that his denunciation of Sunkuli had something to do with the promotion, perhaps because his testimony had proven Sunkuli's loyalty to the country's master. Shortly afterward, the priest came upon a school fund-raiser where Sunkuli was being honored, and according to one report, the following exchange occurred:

Kaiser: "You owe me a beer."

Sunkuli: "No. I owe you three."

11

THE GIRLS

AROUND DUSK ONE day in March 1999, a month after Kaiser's testimony before the tribunal, he found himself behind the wheel of his Toyota pickup, Father Keane riding beside him, as they set out from Kilgoris toward Lolgorien. The day's pastoral work was done, and before them was a drive of two hours. Connecting the two towns was a single gravelly red road that curved without forks through a verdant desolation of rolling grasslands. To break down out here was a bad prospect; you might wait for hours before help came along, and many of the travelers were government men. The priests had taken this road many times, day and night. Anybody who had been monitoring their movements, and had observed them leave Kilgoris, would know the isolation into which they were now headed.

The priests had not been on the road long when they noticed a white car behind them. *In Kenya*, the wary said, *there is always a white car behind you.* The priests knew it hardly mattered exactly who occupied the car—the Special Branch, the General Services Unit, police, game rangers, Sunkuli's bodyguards, Ntimama or Biwott's enforcers, freelance thugs, bandits. What mattered was that their truck was heading into a deep stretch of darkness in the company of strangers. Inconvenient people died this way, swerving inexplicably off lonely roads into trees or ditches, their corpses cold by morning.

Kaiser must have asked himself whether he was just being paranoid. How many times had his eyes narrowed on a strange car, the hair bristling on the back of his neck, only to watch it pass by harmlessly? How many times had he felt someone's watchful gaze burning between his shoulder blades, only to turn and find emptiness? How many times had he read menace in a benign smile?

No, he had to be sure. He eased his foot off the gas pedal, slowing the truck along the edge of the savanna, and brought it to a stop. He told Keane to step outside and pretend to urinate. If the other car meant no harm, it would pass by.

The white car stopped a short distance behind them, waiting.

Keane jumped into the truck and pulled the door swiftly closed. Kaiser hit the gas hard. They picked up speed on the hard road. The white car gave chase. At one point, it pulled ahead, as if to position itself to block the truck. Kaiser floored the truck and took the lead, kicking up a storm of dust, creating distance between him and the pursuers.

He had a plan. He knew the route's every bend and coil; knew that it narrowed into a single lane where it crossed the little Migore River, a few miles north of the parish house; knew the surrounding terrain was abundant with hiding places for men on foot, the road on each side fronted by thick, dense screens of riverine trees and croton brush.

By the time the bridge lurched into the headlights, the white car was some distance behind. Kaiser hit the brakes, positioning the truck before the bridge: a roadblock.

"Get out," he told Keane.

In the truck was an old ax that he used to chop up animals; Keane took it. Kaiser carried his shotgun. They scrambled up a wooded bank into the trees. They waited, breathing, as the night thickened around them. Crouched in their separate places, they watched and listened. They heard the pursuing car roar up and come to a stop. They waited. It was solid dark. Fifteen or twenty minutes must have passed, each minute interminable. It was common knowledge that Kaiser was armed, a crack shot, a trained soldier. The pursuers must have sensed their disadvantage. Finally, the white car came alive, the tires chewing the dirt, wheeling around, and soon the sound of the tread had vanished down the road.

The priests waited until it felt safe to leave the dark woods, then crept carefully down the bank toward the truck. They rode back to the parish house mostly in silence.

Afterward, they didn't talk about the incident much; there was little to say. Keane could sense Kaiser remained in terrible fear, and talking about the danger only seemed to peel his already-raw nerves. Keane learned to fill the air with small talk. They decided there was no point in reporting the incident to police. They could not prove anything, could not identify the pursuing car or who had been inside it. Perhaps it had just been meant to scare them, after all; perhaps it was just a reminder that they were being watched.

Keane thought: *Kaiser would have pulled the trigger. Absolutely: if not to save himself then to save me.*

He would have been on the right side of doctrine; nobody could call it a sin. If they had come after them into the woods, if there had been no choice, yes, the Irishman believed, the old American soldier would have taken aim, dead-eyed, steady-armed, and erased someone's life.

BY DAY, THE two priests said Mass, blessed houses, and visited the sick, Keane roaming off on the Suzuki motorbike, Kaiser in his truck. Keane perceived a hint of pride in his friend: Kaiser seemed to enjoy the spotlight. He would photocopy newspaper articles about himself and send them to friends and family in the States. Keane thought of him as a "terribly stubborn" man who'd argue all day in defense of the Church's prohibition on birth control. He'd tell village women to "increase and multiply" even when they had seven or eight kids already, and he grew irritated when Keane replied that God had issued that commandment when there were only two people on the earth.

Keane saw a streak of recklessness in Kaiser, an inability to resist pushing his luck. He took pointless risks. It was imprudent to go hunting with his unlicensed .22 rifle, since it provided rangers with a fine pretext to take him in. And yet one rainy day, Kaiser said, "Let's go hunting," and drove Keane to an abandoned, grass-overgrown airstrip a few miles from the parish house. There were hares. Kaiser could have used his shotgun, which was legally registered, but he refused to waste a big shell on small game. As Keane waited in the cab, Kaiser took aim at a hare with his .22 and shot it through the head. Soon a pack of game wardens had materialized around the truck.

They found the hare in the back of the truck. They demanded to know what type of weapon had killed it.

Kaiser indicated the shotgun.

They studied the hole in the hare's head and said, *Give us the rifle.*

There is no rifle.

Give us the rifle.

We don't understand. Pole sana. Just this shotgun.

Inexplicably, they did not check under the passenger seat, where Keane had managed to hide the rifle. They let the priests drive home.

The priests waited until night and dismantled the rifle, then buried its pieces around the church compound, and when the wardens returned the next day, the priests said, *Search.*

Keane tried to figure out how the wardens had known where they were. It was as if they had been waiting nearby. Had they been tipped off to their presence at the airstrip? He believed only two people had known. The first was Maria Mokona, the housekeeper, but Keane dismissed the idea out of hand: She would never betray Kaiser.

The second person was Francis Kantai, the catechist, whom Keane had never trusted. He suspected, in fact, that Sunkuli had planted him in the house as a spy. Keane had tried to tell Kaiser that Kantai gave him a bad feeling, that he was a liar, that he was taking him for a ride.

Kaiser would jump to his catechist's defense. His temper flared. He brought his fist down on a coffee table, smashing it.

In the months after Kaiser's testimony at the tribunal, he seemed to be sleeping again at night. But his memory was fading; he'd leave money on the table and forget about it. He neglected himself physically. His diet was *ugali* and whatever game meat he'd shot.

His sense of danger had abated but not vanished. At one point, by

Keane's account, Kaiser came down with typhoid fever and drove himself to the Kilgoris hospital. Waiting for an injection, he somehow discovered that the physician was a friend or relative of Sunkuli; or at least Kaiser, racked with fever, came to believe this was the case. He hurried out of the hospital and into his truck. Even in the grip of typhoid, he navigated the two-hour drive back to his parish, and explained to Keane: *The man could have killed me with an injection.*

It was time for Keane to leave. It was June. He'd been in Lolgorien for seven months. He said good-bye to his friend and rode off with mixed emotions. He did not like the idea of leaving Kaiser out there with Kantai.

AT SOME POINT that summer, Kantai brought a family friend from Kilgoris to see the priest. Her name was Anne Sawoyo, a beautiful Masai in her early twenties. Kaiser knew her face: She had been one of his parishioners for years, and had two young children.

As she sat before him now, she told a terrible story. It was five years ago, she said. Her family was very poor, she explained, with no money to pay her high school tuition, and they'd turned to Sunkuli in desperation. Sunkuli agreed to help, explaining: You elected me to serve you.

Her account of what happened next would later become public. According to her, Sunkuli arrived at her house near Kilgoris wearing a black cap and a long *kabuti,* or coat. He wanted her to accompany him to his home, where she and some other girls would help serve a large delegation of guests the next day. He reassured her by saying the other girls were already there. She reluctantly got into his car, and as they drove, they picked people up and dropped them off. It was dark, near midnight, when he turned off the road leading to his home and stopped the car near a bridge. He and his bodyguard, a man she knew only as Moses, left the car and vanished into the dark. She said that Sunkuli returned and pretended the car would not start, saying it was probably the battery. She said that she was exhausted by then, so she lay back on the seat to sleep, and when she awoke, she found him on top of her.

"I begged him not to harm me, but he did not listen to me. I remember pleading with him not to kill me. He told me that if I became pregnant, he would take me to Nairobi where a doctor would carry out an abortion." She said that Sunkuli covered her mouth to stifle her screaming, and that when it was over, past midnight by then, Sunkuli started the engine and his bodyguard climbed back inside the car. They arrived about 1:30 A.M. at Sunkuli's home, where she was led to a room in which two children—possibly Sunkuli's own—were sleeping. She said that she heard Sunkuli pacing about the house, and when his wife asked him why he wasn't sleeping, she heard him say, "Leave me alone." She locked the door in case Sunkuli came after her again, she said, and at one point she heard him touch it from the other side. She opened a window in case she might need to escape, having determined that "I would not allow him to rape me a second time." She didn't sleep that night, and about six o'clock the next morning, Sunkuli's driver led her to the car and took her home. She said that she kept the ordeal from her mother, and that after she discovered she was pregnant, Sunkuli sent a cousin with a message: The minister would pay the child's school fees and expenses, provided she keep the father's name a secret.

She gave birth at age seventeen, still a high school student, and missed three years of school before returning. She had kept quiet all this time but now wanted to sue Sunkuli, saying he'd abandoned his promise to take care of their child.

Kaiser clearly believed that her account was credible. He gave her money for school and drove her to a lawyer in Kisii to seek advice. The lawyer balked; Sunkuli was a powerful man.

Kaiser told Kantai to accompany her and the child to Nairobi. There, he explained, they should tell their story to the International Federation of Women Lawyers, or FIDA.

FIDA was representing a second young Masai woman who alleged Sunkuli had raped and impregnated her. Her name was Florence Mpayei, a sixteen-year-old Protestant from Kilgoris, who was described in a newspaper report as Sunkuli's first cousin. Like Sawoyo, Mpayei said poverty had forced her into an arrangement with Sunkuli. At one point, by her account, he'd given her a bed in his family home. One day when she was fourteen, she said, Sunkuli took her to his Harambee House office in Nairobi, locked the door, and raped her on the red carpet. When the minister learned she was pregnant, he sent money for an abortion, she said; instead, she gave birth to a son, Dennis.

Her accusations became public that July, when FIDA backed her appearance before the United Nations–sponsored African Court. "A minister raped me and he said there is nothing a poor person like myself can do to him," she said, racked by sobs at the podium. She said she had wanted to kill her son, the product of the rape, but faltered when she looked in his eyes. She said the minister had reneged on promises to pay for the baby's upkeep and her school fees, and had raped her a second time.

Martha Koome, the local FIDA chair, said that Sunkuli arranged a meeting with her in the company of his lawyers and did not deny responsibility for fathering Mpayei's child but offered to cut a deal. Koome replied that they couldn't negotiate on a minor's rape, leaving the minister "very agitated and angry," she recalled. "He told us that Father Kaiser was fueling the whole case." According to a press account, Sunkuli admitted to an affair with Mpayei but characterized her as a spurned lover who had wanted to be his wife.

With Kaiser's urging, FIDA hid both of Sunkuli's accusers in a house amid a row of gated homes in Nairobi. Kaiser was aware of the location. The girls had not been ensconced there long when, in the first week of September, a Land Rover pulled up to the gate. From the vehicle spilled a cadre of Sunkuli loyalists, including plainclothes police. Accompanying them were the girls' parents. By Sawoyo's account, she was outdoors, hanging out wet clothes to dry, when she saw a Transmara councilor watching the house. She also saw her mother beyond the fence perimeter. Sawoyo ran upstairs to hide. Policemen appeared at the door and demanded to be let in: *Give us the girls.* The woman who ran the safe house, Edith Kirugumi, insisted there were no girls there. The police made threats. The door was opened.

Soon Sunkuli's accusers were being led to the Land Rover in the company of their parents. They were taken to a police station, where, by Sawoyo's account, she was asked to sign a statement that FIDA had abducted her. She refused. She and Mpayei were soon released, but the message had been chilling: *We can find you anywhere.*

There was little mystery about how the location of the safe house was discovered: Kantai admitted to giving it up. They came for me, Kantai explained later. They held a gun to the back of my head and said, Show us. They gave me no choice, he said.

Later, Sunkuli portrayed the raid as a "rescue." He said he had given the "opportunist" Kantai ten thousand Kenyan shillings—a little more than one hundred U.S. dollars—to lead his men to the safe house, and that Kantai had volunteered to be handcuffed. Such a touch would have created the impression of coercion.

BY NOW, KAISER had become nettlesome enough to warrant special attention. No one would claim responsibility for what happened next, but the order clearly originated on high. Someone passed word to someone, who passed word to someone else, and in late October, police were searching the country for John Kaiser, with the aim of planting him on an airplane out of the country. The pretext: He was three months late in renewing his visa. It was not the first time he had been late. But now, according to the immigration office, he was to be regarded as a "prohibited immigrant." Kaiser was at his bishop's compound in Ngong when a group of plainclothesmen pounded on the door. How he escaped is unclear—one story has him shimmying down a pipe while nuns held the police at bay. The priest was soon shuttling between safe houses, moving from city to city, village to village. For a time, he hid in Kisii, the place from which he'd been exiled, the place he knew intimately. Those closest to Kaiser believed he feared deportation more than death. To be sent home would mean he wouldn't be able to finish his work.

At one point, Kaiser appeared in Gathenji's lobby near the Nairobi Law

Courts and said, "*Jambo,* Mr. Gathenji." He was dusty, unkempt, standing in the half-open door to his office with a dejected mien. He wanted to
say good-bye. He figured there was a good chance they would catch him.
He stood at the lawyer's door and said, "I may not see you again."

Gathenji stood up from his desk and went to shake his hand.

"You don't have to say good-bye," Gathenji said.

Kaiser held his shoulder and told him to persevere, to be brave, and to
remember the example his father had set. Martyred thirty years earlier,
Samuel Gathenji had seen death from a great distance and refused to
budge. It seemed possible that Kaiser, on some level, perceived that his
life was emulating that trajectory, and did not entirely mind it.

NEWSPAPERS PICKED UP the story of Kaiser's disappearance, noting his link to the sex case against Sunkuli. MYSTERY DEEPENS OVER MISS-
ING AMERICAN PRIEST, read one headline. An article described him as "a
defender of clash victims." The *Daily Nation* was bold enough to charac-
terize the government's gesture as "a mockery of the law." The Church,
claiming not to know where he was, denounced the deportation order as
a vendetta, while the Kenya Human Rights Commission announced that
his only crime had been linking a minister to the rape of two minors.

Most significant was the intervention of the then U.S. ambassador,
Johnnie Carson, a senior diplomat who had been America's face in Kenya
for three months. Like many, Carson believed Sunkuli was behind the
order, and he told Kenya's foreign minister, Bonaya Godana, that he was
puzzled by the attempt to oust a missionary who'd called Kenya home
for thirty-five years. He warned, in his measured ambassadorial manner, that the move "could have a negative impact on bilateral relations."
By Carson's account, Godana said the matter was above his head—an
audience might be required with Moi himself. Yet hours later, at a news
conference, the deportation order was rescinded. An embassy memo
reflected Carson's view of the episode: "The foreign minister's initial suggestion that we take our concerns to the president reveals how seriously

the Kenyans took the case, and the power of the forces arrayed against this troublesome priest."

When Kaiser reemerged after ten days in hiding, one newspaper called him "a beacon of hope in a sea of misery." The regime had managed to do several things with its clumsy stratagem. It had given the opposition a cause, catalyzed the Church's will, and supplied the press with an excuse to resurrect Kaiser's Akiwumi testimony. Kaiser himself considered the episode a great victory.

Sunkuli was unbowed. In remarks to the press, he accused Kaiser of having "designed and executed a plan to bring out what he intended to be a sex scandal," and called the rape accusations "all politics," the work of enemies looking to smear him. He added, "Father John Kaiser hates me like poison." Having just articulated a clear motive for wanting Kaiser gone, he nevertheless denied that he had been behind the order to deport him.

With timing worthy of an orchestrated PR campaign, the *Daily Nation* ran a flattering profile featuring a large photograph of the smiling thirty-eight-year-old minister, who happened to be Kenya's youngest cabinet member, and described his longtime status as "a beacon of Christian moral values": in high school, an altar boy; in college, national chairman of a Catholic student group; in law school, choirmaster at St. Paul's Chapel; as an adult, one who abjured drink and cigarettes.

"The fact that I love women does not mean that I have loose morals," he was quoted as saying.

A *Daily Nation* reporter trekked to Lolgorien and found Kaiser looking haggard and weary, clad in a dusty outfit, a man "perhaps too prosaic in appearance for his station." The reporter described Kaiser as grumbling and moving about, avoiding the camera, responding "peevishly" to questions. Why Kaiser might have found the encounter irritating, if not dangerous, is clear from the drift of the questions: Was he a CIA spy? Would he reply to allegations that he had been smuggling gold? His patience seemed exhausted. "Do not ask me anything about gold," he snapped. He was busy preparing Mass. "Nobody will ever frighten me out of my priestly obligation of condemning injustice and evil, even if it means being persecuted by those who thrive on earthly powers," he said. He described Sunkuli as "a brother in Christ" and said he prayed for him every day. "I have been mistaken by my enemies for a civil rights worker while, in essence, I am just a simple parish priest," the story quoted him as saying.

"Here in Kenya I still get some press coverage which is nice for the ego," he wrote to his sister soon after. A reporter had arrived in a Land Rover with government men: "They hid the vehicle in town & came on foot & pretended they were Press reporters from Nairobi. But 3 of them were police plain-clothes thugs sent by Sunkuli and only one Nation reporter. I only talked to them for about 5 minutes because I wanted Sunkuli to get the message he can come & talk to me if he wants."

Contemplating the state of the country, and a parliament that seemed increasingly bold in asserting its powers, Kaiser wrote, "I think the President feels like a man on a small island of sand with heavy seas eating his footing away." Possibly, Kaiser was also describing himself. Bishop Davies had received anonymous messages threatening Kaiser's life if he remained in Lolgorien. "I think a *real* professional killer would not warn you in advance," Kaiser wrote to a friend in the States. "Also I retain my trusty 12 bore."

It's difficult to say whether Kaiser took the threats as lightly as he tried to make it appear. His letters had an aura of depletion—he acknowledged feeling "rather weak and tired"—which likely reflected the toll of perpetual raw-nerved vigilance.

He urged friends from the States to visit him; he didn't seem to think he'd be around much longer. Considering how closely he was being watched, he wrote to Don Beumer, a friend and benefactor in Minnesota, nothing would happen to a visitor. "If the police come with a trumped up reason to confiscate my shotgun then I will know a raid by thugs is in the near future. These rats are good at beating up on unarmed old man and raping young girls but they will not risk a backside full of buckshot." Three weeks later, he reiterated his desire that Beumer and his family visit "before we all hang up our boots."

12

WE WILL ALL BE SORTED OUT

FOR THOSE WORKING to hasten the end of Moi's interminable epoch, Kaiser had become a useful symbol. On March 11, 2000, the Law Society of Kenya, a stronghold of the pro-democracy movement, booked the posh banquet hall of the Intercontinental Hotel to honor him with a human rights award. He'd refused the award the year before, with the explanation that he was sure others had done more valuable work. He accepted this time, he told people, figuring that a higher profile would make him harder to kill. And he would have another platform. "I hope we aren't all rounded up," Kaiser wrote to his sister hours before the event. He expected the American ambassador, Johnnie Carson, to be there. This was a mistaken hope. A scheduling conflict, Carson said, though few were surprised that he didn't appear.

The banquet hall was a sea of tuxes. There were ice sculptures and a salmon buffet. At the center of the opulence stood a guilt-tinged Minnesotan in a Roman collar and a pair of ten-dollar pants he'd purchased at an American Goodwill. Lawyers and foreign diplomats lined up to shake his hand. In the crowd were other dissidents, some of whom had been beaten, arrested, and tortured. Kaiser suspected the Law Society had given him the award to prod more clergymen into political action. Reading the citation aloud, a lawyer described Kaiser as a "man of God who, like the Biblical Elijah, is a voice of stern rebuke to all those that trouble the people," and "a stalwart defender of the defenseless." Kaiser, the speaker continued, did not go out of his way to find trouble. "To the contrary, he is a retiring, humble and soft-spoken *mzee*. He is a simple man without pretensions. Seeing him on a normal day one could easily dismiss him for just another tired old man—though a tall one."

Reportedly, Kaiser wept. He stood before the assemblage, which almost certainly included agents from the Special Branch, and announced that Moi should be tried at the Hague for crimes against humanity. He urged the Law Society to take up the cause.

After the banquet, Kaiser left the hotel with Don Beumer, a longtime Minnesota friend who had taken up his request to visit. The priest spotted a burly plainclothesman across the street who appeared to be following them. "That's one of those thugs," he said matter-of-factly, and told his friend not to be surprised if he was killed. "They'll say I committed suicide. Don't believe it."

It was late, near midnight, and they were walking in a bad part of town, a few blocks from the hotel. A teenage boy accosted them, begging. Kaiser took the boy's arm and turned it around, looking for needle tracks. He would not give money to a junkie. The boy's hand flashed up and grabbed the glasses tucked in Kaiser's shirt pocket. The boy fled. Kaiser gave chase, and a nervous Beumer watched them disappear into an alley. A few moments later, Kaiser came walking back. Even now in his late sixties, it was not in his nature to reflect long on the danger of a dark alley before plunging ahead.

Back at the Mill Hill house in Nairobi, Kaiser told Beumer, "The boys want to talk to me." The other priests had summoned Kaiser for a private word. They were worried. To call for Moi's prosecution was to invite retribution. *They could kill us,* the priests said. *Can't you ease off, John?*

Afterward, Kaiser reported this encounter to Beumer and told him that he was conflicted. "I took a vow of obedience," he said. Both his bishop and his Mill Hill brothers were asking him to tone down his rhetoric, and if a superior ordered him to stop, he would. But until it was an order, he explained, his conscience compelled him to speak.

Kaiser drove Beumer back to Lolgorien. "If something happens, get in the hallway quick," he told Beumer. "We have thick walls to protect us." He went through the house, making sure the windows were closed and the drapes drawn. Normally, he liked to keep the windows open. But many of the game wardens and police belonged to Sunkuli. He explained that they would take him into the bush and feed him to the hyenas if they got a chance.

Beumer asked what everyone asked: *Why not go back to the States, John?*

Kaiser said his work was unfinished. There was the case against Sunkuli, as well as the case he was trying to build against Moi in international court, and there was another government commission in the works, the Njonjo Commission, where he hoped to give testimony. If he left now, he'd never get back in.

Several weeks later, Kaiser traveled to Homa Bay to give a presentation about the country's history to a church delegation from the States. The delegation was being hosted by Bill Vos, Kaiser's old friend, a Minnesota priest and missionary. Afterward, as Kaiser was walking to his truck, a pair of plainclothesmen approached him. They had some questions. Later, Kaiser told Vos that they were from CID. They wanted to know why he was talking to the Americans.

At one point, Sister Nuala Brangan told Kaiser that trying to bring Moi to the Hague would get him deported or killed.

"You know if you go, you won't get away with it," Nuala said.

"I know," he said. She heard no bravado in his reply.

That April, Paul Muite, the lawyer and parliamentarian whom Kaiser had known since Maela, announced with fanfare that he had enlisted lawyers in London to explore criminal proceedings against Moi in connection with election-related violence. In an enthusiastic letter to Muite, Kaiser offered to assemble witnesses, writing, "I very much wish to support you in this good work and to collaborate in it."

Meanwhile, Kaiser continued urging FIDA to pursue its case against Sunkuli. "It's a just war and I am on the right side," he wrote to his sister.

Mpayei's filing of a private prosecution in late May brought a front-page headline in the *Daily Nation*: SUNKULI ACCUSED OF SEX ATTACK. The story carried a picture of the seventeen-year-old Mpayei with her three-year-old son. She claimed that Sunkuli and two of his men had held her prisoner and forced her to withdraw charges against him. Two weeks later, in a courtroom Sunkuli had packed with Masai supporters in full tribal regalia, Nairobi's chief magistrate ordered that Sunkuli—along with a policeman and a Transmara chief accused of kidnapping Mpayei—appear in court to face charges.

This was hardly a decisive victory. The legal threshold had been low. Among FIDA lawyers, however, it was regarded as a major achievement that a case against so powerful a man had advanced even this far.

KAISER HAD A guest that summer: Camille Kleinschmit, a twenty-three-year-old cousin from Nebraska. She taught math to the local kids and slept in a little room across the hall from the priest, who described her as "a wonder." Some of the kids' parents thought she was a CIA agent, which made her chuckle, and some assumed she was a prostitute, because she wore shorts outdoors. Kaiser worried his enemies might hurt her to get at him.

"You'll be taken and killed," he scolded her when she walked alone. "They'll say 'Stupid American, she ran off into the jungle and got eaten by the lions.' "

When Kaiser talked about politics around other Mill Hill priests, Camille noticed how urgently they tried to hush him. She traveled with him in his pickup, carrying firewood or cement for the medical building he was constructing on the parish grounds, and she watched people running from every direction to greet him.

Throughout the summer, Camille spent a great deal of time with Francis Kantai, the young catechist so many people distrusted. He was kind to her. She found him charming. She was falling in love.

Someone hurled a twenty-five-pound rock through Kaiser's bedroom window in late June. The priest had been out, and when he returned, he found glass shattered on the floor. He hung up a blanket. "I would like to grow old gracefully," he wrote to his sister, "but the government keeps me hoping."

One day, Kaiser got word that Anne Sawoyo was being held against her will at the Mara Serena Safari Lodge in the enormous Masai Mara game park. The lodge, a two-hour drive from the parish house, was a Sunkuli stronghold, and a prison as formidable as Alcatraz; there were miles of savanna in every direction, with lions, hyenas, and crocodile-infested rivers.

He decided to rescue her. It was July 10. Into his truck he piled Kantai, Camille, and, for protection, three other local Masais. The truck lurched down the rocky, winding hill onto the Mara plain. They passed through a gate at the park entrance and cut inward through the interminable expanse of grassland, past croton thickets and fever trees, whistling thorns and scattered flat-topped acacias. At last, the lodge came into view atop an incline. It was a well-appointed resort designed to attract affluent tourists. A gift shop sold expensive Masai souvenirs. A restaurant patio overlooked a breath-catching primeval vista.

Kaiser found Sawoyo "depressed and fearful." She was resistant to their overtures that she leave with them. Camille suggested that she make her escape by lying low in the back of Kaiser's truck.

People are watching, Sawoyo said. *They'll stop me. If they find me they'll shoot all of us.*

Kaiser promised he'd think of a plan to free her. He gave her a rosary. He looked scared.

Pray for me, my daughter. My life is in danger.

Back in Nairobi, Kaiser pressed FIDA to undertake a rescue operation, and he was frustrated at their failure to launch one immediately.

Soon after, Kaiser was having tea in the Kilgoris parish house with its pastor, Father James Juma. Juma told him that he had seen Sawoyo in the town, and that others had spotted her walking freely in Nairobi.

"She is not in prison" in the Mara, Juma said. "She could be playing a game with you. I would be careful fully trusting that girl."

Kaiser jumped to his feet and began pacing in agitation around the house. If she was free, why hadn't she contacted him?

"She has been bought," Kaiser said, furious. He asked to borrow Juma's cell phone and placed a quick call, apparently to tell FIDA not to pursue the second rescue attempt.

Still, Juma noticed, Kaiser remained preoccupied by the notion that he must somehow help her. There was a puzzling naïveté about the American, Juma thought. Once he fixed his mind on something, he was almost impossible to budge. Like his belief in the good intentions of Kantai. Juma had told Kaiser that he'd spotted Kantai more than once in the company of Sunkuli's bodyguards—had witnessed him getting in and out of the minister's cars when the caravan rolled into town—and yet Kaiser inexplicably brushed it off. He believed, somehow, that he needed to protect his catechist.

Back at his parish, Kaiser discovered that checks had been stolen from his mailbox and cashed. He believed it the work of Sunkuli's people.

"I am considered enemy no. one by the Kenyan government and my letters are often opened," he wrote. Sunkuli had "declared open season on me," though it would not deter him from pursuing the court case. "Our chances of winning are slim because our courts are corrupt but at least we are fighting back. They have tried to deport me & failed & have made death threats but what is that to a 67 year old has been."

ONE AFTER ANOTHER, they came to him, the gentle men of good sense, making their futile pilgrimages. In his courtyard, there would be the sound of tires, a slamming door, and another churchman stepping onto the gravel after a bone-jarring crossland journey to Lolgorien. Father Cornelius Schilder, director of Mill Hill in East Africa, stayed for three days. He found the normally sociable American was not acting like himself. He was jumpy, alert to every noise, suspicious of everyone who passed the house at night.

The two priests walked the parish grounds, among the brick shells of the buildings Kaiser said he knew he wouldn't live to complete. "They are going to kill me," he said. "I know I will not get away with this."

To Schilder's eyes, Kaiser was a "ruffian," his clothes shabby, his shoes forever unpolished. He was also "more Catholic than the pope," a man "exasperatingly difficult" to argue with on matters of theology. He saw no gray where other priests did, as with the church ban on birth control. He did not wrestle with such questions as the existence of a literal hell and a literal devil. Kaiser had certainty. He was a throwback, "headstrong as a bull" in his beliefs. So Schilder had small expectations when he urged Kaiser to leave Kenya for a while. *Go back to America, John. Rest.*

Schilder knew that Kaiser would obey a direct order, but he couldn't quite bring himself to give it. He believed that forcing Kaiser to leave would crush him. He admired Kaiser's crusade. He reasoned that he didn't have the right to remove him, if the priest had resigned himself clear-eyed to his death. He was doing an extraordinary thing, he figured, something other people didn't dare. Schilder thought, *Who am I to order him not to?*

Along came Bernard Phelan, who'd been Kaiser's regional Mill Hill superior for the last three years. He'd visited Kaiser before, and it was always the same: awful food, clothes strewn about, unwashed sheets that may or may not have bugs in them. That was John. You had to put up with it.

"This is a very dangerous time," Phelan told him. "It'd be better if you went back to the States till it cools down."

Phelan, too, left without having given him a direct order. He doubted that Kaiser would have obeyed it anyway.

There came still another entreaty to leave Kenya, this time from Mill Hill headquarters in England. It was not quite an order. He ignored it.

RATCHETING UP HIS battle against Sunkuli, Kaiser gave two thousand shillings to Helen Katim, a women's rights activist in the transmara who organized busloads of women to travel to Nairobi to protest Sunkuli's treatment of schoolgirls. It received little attention. A village chief had warned her: *If you go, you'll return in a coffin.* She was one of Kaiser's best sources. She lived on a small farm in the hills outside Kilgoris, in the dangerous borderlands between the Masai and the Kisii. By her account, more than ten girls, ages fourteen to eighteen, had approached her to report that they had been impregnated, after rape or seduction, by Sunkuli. There was a pattern, she said: Poor families brought the girls to

Sunkuli, asking for help with their schooling. Sometimes, she said, he'd visit elementary schools, promising funds or a promotion for the school director, and in exchange he would receive carte blanche to stroll the grounds, taking his pick of the girls. She regarded Sunkuli as "a very evil man who can do anything."

That summer, Kaiser got a personal warning from a sympathetic informant on the government payroll: There was a plan to shoot him and plant a dead animal beside him, so it would appear he had been gunned down as a poacher. One witness said the warning came from a game warden. Another, relying on Kaiser's account, said the warning had come from "government security officers."

Kaiser complained to one of his catechists, Romulus Ochieng, that his room—the sanctum he kept under lock and key, the place he allowed no one—had been opened. His room held sensitive documents: affidavits from victims and perpetrators of violence in Enoosupukia and Kilgoris, statements from women accusing Sunkuli of rape. Ochieng suspected that Kantai, one of the few people who could get hold of a key, had waited until the priest had left the house and then invited Sunkuli loyalists inside. At one point, Kaiser's housekeeper heard him rebuking Kantai for letting people into his room.

In early August came the anonymous note: *Utaona moto.* You will see fire.

According to Kantai, who claimed he was present when Kaiser received the note, the priest's face changed on reading it. "I don't give a damn," the priest said.

ON AUGUST 15, Kaiser wrote a peculiar letter to his friend Martin van Leeuwen, a Catholic brother from Holland who was working in Nairobi. "At present our Honorable Minister is a minor obstacle but he will soon be sorted out," he wrote, referring to Sunkuli. "Here in Trans-Mara the only real support for our Honorable Minister is our Honorable President, but he too will soon be sorted out." Two paragraphs later, after some remarks on routine church business, Kaiser invoked a theological debate that he and van Leeuwen had been having about the nature of eternal punishment. Van Leeuwen, a progressive Christian, reasoned that there could be no hell, since Christ had died for everyone. Kaiser believed in real damnation, but he was not in an argumentative mood. "As far as your theological opinion regarding the permanence of Hell I do not entirely agree but you and I will also soon be sorted out." There was that phrase again—three times in a few paragraphs—as if he were already watching the transient pageant of human striving and folly, including his own, from somewhere else.

THE LETTER THAT would summon him from Lolgorien for the last time came on Saturday, August 19, 2000. It had been passed between church members all the way from Nairobi, and one of his catechists, Lucas Agan, delivered the envelope into his hands. The letter's author was Giovanni Tonucci, the Pope's appointed representative in Kenya, known as the papal nuncio. He wanted to see Kaiser in Nairobi on an urgent but unspecified matter.

Kaiser knew the nuncio did not send a summons casually, and he believed he would now be ordered out of the country, exiled for good. He wept during early-morning Mass on Monday, August 21. He was to depart for Nairobi that day. To his friend Melchizedek Ondieki, he seemed in the grip of a fear he'd never seen. To leave now, the priest said, would be to fail his people. It would show cowardice. "Melchizedek, I'm on a very difficult journey," he said. "Pray for me."

The night of the twenty-first, he arrived in his Toyota double-cab pickup truck at the bishop's house on the edge of Nairobi, near a slum at the foot of the knuckled Ngong Hills. He seemed unhinged, fearful. He spoke of being followed. He complained of not having slept in three days. At dinner, his mood seemed to improve. He traded lighthearted reminiscences with a former seminary classmate, Father Leo. They talked about getting their old Mill Hill classmates together.

Someone gave Kaiser a newspaper that said Florence Mpayei was firing her lawyers and dropping the charges against Sunkuli. She dutifully recited Sunkuli's claim that FIDA was exploiting her case as a fund-raising tool and using it to smear his name. Kaiser reacted with anger and disappointment. Had she been bought off? The two best cases against Sunkuli were collapsing.

That night, Kaiser called the nuncio to say that he had made it to Nairobi and would be dropping by the next morning. He told the nuncio that he had not been sleeping well. The nuncio asked why. It was not every day, Kaiser replied, that one was called by so eminent a personage. The nuncio told him not to be afraid: He hadn't been named a cardinal. They laughed together. The conversation ended "in a humorous mood," by the nuncio's account.

After dinner, Kaiser approached Bishop Davies, who was leaving on a safari early the next morning, and asked to make his confession. Later, in remarks to the BBC, Davies said that Kaiser told him that he was in mortal peril. "People only go to confession at that time of night if they feel there's a real danger they're not going to live very long," Davies said. Later still, Davies would insist that Kaiser's arrival, and the confession, had been unremarkable. "I didn't take any real notice of his coming," he said. "Everything was fine. . . . I didn't suspect anything at all that was on his mind."

At some point on the twenty-first, he dashed off a letter to his Minnesota friends Helen and Peter Housman. He did not know why he'd been summoned, he said, "but if it's urgent then it must be Politics." The Sunkuli case was on his mind. "It seems they will try to stop the case against Julius Sunkuli in spite of a group of Masai mothers who went to Press House in Nairobi denouncing Sunkuli as a defiler of schoolgirls. Pray that I can do something to protect our little girls."

The next morning was Tuesday, August 22. Father Francis Mwangi held a 6:45 A.M. Mass, with a short homily on Jomo Kenyatta; it was the anniversary of his death. Kaiser arrived late.

Over breakfast with Mwangi, Kaiser said he hadn't slept again. He spoke of the stone hurled through his parish-house window.

"Why am I so paranoid?" he asked.

Mwangi had never seen Kaiser so nervous, not even in the crucible of the Maela camp. Kaiser seemed preoccupied with Kantai. "Why did I leave Francis behind?" It was not clear what he meant.

That morning, Kaiser drove to the Mill Hill house a few miles away, where Brother Alphonse Borgman found him pacing in the parking lot. Despite having already arranged a pickup from Mwangi, Kaiser asked Borgman to take him to his meeting with the nuncio. It was not clear why Kaiser didn't drive himself—it was just a few miles to the nuncio's house in Westlands. On the drive, Kaiser slumped low in Borgman's back seat, his jacket covering his face, either from exhaustion, fear, or both. Kaiser said he was close to a breakdown.

Kaiser nervously entered the meeting with Tonucci, but he was soon "completely relaxed," by the nuncio's account. The nuncio reassured him that he was not being exiled. Instead, he wanted his recommendation for a successor to Bishop Davies, who was approaching the mandatory retirement age of seventy-five. During the meeting, Kaiser spoke "without bitterness" of his trouble with certain political figures, and talked about the future of the Ngong Diocese, as if he'd play a part in it.

Afterward, picking him up, Borgman noticed the relief on Kaiser's face. He seemed to be in good spirits. Back at Mill Hill house, he played a cheerful game of croquet in the compound's walled courtyard, a spacious, sweetly shaded garden of oleander and jacaranda, plumeria and hibiscus. As mission guests gathered for a predinner drink, Kaiser reportedly said, "Isn't it great that we have a place where we can all come as a group and drink a beer and share a meal?"

That night, Sister Dominica McQue saw Kaiser in the chapel, bent on one knee, his head in his hands. She also saw him fumbling with his key while trying to open his room.

The next day was Wednesday, August 23. He was spotted in the chapel before breakfast. He drove to the nuncio's house without an appointment, gave him a thin envelope—its contents would never be made public—and declined an offer to stay and talk. About 10:00 A.M. he drove to the nearby

Maryknoll missionary society, where he dropped off a letter to a priest, Bob Jalbert, who had taught him Swahili.

"Greetings, I just want to say a belated thanks for the great Swahili course in 1994. It was a great Blessing for me. Hope we run into each other soon." The letter was signed, "In Domino, John A. Kaiser, M.H.M."

Kaiser joined eight or nine others for lunch at the Mill Hill house. He wept at the table. "I hope it wasn't something I said," a priest told Martin van Leeuwen.

"Don't worry," van Leeuwen replied, "Father Kaiser is not himself."

During afternoon tea, Kaiser sat, withdrawn and silent, in the common room. At some point, he approached a fellow missionary, Paul Boyle, to announce that he'd be dead the next day. Boyle did not know what he meant, but he saw in his face a look of bottomless weariness.

The phone rang, and one of the other missionaries picked it up and began talking. Kaiser stood up and excused himself, saying, "I don't want to listen to the conversation, so I will drink my tea in my room."

Van Leeuwen was worried about Kaiser and thought he should stay close to him. He took him to a construction site a few blocks from the Mill Hill house, where van Leeuwen was supervising the building of a three-story retreat for nuns. He knew of Kaiser's passion for building and thought it might interest him.

At the site, they had tea with the sisters, and Kaiser pumped the hands of all the workmen he could find. He seemed to want to meet everyone. Gently, van Leeuwen tried to restrain his enthusiasm.

"You can't stop everybody from working," van Leeuwen said. "These people are paid by the day."

By midafternoon, Kaiser was eager to return to Lolgorien, but van Leeuwen urged him not to make the trip just then: he would be driving through the dark. Kaiser agreed to spend another night in Nairobi and leave early the next morning. Van Leeuwen dropped him off at the Mill Hill house about 4:00 P.M. About two hours later, he noticed, with concern, that he had vanished.

Kaiser next materialized at the bishop's house around 6:00 P.M. Father

Francis Mwangi was sitting in a small room near the entrance, counseling a couple about to get married. He saw Kaiser pull up in his truck.

Kaiser was brusque. He was in no mood to talk. He wanted a room. He said he needed rest.

Mwangi told him to take the second-floor room he'd used the other night. He informed him that he'd received a call from Sister Nuala, who was looking for him. She was working with the group of Transmara women who were in town to stage another protest against Sunkuli, and Kaiser had intended to meet them, but now he seemed indifferent to the call. Instead, he told Mwangi, "Ring Sister Nuala and thank her for all of the good work she has done."

Kaiser seemed in no state of mind to be pushed. Later, Mwangi said that he feared Kaiser might slap him if he said the wrong thing.

Mwangi watched Kaiser head upstairs to the second-floor landing of the bishop's house. His quarters were a plain, cell-size room with light blue walls, a wood-frame bed, a desk, and a chair. Over the next few minutes, Mwangi would say, he heard what sounded to him like Kaiser pacing upstairs.

It was getting dark when Mwangi heard footsteps descend the stairs. He heard the front door open and close. He heard Kaiser's truck leave the gated compound. When he went to check, he found Kaiser's room empty, the bedding stripped.

ABOUT SIX O'CLOCK the next morning, a watchman was hurrying to work at the Kenya Cooperative Creameries farm about forty miles northwest of Nairobi. It was a large compound encompassing flower, macadamia nut, and cattle operations near the junction of the Naivasha and Nakuru roads. The watchman noticed a truck slanting against a cement culvert in a roadside ditch near the farm entrance. He saw some bedding on the ground, and a human shape. He came within seven or eight feet but didn't stop, assuming, he would later claim, that it was a driver who had spent the night beside his broken-down truck.

Soon after, a butcher truck approached the farm to pick up cows for the slaughterhouse. The butchers, too, noticed the truck and the body, and the fact that a handful of people—the workers who usually gathered near the farm's entrance to await rides to the interior—had assembled around the scene.

The truck was a Toyota double-cab pickup, and the driver's side window was smashed. The set of bedsheets on the ground nearby had been neatly spread out. In the dirt lay the body of the truck's owner, John Kaiser, faceup. He wore gray pants and a black leather jacket. The back of his head had been obliterated. Nearby lay his shotgun.

The butchers drove to a nearby police roadblock and returned with two policemen. By 7:00 A.M., a sizable crowd had formed, and an untold number of the curious had crossed the scene; how badly they might have disturbed the scene, and in which ways, would never be clear. This left the most basic facts about the case—such as what position the body had been in, and where the shotgun lay in relation to it—irretrievably lost.

When Kenyan investigators arrived, they found a twelve-gauge shotgun shell and a pair of glasses in the priest's left shirt pocket. The shotgun's left barrel contained a spent shell, while the right barrel was empty. On the priest's body and in his truck, police found a stack of Kenyan shillings equaling about 250 U.S. dollars, along with a report on tribal clashes, letters he'd written to the World Bank and government officials protesting Moi's policies, and an application he apparently meant to take to the Njonjo Commission (another government panel, ostensibly to probe land grabbing, at which he hoped to testify).

At 11:30 A.M., the body was taken from the scene, en route to the Lee Funeral Home in Nairobi. The chief government pathologist, Dr. Alex Olumbe, was furious that he had not been summoned to examine the body at the scene, though the oversight was a common one in homicide cases. At the autopsy, Olumbe observed that the fatal blast had entered behind Kaiser's right ear. He noted stippling, or powder tattoos, on the scalp, suggesting a "close-range wound"; it lacked the singed hair, soot, or seared skin normally associated with a contact wound. There were no shotgun pellets or wadding in what was left of the cranium, nor had any been found at the scene. There was blood spatter on the lower left front of the priest's pants, drops of blood on the right back pocket, and more spatter on the left shoe.

Also present at the autopsy, having been summoned by the church, was Dr. Ling Kituyi, the Norwegian director of the Independent Medico-Legal Unit, a human rights group that documented torture. When she studied photos of the crime scene taken by Kenyan police, something seemed wrong in the position of the body as it had supposedly been found: The priest was lying on his left side, a little too neatly, with his arms in front of him. At some point, she was convinced, the posture had been altered. Anyone who'd been on the scene, police or passersby, could have done this. Or his killers might have done it. It was not even clear to her whether the priest had died at the site or had been dumped there.

Now, as she examined the body, she, too, noted the stippling and the absence of burned skin, and concluded the shotgun had discharged at a distance of between six inches and three feet from the skull.

She observed scratch marks on the priest's left wrist and blood under his fingernails. She saw a trail of blood running down the back of his right hand, and bloody fingerprints above his right pants pocket. She had an image of how this had happened: Sometime before his death, an attacker had struck Kaiser in the head, which Kaiser had clutched with his right hand, which, in turn, touched the pants. In her mind, the bloody prints ruled out the possibility, which sooner or later would have to be addressed, of suicide. She thought, *How can you shoot yourself and then put your hand in your pocket?* She observed bruises on the knees and shins. This added another element to the murder sequence forming in her mind: At some point before the fatal shot, Kaiser had fallen or been shoved to his knees.

13

THE BUREAU

FOR JOHNNIE CARSON, U.S. ambassador to Kenya, the priest's death was a tinderbox. As he told his staff, it might "change the normal orbit of U.S. and Kenyan bilateral relations." Carson regarded Kenya as the most important American ally in the region, the essential "anchor state" in East Africa. It had functioned as a base for the evacuation of American troops from their disastrous early-1990s engagement in Somalia, and had remained the only country on the continent with which the United States had a military-access agreement. The United States and Kenya also shared "one of the larger and more effective joint counter-terrorist programs in the world," as the State Department put it. Moi had allowed the embassy bombers to be shipped off to the United States for trial, and had been helpful in "several other high-value terrorist renditions."

Carson prided himself on his patience and discretion. In temperament and approach, he was poles apart from his most famous predecessor, the sharp-elbowed Smith Hempstone. Some in Kenya's pro-democracy crowd considered Carson unduly cozy with Moi, but Carson believed that his approach gave him access to the top when he needed it.

Now was such a time. The dead man was an American citizen and a leading dissident. He had been well-known to Carson's staff for several years, though with a reputation as a deep eccentric. One American diplomat privately described Kaiser as "an unguided missile" and "a self-promoter," one who "sought out confrontation for its own sake, frequently casting himself in the role of martyr."

The news of Kaiser's death had come to Carson around 10:00 or 10:30

that morning, and the details were vague—there was the suggestion it had been an accident—but within hours there was confirmation of a weapon, and the possibility of foul play. Carson, who had monitored the deportation attempt closely, knew Sunkuli and other members of Moi's circle would be natural suspects. If this proved to be a government-sponsored assassination, Carson knew it promised "huge ramifications" for U.S.-Kenyan relations.

And so late on the afternoon of August 24, 2000, hours after Kaiser's body was found, Carson marched into the stately Nairobi offices of Kenya's attorney general, Amos Wako. The office, in Sharia House, near the parliament building, bore resemblance to a prosperous British barrister's chambers, with its wood paneling, rows of law books, and photographs of powder-wigged men.

Let the FBI help investigate, Carson urged. The FBI had forensic expertise, he argued, and its presence would show that the Kenyan regime had nothing to hide.

The FBI's legal attaché in Kenya, a former Marine Corps pilot named William Corbett, was in the room that day and recalled Carson's words: "The Bureau has to be able to follow the facts wherever they go." It was a point Carson repeated.

The attorney general said he would need to consult. Of course, His Excellency the President would have to approve.

That evening, just as the ambassador was boarding a plane for a previously scheduled trip to Washington, Corbett received a letter on official Kenyan letterhead, inviting the FBI's assistance. He chased the ambassador to the airport, onto the tarmac, and onto the plane to hand him the envelope.

Carson was pleased. Whatever the truth proved to be, the FBI's involvement would allay suspicions of a cover-up, he reasoned. In this, he was mistaken.

THE CHURCH THAT had considered Kaiser such a troublemaker did not delay in lionizing him. He was easy to revere now, as he lay in his brass-and-teak coffin, robed, wearing a necklace of Masai beads in the shape of a cross. A host of the country's Catholic bishops joined three thousand other mourners at the Holy Family Basilica for the memorial service on August 30, where the nuncio declared him a martyr to the faith and said, "Those who killed him, those who planned his killing, wanted to silence the voice of the gospel." A representative from the U.S. embassy declared that whoever had perpetrated "this terrible crime" would be brought to justice. Outside the basilica, thousands crammed the streets of Nairobi in mourning and in rage. Students and members of the Kenya Human Rights Network took part in protests. Among the signs: KILLERS OF FATHER KAISER ARE ASSASSINS OF TRUTH AND LIBERTY.

For a time, it was unclear whether Kaiser would be buried in Kisiiland or Masailand. An argument had erupted over the question: both groups considered him one of their own and wanted him in their soil. At one point, Bill Vos, the Minnesota priest who had flown in for the services, was buttonholed by a Kisii priest who expressed his fear about a burial in Lolgorien: The primitive Masai could not be trusted; they would surely dig up his grave. Bishop Davies struck a compromise: The Kisii would get the body for an all-night service, and then it would be taken to Lolgorien for burial.

After the memorial Mass, a church van carried Kaiser's body onto the bad roads that led through the grasslands and into the remote western parishes he had served for decades. Villagers streamed forth from their farms and mud-walled huts, waving verdant branches—a sign of peace— as they ran alongside the procession.

It was dark when the caravan arrived in Nyangusu, in Kisiiland, for a second Mass. Some five thousand people waited along the roads, the crowd chanting his name. The churchmen carried the coffin into a small room to neaten the body, which had been jostled by the hard roads. Vos was struck by the incredible damage to Kaiser's head, which morticians had stuffed with cotton. He cut off a small portion of Kaiser's thinning white hair and put it in an envelope, which he would take back home and keep on his desk, a memento of a martyr.

In the unfinished concrete church where the body was next displayed, illuminated by kerosene lanterns, people crowded along the scaffolding for a look. There was singing and dancing until morning, and the children found places to sleep in the church and on the surrounding grass. In the morning, the coffin traveled to a third Mass in Kilgoris. Anne Sawoyo, apparently no longer Sunkuli's captive, if she ever had been, was in attendance. She wept and draped herself over the coffin and appeared to faint. One nun said, "I could just slap her." Some thought her mourning had a theatrical quality; some thought she might feel guilty for what had happened to the priest.

After Kilgoris, the coffin traveled to the hilly green country of Lolgorien. Just outside town, at the Migore River, crowds greeted the caravan, waving branches, running alongside. Masai warriors in bright red wrappings leaned against their spears and watched as the hole was shoveled out a few feet in front of the last church Kaiser had built. The hole was twelve feet deep to deter the beasts of the veldt. The men lowered the coffin with ropes. Children of the parish who used to swarm around the priest now climbed into a big ficus tree overhanging his grave. They squeezed side by side, until it seemed impossible that the branches could support so many of them, to see him sent into the clay.

THAT DAY, FLORENCE MPAYEI appeared in a Nairobi courtroom, surrounded by new lawyers, to withdraw her complaint against Sunkuli. She reiterated her claim that FIDA had been using her to make money. Speaking to Rift Valley police, Mpayei would give an explanation for her new allegiance to Sunkuli: He, not FIDA, was paying for her son's upkeep. "I love him, and he is assisting me," the report quoted her as saying. "My dowry has been duly paid to my parents. I do not know Father Kaiser, neither do I know how he met his death."

Sunkuli had distributed a press release, announcing he would cooperate with the death investigation. "My conscience is clear and I have nothing to hide in this matter," he said. He admitted he had had differences with the priest. "For this reason, I more than anybody else would like to see an in-depth inquiry into what and who killed him, so that my political enemies do not take advantage of those known differences between me and the late Fr. Kaiser to divert the course of the investigation."

Sunkuli did not avoid opportunities to profess his innocence. He took to buttonholing Western diplomats to plead his case, and consented to a filmed interview with the BBC. In an exchange with reporter Andrew Harding, Sunkuli seemed anything but smooth. He had a broad, pudgy face and small, darting eyes; his smile seemed nervous and forced.

Harding: "Who killed Father Kaiser?"

Sunkuli: "How would I know?"

"You didn't kill Father Kaiser?"

"Me?"

"You didn't organize his death?"

"Is there such a possibility?"

Harding kept pressing, and Sunkuli said, "Father was not even one of my prominent enemies. . . . He just, I know, hated me."

Rumors and counterrumors proliferated furiously. Had Kaiser been a CIA operative, and murdered as a result? Why, asked *Newsline* magazine, would Moi kill a well-known American even as Kenyan officials were lobbying Bill Clinton to visit Kenya? Wouldn't Moi, a ruler desperate to show the world a positive face, know the finger of suspicion would point toward him? Wouldn't a murder bring more attention to Kaiser's efforts to bring him before the Hague? "It simply looks too perfect a murder to fit that bill," the article said. "It would take an extremely naive and myopic regime to decide to bump off a priest who was engaged in such an undertaking." Perhaps someone had killed Kaiser "to dim the political star of the so-far fast-rising" Sunkuli.

Kenya's twenty-three Catholic bishops endorsed a statement that they were "seriously troubled" by Kaiser's death, and Bishop John Njue, head of the country's Roman Catholic Episcopal Conference, said the government "cannot be excluded" from suspicion. Moi's minister of state, Marsden Madoka, had a sharp reply. "No one has any moral right to start blaming the government. If the bishops have any evidence implicating anyone, they should report to the investigating officers instead of making unfounded malicious claims. The Catholic bishops should stop their holier-than-thou attitude. We know what goes on in the Vatican."

President Moi angrily dismissed the notion that he or his men bore any blame. "When deaths occur, people say many things. But it is not good for people to politicize the death of the Catholic priest," he said at a Mombasa rally. "I am asking anyone with any vital information in connection with the death to volunteer it to the police."

THE FBI TEAM, led by agent Thomas Graney of the Washington Field Office, had arrived in Kenya on August 27, three days before the memorial service. They unpacked their bags at the elegant Serena Hotel. The agents would be based off Mombasa Road, at the temporary headquarters of the U.S. embassy, where they received detailed warnings about the country. Among them: Don't walk at night downtown. Don't walk alone. Don't let a crowd of beggars surround you. Keep passports and plane tickets in your hotel safe. Drive with your doors locked and your windows up. Don't forget insect repellent. Don't drink tap water. Watch out for bandits should you venture to the border regions. Kenyans drive fast and recklessly, so keep your eyes open on the road. Don't wander into the wild with the lions.

Graney, a Catholic himself, was a sixteen-year FBI veteran who worked for the Bureau's extraterritorial squad, which normally investigated the terrorism-related deaths of Americans overseas. After receiving orders to fly immediately to Kenya, he had visited the Bureau safe and watched the secretary count out ten thousand dollars in cash, which he would carry on the plane and later stash in a safe at the U.S. embassy in Nairobi. This assignment would take him where credit cards could not be relied on. He had traveled to twenty-six countries—he had been a legal attaché in Israel in the late 1990s—but this was his first job in Kenya.

He and other FBI agents fanned out across the country in Land

Rovers, armed with Sig Sauers. They were accompanied by plainclothesmen from the Kenyan police, a group that the American agents were
made to understand represented the cream of the country's detectives. It
was to be a joint investigation. The Kenyans would translate the words of
Swahili-speaking witnesses. They would provide rickety Soviet-era heli-
copters to reach remote villages. They would sit close during interviews.

This presented an obvious problem. Who would risk telling the Americans anything in the presence of Kenyan cops, for decades an integral
part of Moi's apparatus of fear? As Kenya's minister of internal security,
Sunkuli himself oversaw the very police charged with investigating the
case, including the rape allegations against him.

To some, like Kaiser's old friend Melchizedek Ondieki, the presence
of Kenyan police rendered the investigation absurd on its face. By his
account, he refused to talk to the FBI, with the explanation, "You are
already compromised."

BACK IN THE United States, both houses of Congress swiftly passed
resolutions condemning Kaiser's "assassination." David Durenberger, a
former senator from Minnesota, had urged Paul Wellstone, one of the
current senators, to take up the case. Wellstone took the floor of the Sen-
ate and cited the slayings of five other Catholic clerics in Kenya. "Those
who knew Kaiser recall him as humble and soft-spoken with totally self-
less zeal for the service of others," the senator said. He described Kaiser's
confrontations with high-ranking Kenyans, among them "Julius Sunkuli,
considered by many to be the current Kenya President's personal preference as a successor." He cited Kaiser's work championing the rape case
against Sunkuli, adding, "Father Kaiser was killed one week before the
court case was due to begin. A few days later, the young woman dropped
the charge. Father Kaiser's death is a manifestation of the corruption and injustice rampant in Kenya today." Since corruption in Kenya
reached "to the highest level of government"—he noted that Transpar-
ency International had recently ranked it the world's ninth-most corrupt

country—the Kenyans could not be trusted to investigate, and the FBI's investigation was "a good start."

Congress called on Secretary of State Madeleine Albright to report by December 15 on the progress of the investigation. She promised she would monitor it. "Clearly, there are questions that we have about various aspects of how Kenya operates, but it is a country with which we deal," she said.

Her remark encapsulated the U.S. government's attitude toward Kenya. It was impossible to ignore Moi's reliance on brutality. And yet his friendship was as valuable as ever, if not more so. The Al Qaeda operatives who had destroyed the U.S. embassy in Nairobi two years earlier were to stand trial in federal court in New York in a few months. "With the Embassy bombing trial commencing on 01/03/01, the Kenya Police very much remain our vital partners in our aspirations to succeed with what the U.S. Attorney General refers to as the most important DOJ [Department of Justice] prosecution of 2001," an internal FBI memo said.

At the nexus of the two cases stood William Corbett, the Bureau's legal attaché, who had accompanied Carson on his visit to the Kenyan attorney general to request an FBI role in the investigation. He'd been serving on the drug squad in the FBI's Miami Field Office in August 1998 when someone told him the U.S. embassy in Nairobi, where he'd once been stationed as a marine, had been blown up. He turned on the TV and saw the mountains of rubble. In no time, the FBI had him on a plane to Kenya. He was a valuable man, one of the agency's two or three Swahili speakers. He described his Swahili as "functional," not fluent.

As the FBI's point man in Kenya for the last two years, he had forged tight professional friendships with the Kenyan police during the bombing investigation. Now he was central to the Kaiser probe. Corbett, also a Catholic, admired Kaiser's willingness to give up a safe, soft life in the United States to ease the suffering of a troubled country. He had closely followed accounts of Kaiser's duel with the regime. Still, Corbett would say, his job was to remain at arm's length, dispassionate, guided only by the evidence. He believed it was this neutrality, this refusal to draw conclusions before the facts were in, that made him and other agents the target of considerable wrath from the outset. "In the court of public opinion, Kaiser had almost already been canonized," Corbett recalled of the investigation's early days. "John Q. Citizen, members of the Church, they were quite angry we weren't seeing it like they were." At least twice, Corbett recalled, Ambassador Carson noticed frustration simmering among the agents in the face of such hostility. Carson pulled them aside with a gentle reminder: "These are the good folks here, caring for the most forgotten populations in this country. Let's not allow ourselves to be frustrated with them."

Corbett knew the Kenyan government's guilt was widely assumed. He sensed a palpable fear of the regime, even among its representatives. Once, early in the investigation, a Kenyan friend with the Criminal Investigation Department grabbed Corbett's arm and said, "Watch out for yourself."

"Lay it on me here," Corbett said. "Is there something you're aware of that I'm not aware of?" The Kenyan policeman had nothing specific, just a free-floating sense that the powerful men who ran the country must be behind the priest's death.

There was talk, which Corbett began hearing all the time at parties in the following months, that the FBI was intent on giving the Kenyan authorities a pass because of its help on the embassy bombing case. Corbett found himself earnestly insisting that that was not so, not in any shape or form, no: One case had nothing to do with the other. Corbett could imagine a scenario in which Moi had gathered his people and asked them, one by one, if they were behind the killing. No? No? No? Okay, bring in the Americans.

Tom Neer, a profiler with the FBI's Behavioral Analysis Unit, worked on the case out of Kenyan police headquarters, and out of the small legal attaché's office at the makeshift U.S. embassy headquarters, through which "agents galore" were passing as part of the embassy bombing case. "Father Kaiser was just a footnote" amid the bustle, he recalled. "It's not like this was the greatest thing going. This was in the background."

• • •

IT WAS CRUCIAL, first, to reconstruct Kaiser's last days—the circuit that led him from his remote parish house to the ditch about forty miles northwest of Nairobi. Early on, FBI agents received what seemed a stroke of luck. A Kikuyu CID officer, as it happened, had been told by relatives in Kiambu, a remote region north of the capital, that someone resembling the priest had paid them a visit on the last night he was seen alive. The officer had relayed the tip to his superiors at the CID, and the CID had relayed it to the FBI, and the American agents were heading upcountry with their Kenyan counterparts in Land Rovers that very night.

They rumbled for what seemed like forever down a bone-jarring, bladder-pounding road into the darkness, through land as empty as a desert, nowhere itself, the edge of the world. "You go any farther, you're dropping off," Graney would say. "You've never seen dark like you've seen dark there."

They pulled up to a cluster of huts and climbed out with their notepads, using lanterns and truck headlights for illumination. Villagers told a strange story about the night Kaiser had vanished. It was about 8:00 P.M., they said, suppertime and solid dark. They heard an automobile pull up outside. This was an anomaly: No one here had a car, and few vehicles traveled this road. Children ran out to see a white double-cab truck, stopped near one of the houses, lights on, engine running. More villagers ventured out for a look. A white man stepped out of the truck. He looked old. He wore a black jacket and carried a long gun. He walked up a short hill and stared into the darkness, the gun in his right hand, just gazing into the pitch. A villager asked whether there was any trouble. *Hakuna shida,* said the white man. No problem.

Then came the oddest part. A village elder approached, and the white man extended the shotgun, like a gift, asking in English, "Do you want this?"

When the elder refused, the white man apologized in Swahili. *Pole sana.* He carried the gun back to his truck, pitched the vehicle into reverse, and backed past the house so hurriedly that he struck a hedge and scraped a downspout that jutted from one of the buildings. Then he sped off "like he was trying to escape something," like a "mad man."

The white man's visit had lasted no more than five to ten minutes. Everybody in the village, from children to elders, seemed in agreement about his strange behavior. "They told this identical account of this crazy *mzungu* trying to squeeze the truck between two houses that clearly didn't fit," Corbett would say. The investigators asked if they had seen any cars that might have been following the white stranger. The answer was no.

The FBI next picked up the trail at the Moonlight Service Station in the Rift Valley town of Naivasha, not far from where Kaiser's body was found. A man named David Mwania, who worked as a guard at the nearby Naivasha prison and lived on the grounds there, told the FBI that he had pulled into the station about 11:15 P.M. Wednesday to buy gas and was waiting in his Datsun pickup, a pump attendant fueling his tank, when he saw a white man, tall, nearly seventy, oddly wrapped in two blankets, standing nearby next to a white Toyota pickup. Mwania spoke to him in Swahili: "It is very cold." The man responded in English: "It is very cold."

When Mwania asked the white man where he was from, he got this alleged reply: "I am an American from Minnesota." Then the American came up and extended his hand—a struggle, as he had to extricate it from his blankets—and said, "I am glad to meet you, sir."

The investigators produced a picture of Kaiser.

Yes, Mwania told them. That was the American.

Another witness, a gas station employee, reported having seen Kaiser pull up in his pickup. He said Kaiser had walked around his truck, checking for damage, used an ax to hack off a loose-hanging mudguard, and then tossed the mudguard into his flatbed. Kaiser had declined an offer to fill his gas tank, an action the agents thought odd, considering the long trip ahead to his parish.

The interviews ran late that night, and the agents decided not to risk a nighttime drive back to Nairobi. They found a two-dollar-a-night flea-bag motel in Naivasha. Graney thought it prudent to keep the window locked, and he slept with his Sig Sauer on his nightstand.

• • •

THERE WAS A serious time gap—hours—before Kaiser's trail was detected again. The investigators interviewed the guards, or *askaris*, who worked at the Kenya Cooperative Creameries farm, a few hundred yards from where Kaiser's body was found. One guard recalled having heard the rattling, thumping sound of a passing vehicle that night. The guard, fearing attack from one of the area's armed gangs, became hyper-vigilant. The vehicle passed again, and again. He settled back to his fire and grew relaxed. Then, about 2:30 A.M., he heard a loud bang in the darkness. He thought it might be an accident, but he didn't go out to investigate.

The crucial part was what was missing. There had been no sound of a struggle. No voices. No cars in pursuit.

The guard told his story in English, in Swahili, and in Luo, his native tongue. It struck Corbett as credible. The account didn't have the stale, wooden quality of a fabrication. After years on the job, he thought he was a reasonably good judge of these things. "We say the truth has a flavor, and that flavor is very rich in details," Corbett said. "Some of us think we're as good as polygraph machines."

Was it possible, Corbett wondered, that this was some kind of a ruse? Was the guard a plant, a red herring, a diversion orchestrated by some "dark ominous hand" that had arranged Kaiser's death? He found this implausible. The guard had been employed at the farm for some time. How would such a setup have worked?

Crucial as the guard's account would be to the FBI's ultimate con-clusion, his evidence was anything but clear. Graney recalled that the interviews of the farm guards were complicated by language, despite the help of a translator. "We did some of the interviews in Swahili," he said. "These were not easy interviews." And the guard, identified by Kenyan authorities as Paul Omunga, appears to have given a different account to a BBC reporter: Yes, he heard a vehicle circling the area on the night in question, but he was certain it was not the priest's: He glimpsed it and saw that it was a single-cab truck, not a double.

. . .

GIVEN KAISER'S REFUSAL to duck confrontations, the scene where his body was found presented a riddle. If attacked, wouldn't the priest—a former paratrooper and expert shot—have put up a fight? He had been armed with a shotgun and an ax in the truck. Yet there were no signs of struggle: no rips or tears in his clothes, no defensive injuries. Sheets and a blanket had been spread out on the ground, as if for a bed—this would have taken some time in the country dark—and left undisturbed. His wallet, cash, leather jacket, and truck had not been stolen, which seemed to rule out robbery; in Kenya, it was common for a victim to be stripped of everything, even his shoes. No foreign fingerprints were found on the shotgun. He had an extra shotgun shell in his pocket, but he had chosen to load just one barrel of his shotgun. This meant, the FBI reasoned, that he had perceived no danger.

The FBI knew the crime scene itself was heavily compromised. By the time they arrived, days after the body's removal, the area "had been trampled on by a cast of thousands," as Graney put it. It was not even clear who had seen the body first. There had been no lab techs in special suits picking up microfibers. As Corbett phrased it, somewhat euphemistically, "There wasn't that standard First World protocol." There were pieces of physical evidence that remained frustratingly inexplicable, such as a smear of green paint on the side of Kaiser's Toyota. Was it evidence of another car having driven the truck off the road? To Corbett, it didn't look like car paint. Had the priest scraped or rammed a green fence? The agents scoured the area for green fences. No luck. What about the fact that the driver's side window of the truck had been smashed in, apparently from the outside, as suggested by pieces of glass found inside the cab and on his clothing? Had someone smashed it? Had he rammed into a branch?

The FBI men were working sixteen-hour days, crossing the country, missing meals, punchy with sleeplessness. They enjoyed the company of their Kenyan counterparts. Though they were better off than many of their countrymen, the average Kenyan policeman made the equivalent of a few hundred dollars a year. In the morning, when the American and

Kenyan agents met in the hotel lobby, the FBI agents would invite them to breakfast and pick up the tab. The alternative would be to leave them hungry in the lobby. The Bureau men got a glimpse of Kenyan police headquarters and were struck by the disarray of the filing system; it was a pandemonium of papers and boxes. The Kenyan police were chronically short of basic necessities like holsters, and as a consequence their motley assortment of guns, from Glocks to Dirty Harry–style Magnums, would not infrequently go missing. It was hard not to feel sorry for them. At one point in the investigation, during a trip back to the States, Graney gathered a bunch of old holsters and took them to the Kenyan force as gifts.

Through it all, Graney and Corbett were piecing together the time line, mulling over scenarios, bouncing ideas off each other. What were the dynamics of Kaiser's inner life? Had he been as pure and upstanding as appearances indicated? They had to consider every possibility. Had he been some kind of rogue priest? Had he become entangled with women? Had he been dying of AIDS? Had he been transferred to his far-flung parish in an attempt to cover up a scandal, in the wearily familiar pattern of pedophile priests?

Interviews with those who knew Kaiser consistently refuted those scenarios. Sex had never been his vice. As the interviews progressed, Graney developed a clear mental picture of a sixty-seven-year-old-man who in some ways resembled a lot of men at that age, headstrong, set in his ways: "He'd done it all, and he wasn't gonna be argued with."

Why, the agents wondered, had Kaiser left the safety of the bishop's compound that night, a place with two guard dogs and three gates, each manned by a guard? "He seems to be sort of walking into death," as Bishop Davies put it. Wouldn't a man being hunted seek out civilization, rather than darkness and isolation? If Kaiser had somehow been lured away, as Davies believed—lured by someone playing on his gallantry, perhaps, begging for his help—where was he supposed to meet this person? At the side of the unlit road in Naivasha? To the agents, that made no sense; nobody with a modicum of instinct for self-preservation would linger in such an area. Robbers were everywhere, their ruses endless:

They'd plant a fake accident victim in the road to block your car, then rob you and beat you to death.

Why had Kaiser driven to the homestead in Kiambu, way down that impossible dark road? True, he was known to visit Maela survivors in the area, and his habit was to arrive at places unannounced—but why this particular road, this homestead, these strangers? Had he gotten lost? What had he been thinking as he stood on the knoll and looked into what Graney called "the darkest night you've ever imagined in your life"? Maybe he hadn't expected to be discovered. Maybe he'd been seeking the most isolated place possible to kill himself. Why had he attempted to give away his shotgun? Had he been afraid he might take other lives to save his own? Had he been giving away his possessions in the fashion of a man bidding good-bye to the world? Had he sensed himself spiraling into despair and worried that he would use it on himself? Had he just meant to reassure the village elder that he didn't intend to hurt him? Or, Corbett wondered, had a delirious, sleep-deprived Kaiser thought he was surrendering his gun to a pursuing assassin? "Maybe he's tired of running and thinks, *They're here*," Corbett said.

Was it possible to ascribe rationality to his movements at all? If he was being followed, why hadn't he sought the help of the villagers, and—equally crucial—why had no one seen a pursuing car?

The agents knew Kaiser had made powerful enemies, but it seemed that he'd already aired the gist of his claims—involving government-sponsored clashes and ethnic cleansing—at the Akiwumi Commission. As the agents studied his testimony, it struck them as fragmentary, full of bluster and passion but no smoking gun. He had "provided no provable evidence that any high-ranking GOK official had committed a crime," the FBI concluded. "None of the allegations made by Father Kaiser during his testimony were supported in any way by anything resembling fact." His claims, instead, were drawn from his own inferences, from hearsay, and from what he believed to be common knowledge. Had he since come into possession, somehow, of what Corbett called a "eureka nugget of information"? Had he been eliminated because he knew enough to destroy Moi? "The more we investigated, it all kind of led to empty trails," Corbett said. "There was no career-ending information he was sitting on."

NO SMALL PART of the agents' work was separating the genuine leads from the chimeras, the puffs of smoke, the blind alleys. What of Paul Muite's account, for instance? The Nairobi lawyer told the FBI that a policeman—he would not reveal the name—had given him the identities of a "hit team" that had killed Kaiser. It's possible that the FBI's sense of Muite's credibility was colored by the attitude at the U.S. embassy, where some top diplomats regarded him as an opportunist looking to capitalize on the drama to serve his political ambitions. FBI reports suggest the agents interviewed the men on Muite's list and were satisfied with their alibis.

One day, the agents sat in Nairobi's Norfolk Hotel, listening to a man describing in great detail a conversation he claimed to have overheard at a restaurant in Kiambaa—a brief drive from the crime scene—two days before Kaiser vanished. He explained that three strangers pulled up in a dirty white Nissan four-door, its taillight broken, its cab littered with beer cans. The first stranger was a short, muscled, tired-looking man, rumored to be an assassin for hire, whom he referred to as the "Happy Guy." Another was a corpulent man in a black coat who smoked Embassy cigarettes: the "Unhappy Guy." A third was a thin, bearded man with an inflamed eye: the "Driver." The men, who spoke in Swahili, had some meat prepared at a nearby butcher's shop and then took it to the restaurant and found a table. When somebody asked the Happy Guy why the car was so dirty, he replied that he'd just returned from the Mara, where he'd been assigned "a difficult job that would pay very well" and permit him to repay a fifty-thousand shilling debt (about seven hundred U.S. dollars). One of his companions, it emerged, had paid the Happy Guy's bail on a recent arrest, and the Happy Guy owed him. He would pay him back on August 25 or 26, apparently after his mysterious assignment was complete, and then head to Zanzibar, apparently to hide out. The Happy Guy said he was going "to give Kaiser his dues," and displayed five pointed-tip two-and-a-half-inch-long bullets to prove his seriousness.

Would a real assassin display his ammunition and announce his intention so nakedly? Is it possible that such a detailed account could have been fabricated from whole cloth? Was it all an elaborate con to cadge a few dollars from the American agents?

To judge from FBI reports, the agents attempted to pursue the tip but dismissed it as another blind alley among countless others. To pore through the agents' hundreds of FD-302 reports—the documents detailing their daily pursuit of leads and interviews—is to hear an echo of Graham Greene's colonial policeman in *The Heart of the Matter* brooding on the nature of criminal investigations in West Africa: "In European cases there are words one believes and words one distrusts: it is possible to draw a speculative line between the truth and the lies; at least the *cui bono* principle to some extent operates, and it is usually safe to assume, if the accusation is theft and there is no question of insurance, that something has at least been stolen. But here one could make no such assumption: one could draw no lines. He had known police officers whose nerves broke down in the effort to separate a single grain of incontestable truth. . . . " A Western anthropologist who had lived among the Kisii described a similar frustration in her attempt to penetrate facades that seemed deliberately constructed to flummox outsiders: "During our time in Gusiiland, we slowly learned that the most important factor in any given situation is often the one most carefully obscured. . . . Sometimes no one mentions it at all. Neighbors and relatives may know what is going on, what the score is, but outsiders like ourselves remain confused and mystified."

Much later, asked what most surprised him about working in Africa, Graney would reply, "How difficult it is to get them to answer a direct question." There was also the complication of relying on translations of a language vastly different from English. He added, "You throw Swahili into the mix—oh my God, it's a freaking nightmare."

• • •

NO ONE ILLUSTRATED this slipperiness, this maddening ambiguity, more than Francis Kantai. The FBI sat down with him on the morning of September 20, nearly a month after Kaiser's death. Kantai was in hiding at a parish house outside Nairobi. The interview began at 10:00 A.M. Bananas and drinks were served. Kantai said he had known Kaiser for five years. The priest had been looking for a Masai catechist to reach the local people, and had trained him and given him a room. The priest had a temper, he said. He wouldn't yell, but he'd speak his mind and close the door. Kantai said he had been in Lolgorien when Kaiser was killed, had not known of the priest's planned final trip to Nairobi, and had not attended Kaiser's funeral because he feared his life was in danger.

Did Kantai know what Kaiser might have been doing around Naivasha? Kantai said he sometimes visited a widow there. But he said Kaiser did not travel at night and would not sleep outside. If he left Nairobi late for Lolgorien, he'd find a cheap hotel en route. He said Kaiser always checked his truck before he hit the road, and made sure he had a spare tire, a hoe, an ax, a shotgun, and his rosary. When he feared he was being followed, he would drive around and around in circles. Twice that year, Kaiser had spotted a certain mysterious man who seemed to be watching him—seated, always alone, with a medium build, a black coat, a clear face, and a red baseball hat. He'd seen him once in Nakuru in May and again in Ngong in August.

The agents couldn't shake their unease around Kantai. He seemed evasive, and to them his body language screamed duplicity: He repeatedly covered his mouth when he talked, bit his lip, and closed his eyes. He complained that his words were being twisted and that he was being treated as a suspect. He said that people didn't respect him. He said he wished that he'd never met Father Kaiser.

Do you know anyone who would want to hurt Father Kaiser? the agents asked.

As the agents recorded it, Kantai lapsed into silence, looked down, and asked them to repeat the question.

Do you know anyone who would want to hurt Kaiser?

No answer.

"You're not telling us the whole story," Corbett said. "We're just gonna sit here till you tell us the whole story."

There was a much longer silence this time, one the agents made an effort to extend for as long as possible, in the hope that it would make Kantai uncomfortable enough to crack. The agents documented the silence as a full fifteen minutes. Kantai just sat there.

Kantai appeared soft, effeminate, easily breakable. But the agents were already coming to believe that he was tougher than he looked, a manipulator, a survivor. But what was his game, exactly?

In a written statement and perhaps also during the interview, Kantai apparently informed the agents that Sunkuli had tried to get him to poison Kaiser. According to a report of the interview, Kantai also offered the astonishing news that he had been driven to State House in Mombasa to meet President Moi himself. His meeting with the president had lasted a full five minutes, and Moi had asked, Who are these people who have been using you?

The agents took careful notes. What was there to do with *that* story? To the agents, Kantai seemed an opportunist through and through, a man who had found a meal ticket in the priest, and now, apparently, had found a ticket out of Africa: He would soon marry the priest's cousin, Camille, and move to the United States. Years later, speaking of Kantai, Graney's contempt and distrust still burned strong. "A freaking nightmare," Graney called him. "An out-and-out liar."

The interview lasted till 6:45 P.M. They had devoted a full workday to a man whose motives were inexplicable and whose information might send them chasing vapors for years. How Kaiser had treated the catechist presented another puzzle. Kantai had admitted to burning innocent people out of their homes at the government's behest, and yet Kaiser had made him one of his closest confidants. "He confesses to Kaiser and maybe rather astutely thinks Kaiser will forgive him," Graney said. Graney could understand forgiveness: That was a priest's job. "But I'm not going to take him into my inner circle."

• • •

WAS THERE A clue to Kaiser's mental state, perhaps, in the slim letter that he had handed to the papal nuncio the day he vanished? The agents thought there might be. But Tonucci refused to release the letter and insisted it had no bearing on the case. It had been a privileged communication dealing with church business: Kaiser's opinion on who should succeed Davies as bishop. If it became public, who would speak frankly to the nuncio again?

During his interview with the nuncio, in the company of Kenyan police, Corbett sensed that Tonucci was uneasy, that he might have something more to say. Corbett handed him his business card, with a note on the back indicating how to contact him privately if he wished. A couple days later, Tonucci summoned him, and Corbett arrived without his Kenyan counterparts. This amounted to "sort of breaking the rules," Corbett would say, as this was supposed to be a joint investigation.

Some months earlier, the nuncio explained, there had been a break-in at his house. Robbers had vaulted the wall outside and tied up his staff. The nuncio seemed convinced the attack was somehow related to the Kaiser slaying.

Corbett wrote down the information, thanked him, and left. Was it part of the puzzle? Did it fit? There was no evidence in that direction. Corbett knew that street crime was so common and undiscriminating in Nairobi—commonly referred to as "Nairobbery"—that even the police director's home had once been raided by men with machetes. That the nuncio had fallen victim to crime meant only that he enjoyed no special immunity from it. Yet the nuncio's fears bespoke the atmosphere. Here was a man with advanced degrees, smart, rational, the Pope's own man in Kenya, sensing an unseen conspiratorial hand at work.

ONE EVENING, AFTER another eighteen-hour day, Graney was taking a shower when he reached for his back and found his hand full of blood. The doctor at the embassy told him not to worry. He had shingles, a nerve condition. Stress could bring it on, and he was certainly under plenty of stress. There was considerable pressure to bring in defensible facts: This was his case, his responsibility, his burden. He wanted to do the right thing by the brave American priest.

The investigators lined up interviews in Lolgorien and in the Masai Mara. A Kenyan military helicopter set them down in the game park. They stayed in tents. At night, Graney listened to the animal noises across the plains and felt glad to have his Sig Sauer.

They found Anne Sawoyo still working at the Mara Serena lodge. Before they interviewed her, by Corbett's account, they assumed that Sunkuli had sexually assaulted her. They came away with a more ambiguous picture.

"I don't want to say [it was] consensual, but in that culture—it's difficult to describe in Western terms—it's almost a resource issue. When you're very wealthy and there are young gals around, young gals want a better life," Corbett said. Had she been imprisoned at the Mara, as Kaiser had once believed? "Our conclusion was she was far from this person who was in a desperate situation, or was sitting on some story," Corbett said. "What we found was a gal who saw a heck of an opportunity" and enjoyed "the attention of a powerful, wealthy man. The notion of [her] being kidnapped all melted away when we talked to her."

When Kaiser learned that Sawoyo was not being held captive, soon after his failed attempt to whisk her out of the Mara, the emotional effect could have been wrenching. "Father Kaiser had put a heck of a lot of eggs in that basket," Corbett said. "I don't want to make it sound like he was tilting at windmills there, but he had pursued it with a lot of vigor."

Whether Sawoyo had been a prisoner at the Mara would never be completely clear, however. The FBI came across evidence that rangers at the lodge—men with close ties to Sunkuli—were keeping a close watch on her. A young man named Levi Marko told investigators that in July he had spent a few days at the lodge, visiting a cousin who worked there, and in his free time he'd lounged in the canteen, watching TV. There he got to know Anne Sawoyo and attempted to seduce her. On July 11—the day after Kaiser had visited—rangers discovered he'd been talking to Sawoyo and took him into custody, apparently believing he was one of Kaiser's agents, sent to spirit Sawoyo away. He was beaten with one stick until it broke, then a second, then a third, and was left bleeding from the mouth and hands. He claimed he was driven to the Kilgoris police station and tortured again. He was charged with trespassing at the lodge.

Soon, the Americans confronted the accused rangers, identified as Samuel Kortom and Joseph Kupasar, men Graney would later refer to as "those two idiots." The senior figure was Kortom, a physically imposing man with a fourth-grade education. Graney focused on Kupasar, the smaller, quieter, subordinate figure. Had they been watching Sawoyo at Sunkuli's behest? Was there some connection to the priest's death?

"Look at me when I talk to you!" Graney demanded, jabbing his finger accusingly. "Tell me the truth!"

Now and then, Kortom tried to talk, and Graney told him to shut up. Finally, he recalled, Kupasar broke, but he told them only what they'd already heard: that Kortom had beaten Levi with a stick. Kupasar asked for a bathroom break and used the opportunity to disappear. This gave the investigators, American and Kenyan, a good laugh.

Whether anyone would be prosecuted for beating Levi should be up to the Kenyans, the FBI decided. This meant nothing of the sort would happen.

In the end, Graney thought the rangers *had* been watching Sawoyo. But did that mean, strictly speaking, she hadn't been able to escape? He reflected on the priest's attempt to rescue her from the lodge in the company of a pack of Masai. "Does that sound like a guy in touch with reality?" Graney said. "He's gonna go there and do a forcible rendition?" It struck him as outlandish. "What did he see, a bad pirate movie? Kaiser needed a little army of Masai to go with him? There wasn't a single police officer Kaiser could go to and say, 'They're holding this girl against her will'?"

14

MANIC DEPRESSION

A<small>S THE PROBE</small> progressed, investigators found themselves confronting a side of the priest that very few beyond his family, close
friends, and church colleagues had known—a history of manic depression that went back decades. This discovery would profoundly color the
FBI's perception of the case; critics would insist it profoundly deformed
that perception. Kaiser's sister, Carolita Mahoney, a nurse, whom agents
interviewed during her visit to bury her brother in Kenya and again at her
home in Underwood, Minnesota, had volunteered the fact of her brother's illness without realizing that it would become central to the case. For
her brother, she said, the episodes started with sleep deprivation and progressed to extreme agitation and an intense focus on narrow issues.

At least three times, he had been hospitalized in the States. The first
time was in New York in February 1969, while he was working as a rector
at Mill Hill's Albany house, under the supervision of Father Pierre Heymans, the chief of the missionary society's American operation. The FBI
learned little more than the bare outline—that Kaiser clashed with Heymans, leading to his arrest and brief institutionalization—and deemed
the episode an illustration of a volatile temperament and an unhinged
mind. The complete story was impossible to recover; the principals were
dead, and the New York Police Department, the agency that took Kaiser
into custody, had no surviving record of the event. Carolita Mahoney
was tightfisted with details, apparently loath to summon the memory,
though she told the FBI that "he had resisted the NYPD officers because
there was nothing wrong with him."

The particulars of the episode would be revealed in a letter the FBI never saw. Kaiser wrote it in late 1969 and gave it to his friend Tony Barnicle, who kept it secret for decades. In it, Kaiser described Heymans as "a psychopath with dangerous sexual aberrations." He explained that he had grown concerned about the state of the accounting books Heymans was keeping, but had encountered stiff resistance when he suggested an accountant should examine them. He described his discomfort with Heymans's pretensions—he was a diminutive Dutchman who spoke in an ersatz Texas-cowboy drawl and rode a big white horse on the parish grounds. When Heymans, aging and in ill health, was hospitalized, his female Alsatian—reportedly a loud, terror-inducing beast—was left to roam the grounds with its male counterpart. Kaiser visited Heymans at the hospital to tell him he would care for the dogs off the compound. In a fury, Heymans threatened Kaiser "with trouble" and ordered him out of the room. "I then knelt & demanded his blessing which he refused twice but on the 3rd request he gave," Kaiser wrote. Days later, Heymans told Kaiser that he was being too emotional and spoke of his "great respect for certain psychiatrist friends of his in New York" that he wanted Kaiser to see. The vice rector of the Albany house urged Kaiser not to go, warning, Kaiser wrote, "that Fr. Heymans would have a net thrown over me." Nevertheless, Kaiser agreed, taking a bus from Albany to the house of the Capuchin Fathers in New York City. On arrival there, Kaiser wrote, "I could tell from their overly cordial reception & general attentiveness that they were humoring me."

After a brief visit to a Fifth Avenue psychiatrist named Dr. Charles Riordan—Kaiser did not describe what transpired there—he returned to the Capuchin house and was greeted by several policemen. They arrested him, searched him, and took him to Bellevue Hospital, where he was committed to the psychiatric ward. He refused medication. Orderlies forced him to the ground and injected him with tranquilizers and sedatives. From Dr. Riordan, Kaiser learned that Heymans had phoned to say he'd made violent threats and was likely carrying a gun, though Kaiser did not own one.

Kaiser managed to place a call to his sister, who threatened legal action unless he was released from Bellevue. After three days, he was transferred to St. Vincent's Hospital, where, by Kaiser's account, a young Albany nun showed up to protest that Heymans was keeping him hospitalized under false pretenses. She also alleged that Heymans had made "sadomasochistic" sexual advances toward her. Years later, the same woman, living in England and then in her early seventies, elaborated on the nature of Heymans's predilections: He would strip naked and insist that she whip him. Asked if he demanded the same of other nuns, she replied, "I don't think I was special at all."

Tony Barnicle, Kaiser's seminary friend, assumed control of the Albany operation after the 1969 debacle. He had no doubt where blame rested: Heymans was "an absolute nut, certifiably crazy," the kind of man who made the hair rise on the back of your neck. Barnicle said he alerted Mill Hill's superior general to the claims of sexual abuse, but the matter was swept under the rug. "Those were the days before anyone talked about this crap," Barnicle said. It was "the same damn thing that bishops did when pedophile priests appeared. They thought it would go away." To level accusations against a man as prominent as Heymans was to flout a deep-seated institutional taboo. "He's the CEO, the bigwig. If you even suggested anything like that, you've really crossed the line." Heymans flew to California for medical treatment and died soon after. Barnicle lasted at Albany a year, his faith in Mill Hill having eroded beyond repair. "Heymans is probably the least guilty of them all. He had been allowed to just get by with all the crap."

For all that would remain mysterious about Kaiser's brief, disastrous stay in New York, the basic dynamic seemed clear. He'd found himself confronting a sleazy martinet whose abuses were essentially ignored by the Church. Sexual predation, financial impropriety, and a pair of Cerberus-like hounds guarding the demented fiefdom—it was a portrait of ecclesiastical authority allowed to run totally amok. A man like Kaiser would have taken this very hard indeed. As would happen repeatedly throughout Kaiser's life, the institution to which he'd sworn allegiance had failed him. Nevertheless, what mattered to the FBI was that Kaiser had been arrested and institutionalized. It bespoke a certain personality.

AT LEAST TWO other times in his life, the FBI discovered, Kaiser would be hospitalized for psychiatric evaluation. During the early 1970s, Kaiser visited Father Bill Vos, who was then a pastor at St. Cloud State University, in Minnesota. Having spiraled into a profound depression, Kaiser would sit at the table, his head down, tears forming in his eyes, unable to explain what was wrong. For its sufferers, depression often feels divorced from exterior sources—the locus of pain is everywhere and nowhere. The tears were triggered by nothing specific, Vos recalled, "just the black hole he was in." He was listless, withdrawn, incapable of shaking the sadness, and Vos grew so worried that he contacted a local psychiatrist. Kaiser agreed to be hospitalized briefly, and records show that he was treated at St. Joseph's Hospital in St. Paul, Minnesota, in early 1972. He was prescribed lithium. Vos believed Kaiser's depression was linked, in some way, to culture shock. He'd left a starving country where nothing was wasted, where afternoon meals were eliminated in the lean months before the harvest, and had entered the temple of vacuous consumerism and squandered abundance, a land of obscenely overstocked supermarkets, of televisions that bleated with come-ons for a bonanza of pointless products. It was a time of campus unrest and incinerated draft cards. The country was in the throes of cultural and sexual revolutions, and had grown, in some ways, unrecognizable in his absence. Kaiser himself would give the culture-clash explanation to account for his bouts of depression in the States. When Kaiser returned to Africa, he told Vos that he'd stopped taking his lithium because he was past his depression, explaining: It's just the States, Bill. Too many things trigger it there.

Vos wondered whether Kaiser's reservoir of empathy, his inability or unwillingness to distance himself from others' pain, exacerbated his sorrow. Once, he remembered, Kaiser was approached by a girl prostitute in Nairobi. Kaiser had seen these girls before countless times, but her age—and what he grasped instantly as the wretchedness of her life—visibly wounded him. "It got him more in his belly," Vos said. "I think his own personal struggles might have had a lot to do with that."

In the early 1980s, Kaiser was hospitalized a third time for psychiatric care in the States. In this case, it's possible the manic-depressive cycle began in Kenya. Records show that Kaiser, then forty-nine years old, was admitted to Nairobi Hospital in April 1981 in a condition of "extreme fatigue" (for many years a euphemism for deep depression), and complaining that he'd been suffering chest pains for the last four months. He was released three days later. The next month, he wrote to Minnesota friends that he was considering returning to the States for leave earlier than expected, with the explanation that "I am a bit rundown & am not accomplishing much so maybe need a rest."

Once back at his parents' home near Underwood, Minnesota, he grew furious with his younger brother, Joe. Kaiser had returned from several years in Africa, to find his father nearly blind and his mother sinking helplessly into the grip of Alzheimer's and his brother encamped at the house. Saying Joe possessed a "battering kind of personality with his mother," Carolita Mahoney added, "John did question how Joe was handling things in the house." She was there to witness the confrontation escalate. "I thought John and Joe were gonna kill each other, they were so angry with each other. John was so strong. Joe was strong, too. That's when I called the police. I said, 'Nothing is gonna happen that we're gonna regret for the rest of our lives.'"

Recalling the confrontation, Joe Kaiser, in his mid-seventies and still living in Minnesota, said his brother John's behavior had frightened him terribly. "He almost threw me off the roof of the house," Joe said. "He was so much stronger than me. . . . He pulled me up the stairs. He said, 'Joe, show me some authority or I'll throw you off the roof.'" Asked what he might have meant by "authority," Joe replied, "He was just looking for authority, and just wasn't getting it from his order or from Africa." This did not clarify things much, but it hinted at discord between Kaiser and his superiors. "John was kind of halfway loose in his mind," Joe continued. "John was out of his mind. So I got my thirty-thirty out and leveled it at the floor." The law arrived. "The sergeant from Fergus Falls, he put his hand on his three-fifty-seven. He said, 'Father John, if you want some authority, I've got it right here at my side.' John calmed right down."

During this episode, a hefty neighbor named George Hess had intervened to calm Kaiser down, and the priest threw him on his back "like he wasn't even there," Joe said. "He was like Paul Bunyan."

Hess, a retired telephone repairman in his late sixties, could no longer recall many details of the scuffle. "I guess I tried to calm him down," he said. "He was a different person all of a sudden. He was like Jekyll and Hyde. He just changed. When he started getting like that, it was time to get back to Africa."

Deputies took Kaiser to nearby Fergus Falls State Hospital for psychiatric evaluation. When his niece Mary visited his room, the corridor outside echoed with the screams of other patients. Kaiser had a trapped look, and pleaded, "Get me out of here." He was soon transferred to St. Joseph's Hospital in St. Paul, where he was diagnosed with "bipolar illness—manic phase" and treated with lithium, thioridazine, haloperidol, and chlorpromazine.

When the FBI interviewed Francis Kaiser, the priest's brother, in Santa Rosa, California, he denied that his brother had suffered from manic depression, claiming that only the United States had rendered him psychically unhinged—the abundance, the waste. As for the hospitalization at Bellevue, the Church had orchestrated it because he had uncovered Heymans's sexual predations on the nuns. "Within the Catholic Church, priests who expose problems or won't put up with crap become outsiders real quick," according to an FBI summary of its interview with Francis Kaiser. "The Catholic Church has a phrase to describe these priests. They call them priests who are 'out of tether' and need psychological evaluations."

To the FBI, it seemed implausible that Kaiser's periods of mental trouble had only happened in the United States. Were there other instances that family or friends didn't know about, or had kept secret? Had such scenes gone unnoticed in Africa? Had Kenya been a place for Kaiser to hide? He'd certainly found a wide berth, deep in the isolated hill country of Kisiiland and the remote grasslands of Masaiiland. There was endless space to escape in. Who would have perceived the signs of an eccentric white man spiraling into a manic-depressive episode? And even if someone had glimpsed this, who was there to tell? By the mid-1980s, Kenya, though more progressive than its East African neighbors, had just one in-patient mental-health facility, and a handful of psychiatrists ("one for every 2 million persons" by one reckoning). The paucity of Swahili terms for the wild spectrum of emotion a manic-depressive experienced suggested something of the realm in which Kaiser could have shielded himself from scrutiny. "You have to realize, he's the head *mzungu*," Graney said. "He can act irrationally all he wants around the Africans and nobody's gonna question it." Their livelihood was closely tied to Kaiser and the Church, another incentive to ignore erratic spells. "The people who were around him the most, he was their rice bowl," Graney said. "He had hanger-oners. Their job is to sort of carry out the bidding of the *mzungu*."

The autopsy results, which found no trace of lithium in Kaiser's bloodstream, merely confirmed what he'd been telling people for years: He didn't think he needed it.

As the FBI worked with profilers to assess the priest's psychological state, their Kenyan counterparts enlisted a Nairobi psychiatrist named Frank Njenga to perform a "psychological autopsy" on him. He concluded that the priest had been suffering from "acute adjustment disorder," in addition to physical ailments, and that suicide was a "real possibility." He surmised that Kaiser had been devastated by the unraveling of the rape case against Sunkuli, and he offered this observation about the priest's frustrated effort to retrieve Anne Sawoyo from the Mara Serena lodge: "For the first time in their relationship, Fr. Kaiser seemed unable to persuade the young lady to follow a course he believed to be right and just. . . . He had worked so hard for the girl and the course of justice and all his efforts were coming to nothing because this girl could not see things in the same light!" Kaiser had wagered "his name, fame and reputation" on the abortive case.

According to an FBI paraphrase of his conclusions, the psychiatrist found Kaiser was "without companionship or a support system a good deal of the time," and had a "vertical relationship with the people in his parish." He gave them money and other help, but "in turn could ask little in the way of emotional support from them." He was lonely.

The American investigators did not believe, despite the insistence of Kaiser's family, that his manic-depressive episodes could be consigned to the distant past. "Most affective disorders that would warrant institutionalization have a chronic, lifelong property to them," the agents wrote. They noted the "highly unique social structures of Father Kaiser's cultural and religious existence." This undermined "any attempted application of common psychological assessment criteria and generalizations about conventional population groups." In other words, Kaiser was sui generis; the yardstick hadn't been invented to gauge him.

The agents learned of Kaiser's demotion from the rank of sergeant in the U.S. Army in the 1950s, but they found details hard to come by: A fire had destroyed many of the records from the Korean War era. What was clear: He'd clashed with superiors as a young man in a way that seemed to indicate a strong-willed, confrontational, authority-bucking streak, traits that would surface later in conflicts with church superiors.

Even as they sought to uncover the scope of his mental illness, the agents understood that a certain respect for the Kaiser family's privacy had to be preserved. The family, for its part, was reluctant to turn over the priest's full medical records. Carolita Mahoney had been ill at ease almost from the beginning, when she realized that agents were using the term *violent death* rather than the word *murder* to describe the nature of the case; the drift of the questioning, which seemed to focus on her brother's mental state, made her increasingly uncomfortable.

The investigation was classified as a 163, a foreign police cooperation matter. It was technically the Kenyans' case; this meant the FBI couldn't just subpoena the medical files. Graney did, however, prevail upon the

Kenyans to submit their own requests for the files—called "letters of rogatory"—to federal prosecutors in New York and Minneapolis. The process would be a slow one.

Meanwhile, the agents were circling back to a few basic questions: If assassins had been following Kaiser, when did they happen upon him, and where had they been lurking? Where did their vectors intersect, hunters and hunted? How would assassins have followed his erratic, perplexing, hours-long route from Nairobi to the lonely road in Naivasha—what Corbett called a "bumblebee trail"—without being spotted? Would a hit squad have relied on their victim to provide the weapon for the killing? There was a good reason so many assassinations occurred as victims were leaving their homes or offices: The attackers could be ready and waiting. A moving target presented a greater challenge, and a man who came and went with Kaiser's seeming impulsiveness presented a quarry more slippery still.

Yes, the beating of Levi Marko at the Mara Serena lodge pointed to Sunkuli's desire to keep a close watch on Anne Sawoyo. But where was the evidence that the minister had lined up a murder plot so elaborate, so fastidiously orchestrated, that it could have been carried off against such odds? "There would be so much ninjalike activity that would be required. The real world doesn't work like that," Corbett said. "There wasn't a lot to suggest this was predator and prey. What there was to go on was his behavior."

In that behavior, FBI profilers discerned a "manic cycling from high to low," a mind unmoored. Agents saw an uncommonly tough man whose fortitude had nevertheless raveled out over too many hard years. They saw a man in pain who wanted it to end. Corbett wondered if there was any special significance in the location of the gunshot wound at the back of Kaiser's head, as opposed to, say, right at the temple. Did it suggest a man desperate to hide—perhaps even from himself—the fact that he was ending his own life?

In weighing the evidence, Corbett recalled what a prosecutor had once told him about the nature of proof. Picture yourself at the edge of a precipice, with a ten-foot gap separating you from the other side. To get there, you need a plank that is at least ten feet and one inch in length. Two five-foot planks won't do, nor will five two-foot planks.

Murder theories abounded, but did the assembled evidence bridge the chasm? Maybe a simpler explanation would.

The FBI's burden was to persuade people that the priest had done the unthinkable. Everyone at the Bureau knew it would be a hard sell. Denial kicked in when you thought you knew someone and found out you didn't, not really. To the investigators, it was an utterly familiar reaction. "No family of an eighteen-year-old wants to admit he took his life," Corbett said.

By November 2000, some in the Bureau were contemplating "end game and exit strategies," with an eye toward minimizing bad PR. Agents had yet to interview Sunkuli, reportedly because they first "wanted to be prepared with all of the facts," though the Bureau understood how bad this might look.

"Some antagonists are even attempting to advance a [sic] interpretation that portrays the U.S. Embassy and the FBI as giving a willing wink at the savage behavior of the Kenyan Government," according to an internal FBI memo. "Although this may seem outrageously off the mark, one must be cautioned against underestimating the entrenched reluctance of Father Kaiser's supporters to accept anything other than a sinister murder scenario involving elements of the Kenyan government. It is this same uncoupled mindset that provided the inertia [sic] for the irresponsibly inaccurate resolution pushing through both bodies of Congress." (This referred, apparently, to the congressional resolution condemning Kaiser's "assassination.")

The FBI memo warned that "the potential for a sensationally distorted reporting of this case looms menacingly. A worst case scenario storyline would predictably highlight Father Kaiser's life of goodness, the Dictator-like qualities of the Daniel Moi regime and, among other things, the fact that the principal suspect has never been interviewed by FBI investigators." The behavioral profilers had decided on suicide, and further leads were "not expected to avail new evidence." Close the case, the memo urged. The longer the delay, the louder the complaints of a cover-up.

• • •

IN THE FIRST week of December 2000, more than three months into the investigation, the FBI agents and their Kenyan counterparts interrogated Sunkuli at the Nairobi headquarters of the Criminal Investigation Department. Graney appreciated the sensitivity of the situation for the Kenyan police: This was the equivalent of an FBI man like himself sitting down to interrogate, say, the United States deputy defense secretary. They asked Sunkuli a few respectful questions in English and then allowed Graney to lead the questioning. To Graney, Sunkuli seemed strikingly relaxed and untroubled, not at all the demeanor you'd expect from a man accused of rape and suspected of murder.

Tell me about your relationship with Kaiser, Graney asked.

Sunkuli said he had hardly known the priest. Oh, he'd been familiar with Kaiser since the late 1970s and had, in fact, attended his church as a young man. He remembered seeing Kaiser sleeping at the construction site of a church he was building. And he recalled the morning that Kaiser, "badly dressed" and apparently unshowered, came to his home to announce that he would be implicating him at the Akiwumi Commission. After the tribunal, they'd run into each other and exchanged good-natured words. But no, he'd never tried to have the priest deported. Now that the priest was dead, well, his political rivals were having a field day, and Kaiser was probably enjoying it, too, wherever he was.

Asked if he'd had sexual relations with his accusers, Sunkuli replied that what sex had occurred had been consensual. At the mention of Florence Mpayei, Graney would recall, Sunkuli offered a wink and a smile, with the remark, "Hey, what's a man to do? She's so feisty."

The minister struck Graney as a man who used young women sexually because he could. That didn't necessarily make him a murderer.

Sunkuli claimed he had no information about the priest's death. He said he first learned about it as he was boarding a plane in the company of His Excellency the President. Sunkuli offered to take a polygraph examination. There is no evidence that it actually occurred. The questioning lasted just over two hours.

· · ·

AS THE YEAR ended and the investigation dragged on into the next, the U.S. government was feeling keen pressure to publicize its findings. "The mission has taken a hammering in the local press, and those who believe in conspiracy theories and want desperately to see Kaiser's death as a political assassination are in the ascendancy," read an internal January 2001 memo of the U.S. embassy in Nairobi. "USG [United States Government] silence on the investigation is increasingly viewed as cover-up, complicity and conspiracy with the government of Kenya."

Ambassador Carson had spoken with FBI director Louis Freeh, the memo noted, and Freeh had "agreed to expedite remaining laboratory work." Carson had urged Freeh "to allow the fullest report possible to go forward—because otherwise the credibility of the embassy and the good work and name of the FBI would be questioned." Carson expected tough sledding with Congress, especially Senator Wellstone. "After having done so much right, we are on the defensive."

The memo revealed that the United States had dissuaded the Kenyan government from launching a judicial investigation, or inquest, into Kaiser's death. "Such an inquest, in our judgment, would bring the results of the investigation into public light in a manner that would seriously undermine their credibility." The memo did not explicate why such an inquest would have undermined the investigation, but continued: "Given rising level of media interest, we are going to get battered if we are not careful in our future handling of this issue. The facts are with us, but if we do not get them out, misperception and distortion will win the public relations and public opinion battle that is shaping up."

IN FEBRUARY 2001, as the investigation neared completion, Graney was at the tag end of his third trip to Kenya and visiting a priest who ran an orphanage near Naivasha. A pleasant lunch was served in the yard, and Graney watched African boys leaping jubilantly off a mattress into a pile of hay, kicking up storms of bugs. Graney looked down and noticed that his legs were covered with bites. He had not applied mosquito repellant.

Shortly afterward, on an airplane back to the States, he experienced a terrible thirst, which no amount of water could slake. By the time he got home, he was running a bad fever, and the fatigue was overwhelming. He got in the bath but was too weak to extricate himself without his son's help. The next day, his body was racked with cold, an all-consuming chill he couldn't shake. He thought it must be malaria. His wife drove him to the hospital. He got IV fluids. He'd never been sicker. His fever went up to 105 degrees, and persisted for two weeks at a lower grade. He turned fifty in mid-February but was in no shape for a party. One day, the phone rang, and the man on the other end claimed to be Louis Freeh. Graney thought it must be one of the boys from work playing a prank, but it was the FBI director himself, offering his sympathies and the name of a contagious-disease specialist. The diagnosis was dengue fever, also called "broken bone fever" because the joints became swollen and inflamed. It mimicked malaria, and in extreme cases, like this one, could provoke in its sufferers a longing to be dead and have it over with. The disease wiped him out for six weeks, during which time he shed thirty pounds. Later, he would think of the episode as part of the price he paid for his dedication to the Kaiser case, one that would be invisible, like so much else in the investigation, to all the critics.

The case was moving ahead without him. As he recovered, the FBI enlisted Vincent DiMaio, a world authority on firearms forensics, to examine the evidence. Already, two independent pathologists—one enlisted by the Church, the other by a human rights group—had studied the entry wound close-up and concluded that the shot that obliterated the back of Kaiser's head had entered behind his right ear from a distance of at least six inches, and possibly as much as three feet. Since it seemed impossible for Kaiser to have pointed the long-barreled gun at himself from such a range, that meant murder was the only explanation.

Now it was DiMaio's turn. He was the superstar of his field, author of a definitive textbook on gunshot wounds. As chief medical examiner in San Antonio, Texas, for twenty-five years, he had performed some nine thousand autopsies and supervised another thirty thousand.

Studying thirty-six crime-scene photos taken by Kenyan police, an autopsy report, and twenty-seven autopsy photographs, which he described as "unreadable for all practical purposes," he found that the barrel could have been touching Kaiser's head at an angle when the shot was fired. He believed there had been a small gap between the gun barrel and the skin, allowing gunpowder to escape and creating the "powder tattooing," or "stippling," on the scalp. It was not, however, what he called a "dirty" wound—no gun soot, no burned skin.

The lack of "dirtiness" ordinarily suggested a shot of some distance, but here, in his judgment, it was easily explained by the nature of the weapon. Shotguns have long barrels, twenty-four to twenty-six inches, and they fire clean, with most of the material diffusing into the barrel. In his career, he'd seen a number of point-blank, direct-contact shotgun wounds that looked so clean and unsooty, you might at first mistake them for distant shots, until a closer look at the wound showed the imprint of the gun itself.

DiMaio noted that there was blood spatter on the priest's right knee and lower left pant leg, but none on his lap. In his view, this suggested that a standing Kaiser had placed the shotgun butt on the ground, with the barrel angled behind his right ear, and had folded his body forward to reach the trigger, thereby shielding his lap when blood sprayed onto his legs. The FBI's own forensic examiner believed that Kaiser had been sitting down when he pulled the trigger, his knees bent before him, with the right knee closer to his chest, and that blood had gouted from Kaiser's head, struck his right knee, and ricocheted to his left leg and shoe. Whether Kaiser had been sitting down or leaning over, DiMaio concluded, the same blood spatter pattern would have resulted. Strange as the location of Kaiser's wound seemed, DiMaio classified it as a shot to the temple, the second most common gunshot suicide after a shot through the mouth.

He found it significant that the body showed no defensive wounds. He also took into account what struck him as the priest's erratic behavior.

"Virtually no homicides are like books," DiMaio said. "It doesn't work that way, like *Mission Impossible,* where all these wonderful things happen. It's difficult to mimic suicide unless it's very, very simple. The problem that you have here is you can't excuse his conduct prior to that. You'd have to say, 'This is a guy who's bipolar, who's beginning to cycle, and then he just happens to get murdered by his own rifle.'"

The unexplained bloody fingerprints on Kaiser's pants, he guessed, had gotten there when the body was moved; the blood on the right fingers could have resulted, he explained, by the hand resting in blood from the wound. "You want to stage a homicide? You run him off the road. You grab him, hit him over the head, then just get someone to drive him off the road into a ravine. That's the easiest way."

Why had Kaiser tried to give his shotgun away? "I think he was really scared that he was gonna kill himself. It was all coming apart and he knew it was coming apart. They can't control themselves. They know something's wrong. They don't know what to do. The problem is a lot of mental patients stop taking their medication. With bipolar [disorder], you can go a significant amount of time without symptoms, or mild symptoms, then shift into something really bad."

DiMaio dismissed out of hand the theory that Kaiser's body had been dumped at the scene. "He was killed there. The body was not moved. That's easy. You can just tell that by the spray, how the body was lying at the scene." He maintained a tone of utter certainty, despite his reliance on imperfect photographs taken by the Kenyan police. "You can see how the tissue was distributed, how the blood was running." If he'd been moved, DiMaio explained, "you'd be seeing blood patterns going down or sideways, multiple blood pattern contradictions."

Passing off a murder as something else is a complicated business, he said. "People who try to do it virtually always get caught, because you can't."

Yet murders successfully staged as suicides or accidents are forever believed suicides or accidents: They don't make it into the data pool. Suicide remained just an expert's educated guess—and one he acknowledged might change if further evidence materialized—rather than a certainty. He was asked if there was hard evidence to disprove the possibility that Kaiser was forced to his knees, or to a sitting position, and then shot. No, he replied.

DiMaio issued his report in March 2001, with this conclusion: "There is no evidence of any outside intervention."

15

THE VERDICT

WHEN GRANEY GOT back to work from the wasting fever, he started slowly, putting in half days as his strength returned. One day in early April, Tom Carey, an FBI supervisor, informed him that the case had to be concluded immediately. "We're going to Kenya next Monday," Carey said.

That was seven days away. Graney was taken aback. Why the rush? Weren't they going to wait to get Kaiser's medical records? The U.S. attorneys in New York and Minneapolis were reviewing the request for the records, and in another month or two the FBI might get them. Why not wait and see what they contained, rather than surrender the possibility of ever knowing? What if they held evidence of manic-depressive breakdowns that Kaiser's family had not revealed, of a psychic illness even more profound and unmanageable than the available evidence indicated? The records might dispel lingering doubts about the FBI's conclusion and the integrity of the investigation.

Carey, by Graney's account, was adamant: The case needed to be wrapped up. Graney would later say that he disagreed strongly, and told Carey so. "The decision's been made," Graney recalled Carey saying. "Put the report together. You have one week."

It would rankle Graney persistently, the decision not to wait for the records. And yet he was a loyal career Bureau man with orders to follow and a report to buckle down on and write. The deadline meant, inevitably, executing what he called "a cut-and-paste job" on the report. He took the lead in assembling it, with other agents and profilers adding their own chunks. It had a hasty, jerry-rigged feel, with competing typefaces and the occasional factual error. But inside a week it was done, running to eighty pages, with the Bureau's circular emblem, at the center of which were the scales of justice, affixed to the cover sheet like God's own seal.

IN HIGH-PROFILE CASES, it was the Bureau's practice to send in the brass to announce its findings. The press conference was on Thursday, April 19, 2001, at the temporary U.S. embassy at Barclays Plaza in Nairobi. With an American flag behind them, Carey and other FBI agents stood alongside Ambassador Carson, Kenyan police officials, and Attorney General Amos Wako. Carey hailed the investigation as an independent one in which his agents were allowed to "pursue every lead and examine every piece of evidence."

The FBI had conducted seven major searches for evidence and more than two hundred interviews. Statistically speaking, the FBI noted in its report, most American men who kill themselves do it with guns, and 95 percent of suicides happen at the peak of a depressive episode. Kaiser's fear that the nuncio would kick him out of Kenya had been "a significant life stressor," the report noted, and the collapse of the case against Sunkuli had been "a significant disappointment."

Kaiser had "an 'in your face' style" that the Catholic leadership didn't fully approve of, the report noted, and had, at least three times, "reportedly acted aggressively toward others, including law enforcement officers." This referred to two of his U.S. hospitalizations—the Bellevue incident and the confrontation with his brother in Minnesota—and to his tussle with police at Maela.

The report noted the undisturbed bedding at the crime scene, which seemed to indicate that the priest had not been surprised. There was only one set of tire tracks visible in the Kenyan police photos, suggesting no other vehicle had forced him off the road. The lack of damage to the front of his Toyota meant he had driven the truck slowly into the culvert. He had carried both a shotgun and an ax, and yet there were no signs of a struggle. At the gas station, he'd declined an offer of gas, despite a long trip ahead. He had a history of psychiatric hospitalizations, and his health was failing.

The report cited twenty-eight incidents said to demonstrate Kaiser's "peculiar behavior" in the last ninety-six hours of his life, during which witnesses described him as "out of sorts," "tense," "scared," and "haunted." (Among these incidents, as an illustration of the report's sloppiness, were his all-night vigils with his shotgun during the Akiwumi period more than a year earlier.) There was his weeping at Mass, just before he left to meet the nuncio in Nairobi. There was his remark, as he traveled to Nairobi, that he was on a "difficult journey" and required prayers. There was his lack of sleep, as well as his remarks that he was being followed and feeling paranoid. There was his request that Mwangi drive him to the nuncio, even though he had his own truck, and then his failure to wait for Mwangi's arrival, instead of catching a ride with Borgman. There was the way he lay in Borgman's backseat, his head covered. There were his mood swings: his good cheer during the croquet game and his visit to the construction site, contrasted with his weeping at the group lunch and his withdrawn behavior at afternoon tea. There were his remarks that he believed death was imminent. There was his refusal to stay and chat with the nuncio. There was the note he left with the Maryknoll missionary, thanking him for the Swahili course. There was his unexplained departure from the Mill Hill house, and, later, from the bishop's house. There was his remark to Mwangi to thank Sister Nuala for the good work she had done. There was his appearance on the isolated knoll, where he attempted to give away his shotgun.

As the FBI cast it, this all amounted to a man in deteriorating mental health, a man wrapping up his affairs as he prepared to take his life.

The Americans praised the Kenyans for their cooperation and gave their verdict: An emotionally troubled Kaiser had killed himself.

The Kenyan government did not delay in declaring itself exonerated. A front-page story in the *Kenya Times*, the state mouthpiece, announced that the FBI's verdict "drove the final nail" into the coffin of "a sick man."

"The man on the Altar was deranged," the story said. "So when Kaiser left the sanctuary of the Ngong Bishop's house on the day he died, he must have been running away from the enemies he had in his tormented mind."

Back in Minnesota, the FBI sent agents to the home of Kaiser's sister, Carolita Mahoney, to hand-deliver the report. Graney wanted to go personally, but he was still on a four-hour-a-day work schedule in D.C., recovering from his illness. Nevertheless, he called her house that day; he felt he owed it to them. He got Carolita's husband, Joe Mahoney, and found him incandescent with rage. Mahoney called it a whitewash. "You're bought off by Kenya," Graney recalled him snarling. It would be a common sentiment.

WHATEVER ELSE PEOPLE said about Kaiser, there was one point of consensus: His Catholicism was the "terribly old-fashioned" kind. Heaven and hell were not metaphors, but actual locations, and certain sins were inexpiable. Despair was the sin of Judas, of whom Jesus had said, Better that he'd never been born. Francis Kaiser had learned the story as a boy, right alongside his brother, and had been taught what meaning to ascribe: It spoke to the scope of the torment that awaited suicides. Dante had consigned them to the seventh circle of his Inferno, their souls entrapped in thorn trees that were haunted by devouring Harpies.

For a man of old-time religion, damnation for the self-slain was an iron tenet. Kaiser liked to quote from G. K. Chesterton's *Orthodoxy*, a defense of classic Catholicism, in which the author wrote, "Not only is suicide a sin, it is the sin. It is the ultimate and absolute evil, the refusal to take an interest in existence; the refusal to take the oath of loyalty to life. The man who kills a man, kills a man. The man who kills himself, kills all men; as far as he is concerned he wipes out the world. . . . There is not a tiny creature in the cosmos at whom his death is not a sneer."

The Bible itself does not condemn the suicides it records, from those of Samson and Saul to those of Abimelech and Achitophel; even Judas escapes textual judgment for the act. The ecclesiastical sanctions came later. It was martyrdom's early popularity that gave Medieval Christian leaders a fierce incentive to demonize self-murder: The unvarnished creed, taken seriously, could make death much too attractive. Every flea-bitten, hunger-tormented, disease-racked day on earth represented another needless delay in the achievement of salvation. Every sunrise exposed you to further temptation and sin; every breath jeopardized your eternal reward. In the fourth and fifth centuries, the fanatical Donatists took martyr lust to an extreme, flinging themselves off rocks with a great flourish and profaning pagan temples in the hope of inviting murder.

Confronting this horror, Saint Augustine invoked the sixth commandment—Thou shalt not murder—and argued that because life was a gift from God, to take it was to flout divine will. It was not until the sixth century, swayed by this reasoning, that the Church declared suicide a crime. And yet "suicide, thinly disguised as martyrdom, was the rock on which the Church had first been founded," A. Alvarez argued in *The Savage God: A Study of Suicide*. "So perhaps the absoluteness with which the sin was condemned and the horrors of the vengeance visited on the dead bodies of the suicides were directly proportional to the power the act exerted on the Christian imagination, and to the lingering temptation to escape the snares of the flesh by the shortest, most certain way."

During the European Middle Ages, the Church's revulsion reached a ghastly pitch. Suicides were not just denied burial rites, their property confiscated, their names defamed. Their bodies were also dragged by horse through the streets and hung on gibbets; thrown in sewers and on refuse heaps; stuffed into barrels and floated down the river; buried at a crossroads with a stake through the body and a stone over the face.

Such grisly rituals were not without "rational and philosophic truth," as Chesterton saw it. "There is a meaning in burying the suicide apart. The man's crime is different from other crimes—for it makes even crimes impossible." A martyr and a suicide were not cousins, but occupied "opposite ends of heaven and hell," Chesterton wrote. "One man flung away his life; he was so good that his dry bones could heal cities in pestilence. Another man flung away life; he was so bad that his bones would pollute his brethren's."

By that logic, Kaiser had tumbled from heaven to hell at the stroke of the FBI's pen, plunged from the most exalted figure in Christendom to the most reviled. After a lifetime of self-abnegation and good works, he'd entered eternal torment—passed beyond the possibility of salvation—through the mouth of his own gun. He'd incinerated the immense Minnesota skies and every summer june bug. He'd placed himself beyond grace, beyond the possibility of redemption; there was no opportunity to repent.

It is true that the Catholic stance on suicide had evolved from the doctrines Kaiser imbibed as a child. In the early 1980s, the Church, belatedly acknowledging the contributions of psychiatry and the severity of mental illness, removed suicide from its list of unpardonable sins. When a member of Pope John Paul II's Swiss Guard killed his commander, the commander's wife, and then himself in 1998, he received a Vatican funeral service with an honor guard, indicating the dramatic distance the Church had traveled from the epoch of the staked heart at the crossroads. But the message would be slow to percolate to millions of Catholics, and by all accounts, Kaiser's view never wavered from the old one.

David Durenberger, a former Minnesota senator who knew Kaiser in high school, was in disbelief at the FBI's finding. "There's something about 'The FBI says,' 'The FBI declares'—it's pretty hard to overcome that one," he said. "You can't change the gravestone once you've carved it."

Few who knew Kaiser could bear the verdict. Everything Kaiser was supposed to have been—devout, brave, a tough-minded paratrooper who'd been prepared to lead men into battle—seemed to militate against the possibility of suicide. As another high school classmate, Don Montgomery, put it, "It's just completely alien to his constitution and his training and his upbringing." Said his sister, Carolita, "It would be the unforgivable sin. It would not be in John's makeup." Cornelius Schilder, one of his Mill Hill bosses, recalled that Kaiser had told him he'd rather be killed one hundred times than take his own life.

There were other skeptics. On April 26, 2001, a week after the FBI released its report, Paul Wellstone—the Minnesota senator who was as liberal as Kaiser was conservative—summoned some of the FBI agents to his Washington, D.C., office to question them. Wellstone believed their conclusion implausible, as did his chief of staff, Colin McGinnis, a midwestern Catholic familiar with shotguns.

To McGinnis, a man shooting himself in the back of the head, with the gun butt resting on the ground, beggared credulity. Why not put it under your chin, or in your mouth? McGinnis found a long stick and, in front of his boss, attempted to reproduce Kaiser's alleged position. "It requires physical gymnastics," McGinnis said later. "It didn't make sense."

For more than an hour, assembled around a conference table with the crime-scene photos, Wellstone and McGinnis questioned the agents. The agents acknowledged that Sunkuli had admitted to sex with his accusers, and that their probe had uncovered the brutal beating of Levi Marko at the Mara Serena lodge. But it didn't follow that Kaiser had been murdered. They were undisturbed by the gun's position—they'd seen all kinds of bizarre things in their time, and this was not impossible.

Wellstone wanted to know if witnesses had felt free to talk. The agents replied that they had interviewed two hundred people and that only three had declined to talk in the presence of the Kenyan police.

Still, the agents acknowledged, in certain matters their hands had been tied: The crime scene had been disturbed. To McGinnis, there seemed obvious limitations to the investigation. "They weren't as provisional as I thought they would be in their investigative conclusions, given these ambiguities, " he said later. "There were a lot of questions that were just insoluble."

The meeting left Wellstone unpersuaded, prompting him to write to Attorney General John Ashcroft, saying he remained "deeply skeptical" about the FBI's conclusions. He believed the agency had "failed to give sufficient weight to the considerable harassment, intimidation, and death

threats Father Kaiser faced as he challenged officials of the Moi regime."
He characterized the FBI report as "incomplete": Though agents told
him Sunkuli had "conceded the substance" of the sex allegations, their
report contained no mention of it. He urged Ashcroft to direct the Justice
Department to review the FBI's report. The request went nowhere.

A month after the FBI's verdict, *60 Minutes* aired a segment that cast
doubt on the investigation and suggested Kaiser's death was linked to
his efforts to bring charges against Moi. (During their research, the *60
Minutes* crew had rented a small plane to fly to Lolgorien and discovered
something ominous: an AK-47 shell, apparently planted on the plane,
that the U.S.-trained pilot and the airport captain interpreted as a warning from the government.) In a letter to the show's producer, Don Hewitt,
the FBI's acting director, Thomas Pickard, complained the segment contained "misconceptions." The case had been "one of the largest international police cooperation cases ever," and "no credible information was
developed that indicated Father Kaiser was the victim of foul play."

In light of Kaiser's almost single-minded devotion to bringing Moi
to justice by whatever means he could seize, Pickard's most astonishing
sentence was this one: "While Father Kaiser may have wished to present evidence before an international tribunal, our investigation found
no evidence that he took any steps to do so."

16

THE END OF THE TIME OF MOI

AT HIS NAIROBI office, Charles Mbuthi Gathenji worked his way carefully through the FBI report, taking notes. Kenya's Catholic bishops knew him as one of the few lawyers willing to take such a case, and one of the few who could be trusted with it. Asked to make recommendations on how to proceed, he read the report through once, then a second time, and then a third.

He was incredulous. The American agents' work, to him, gave off a whiff of bad faith and betrayal. They had never interviewed him, despite his close work with Kaiser and his deep knowledge of the political landscape. The report they touted as definitive lacked both full witness statements and a summary of those it had interviewed. It gave no explanation for the months-long delay in interviewing Sunkuli. It gave little credence to the fact that Kaiser had been closely followed by the government. It seemed a patchwork of bad inferences and tunnel-vision analysis, animated by an eagerness to distort the meaning of Kaiser's behavior to fit its conclusion.

The notion that Kaiser's conduct in his last days bespoke a mental unraveling seemed ludicrous. Instead, it seemed clear, Kaiser's behavior reflected a man who had good reason to believe that killers were hunting him. He had faced arrest, deportation, death threats. He'd been chased, harassed, urged to flee. He'd predicted his death, over and over, and had warned people that his enemies would make it look like a suicide. That he had wept at Mass in Lolgorien, and told people he was preparing for a long journey, seemed less the behavior of a suicidal man than of one saddened by the prospect of leaving the country he loved. And what the FBI called his erratic behavior—leaving abruptly from church compounds, traveling at night to the remote village of Kiambu—seemed more likely the stratagems of a former paratrooper who was trying to shake his pursuers.

Gathenji searched the report for a ballistics study on the shotgun that had supposedly killed the priest. There was none. Nor were there measurements of the shotgun's trigger-to-muzzle length in comparison with the reach of Kaiser's arm. Why hadn't such a basic thing been ascertained? Would it have even been physically possible for the arthritic priest to position himself with the long barrel behind his ear and pull the trigger? Were they supposed to take the FBI's word for it?

As Gathenji saw it, something crucial was missing from the scene where Kaiser's body had been discovered: the pellets and the wadding that his shotgun would have discharged when he was killed. To judge from other shells found in Kaiser's desk drawers, which contained twelve or thirteen pellets of double-ought buckshot, there were plausibly about a dozen pellets in the shell that supposedly killed him. They weren't found in the remains of his cranium or, despite searches over a wide radius, in the surrounding dirt and shrubs. The report carried no explanation for this, either.

It was difficult to tell, Gathenji thought, whether the report stemmed from the combined incompetence of the Kenyan police and the FBI, or whether there had been a deliberate cover-up. True, the FBI had been hamstrung from the outset: They had not arrived on the crime scene until days after Kaiser's death, and by then the Kenyan police had already allowed it to become irreversibly compromised. Though the body remained by the roadside for five hours after police arrived, the pathologist who performed the autopsy had never been summoned to the scene. It was a common misstep in Kenyan homicides—perhaps it would have seemed more unusual if the pathologist *had* been summoned. Nevertheless, the absence of an on-scene pathologist was an incalculable evidentiary loss.

Gathenji thought of Robert Ouko, the Kenyan foreign minister found in a ravine a decade earlier, a gun beside his charred, mutilated body. He thought of how Moi had manipulated New Scotland Yard, of how there had been official inquiries and further inquiries, voluminous reports, witnesses who died year after year, of how the case had become a template in national memory, a byword for government murder and for investigations that were never meant to find the truth, but, rather, to ensure that it vanished into the abyss of Kenyan history.

Gathenji, once so optimistic about the FBI involvement, now believed that Moi had invited the U.S. agency with the knowledge that its inquiry would be sharply circumscribed. Moi knew how much America needed his cooperation in the prosecution of the embassy bombers. If the FBI had been after the truth, Gathenji asked himself, why hadn't they demanded the file that Moi's Special Branch had certainly been keeping on Kaiser, the kind the state spy agency assembled on dissidents of any profile? And if the Special Branch had refused to divulge the file, why hadn't the FBI raised an outcry? To have done that, the lawyer reasoned, would have blown a hole in the facade of Kenyan cooperation. If the Americans had found Moi's people completely cooperative, as they claimed, perhaps that was because they hadn't pushed them hard enough where it mattered.

From the start, the priest's death had felt coldly familiar to Gathenji. His own father's death had been both politically charged and unpunished, and, like Kaiser's, it had had a feeling of inevitability: Despite clear threats and repeated warnings to desist, a stubbornly idealistic churchman had refused to flinch as he marched toward martyrdom.

Studying photographs of the Kaiser crime scene, Gathenji noticed how carefully the set of bedding had been arranged on the ground near Kaiser's body, as if the priest had been planning to sleep there. The neatness of the bedding seemed to reflect a Kenyan's conception of a punctilious Englishman. It didn't look like the handiwork of the priest he knew as "essentially a cowboy" in the American mold, a man who, his church friends insisted, was well-nigh incapable of laying out neat sheets and blankets. "In this country, they think a white man is perfect, is tidy,"

Gathenji would say. "It was arranged by someone with very foreign ideas about Father Kaiser."

Had Kaiser suffered manic depression, as his hospitalizations and occasional use of lithium suggested? Gathenji could acknowledge the possibility, but he considered it a moot point. Kaiser had always struck the lawyer as mentally tough, even in the face of terrible stress, and nothing in his final letters suggested derangement. He'd never been known to attempt suicide. He'd left no note. No one had seen him shoot himself.

Officialdom had put its stamp on the suicide theory. They had succeeded in casting the narrative of Kaiser's last days, and chances of replacing it with an alternate one seemed slim. For anyone looking to justify passivity, the FBI's conclusion was a boon. "A lot of people said, 'It doesn't concern me, if that's what they say happened,' " Gathenji said.

He called a meeting with the Kenyan bishops and laid out his conclusions. He believed the Church should launch its own investigation. This, he cautioned, was a dangerous tack. Once they took witness statements and passed them on to the police, the witnesses would be easy targets. They might end up dead.

The only apparent remedy lay in a vestige of British colonial law, which provided for an inquest—an inquisitorial proceeding in open court—in the case of mysterious deaths. To the Church and Kaiser's family, it represented the best hope of casting light on evidence the FBI might have missed or ignored. A magistrate would preside. They could call witnesses. The rules of evidence were loose, so even rumors and hearsay could be explored. It would be accessible to the press; daylight meant a measure of protection.

Gathenji was hardly surprised, however, when his request for an inquest was rebuffed by Attorney General Amos Wako. Neither the Kenyan nor U.S. governments wanted the matter reopened. The FBI had spoken. The American agents had flown home. The investigation was over, the case closed, the regime officially exonerated. Whatever private doubts Kenyans harbored, that was now the official history, one that Gathenji feared might stand forever.

Gathenji received regular calls from Francis Kaiser, the priest's elder brother, eager for updates. Francis had flown to Kenya for the funeral, but he was seven thousand miles away again now, at home in Santa Rosa, California, growing old, harboring a helpless feeling. It was not easy for him to communicate with Gathenji, whose Kenyan accent was thick. As best he could over the phone, frequently pausing to repeat his words, Gathenji tried to explain the nature of the political situation. Moi ran the country. He controlled parliament. He controlled the courts. As internal security minister and a rumored successor to Moi, Sunkuli was untouchable, and he bragged that KANU would rule for one hundred years. There was little to do, in such a climate, except wait.

THE CASE DEAREST to the U.S. Department of Justice, meanwhile, was about to go to trial. In contrast to the small team deployed for the Kaiser investigation, the probe into the East African embassy bombings that killed 224 people had represented what the FBI claimed was the largest foreign deployment in its history. Moi had obligingly waived rights to the suspects, and on January 3, 2001, in a fortified Manhattan courtroom surrounded by concrete barriers, jury selection began in the case against four of the accused conspirators. To countless observers, the five-month trial introduced a theme still novel in the months before 9/11: Osama bin Laden's plan to kill Americans everywhere. The trial yielded guilty verdicts against the four bin Laden followers, who received life in prison without parole. The Justice Department had its victory—it was the first time a U.S. court had convicted terrorists for attacks against Americans abroad—though thirteen others indicted in the bombings, including bin Laden himself, remained fugitives.

The one-year anniversary of Kaiser's death refocused attention on a case officials wished would simply vanish: There was a memorial Mass, a rally, and renewed calls for an inquest. The clamor seemed to be building. "No one at the embassy or in CID wants a public inquest. We do not foresee it," read an August 2001 memo from the FBI's Office of the

Legal Attache (Legat) in Nairobi. "However, since it would be an independent move by the GOK [Government of Kenya], we would have to say we would cooperate. As far as Legat is concerned, the investigation is over and we stand by the report."

There was no need for the FBI to fear an inquest so long as Moi stayed at the helm. But the "Professor of Politics" was nearly eighty, and increasingly prone to miscalculation. As the 2002 elections approached, the damage he'd wrought was evident everywhere: Bandits ran amok, angry idlers crowded the streets, schools and pavement were disintegrating, and foreign investors, battered by an endless gauntlet of graft, had fled. Across the country, the anger was barely containable. Having looted the treasury for so long—having transformed banks, import and export licenses, government-owned railways and telecommunications networks into streams of steady cash—Moi had made himself one of the continent's wealthiest men, even as he presided over the pauperization and gangsterization of a country once regarded as the region's great promise. Among the capital's two million inhabitants, 60 percent were confined to fetid slums redolent of garbage bonfires and open sewers. Below his Nairobi mansion sprawled the rust-colored galvanized-roof shanties of what had become, under his watch, East Africa's largest slum, Kibera, an immense, lawless labyrinth of narrow, muddy roads where murder and extortion gangs ruled largely unchallenged. Such gangs, rumored to be protected by Moi's machine, now comprised what some called a shadow government.

Gathenji, still in a kind of legal exile, was watching the political scene closely. He was working with an unlisted number in a peeling limestone bungalow with a leaking roof. He had a security gate in front and an escape route through the back door. He kept a guard, who lived on the site and carried a cell phone, to alert him if government men arrived and demanded entry.

The approaching election, as everyone understood, would be a referendum on Moi, who had been president so long, most Kenyans had not been alive to remember another. Because of a 1992 amendment, the

Kenyan constitution forbade a president from being elected to more than two five-year terms. Moi's term would expire in January 2003—provided, of course, he opted not to alter the constitution.

Though Moi had served American interests, and was still perceived as a relatively reliable partner in the campaign against Islamist terror, Washington now wanted a change. Secretary of State Colin Powell and Ambassador Carson urged Moi to honor the constitution and step aside, with a strategy built around "positive reinforcement of Moi's statesmanship." Flattery seemed the core of the policy, as reflected in U.S. State Department correspondence: "We should appeal to Moi's desire to establish a lasting legacy, securing democracy for his people and setting a regional and global example. . . . We can also underscore appreciation for Moi's commitment to peace in Sudan and Somalia. . . . For all his faults, we recall he has stood as a friend to the United States in both the Cold War and the Global War on Terrorism and that he values our historically strong bilateral relations."

This would be "the most important year in Kenya's post-independence history," U.S. diplomats believed, though it could "degenerate into confusion and crisis." Would the president foment chaos, only to declare a national emergency and cleave to power? Would he bow out, only to extend his rule indefinitely by proxies? For years, he'd been sending deliberately ambiguous signals about his intentions. "I cannot just jump ship because my term is about to end," he'd say, even as he suggested it was time to bequeath his rule to younger men. Sowing confusion was his metier. "The old man's well-honed skills are dazzling," gushed a U.S. embassy memo. "It is not clear, however, how long he can keep up the display without telling Kenyans, or at least party insiders, his preference for a successor."

Sunkuli remained one of the five "young Turks" in contention. "No one in Kenya—perhaps including Moi himself—knows exactly when or how Moi will depart," wrote an embassy observer. "If history is a guide, Moi will continue to keep his own counsel until the end. . . . Moi does not relish retirement, in our judgement, but he is probably enough of a realist to recognize that his time is up."

Though Moi had assured U.S. diplomats that he would leave at the end of his term, embassy staff observed that "he has entertained all manner of dubious ideas about when that term will end. Moi faces significant pressure—from some of Kenya's worst political elements—to stay in office for another year or so. Judging from his private remarks, Moi would like to do just that."

Among the rumors: Moi would suspend elections on the pretext of completing a constitutional review, with the aim of staying at least until August 2003, so that he could round out a symbolic twenty-five years in power, a plan he had "explicitly endorsed" in a meeting with Carson. Fearing that delayed elections would embolden other African rulers to extend their terms, U.S. diplomats intensified their lobbying.

Finally, Moi declared his heir: forty-one-year-old Uhuru Kenyatta, the first president's son, a political neophyte who was Moi's minister of local government and who had been trounced by voters in a bid for parliament. There was a strategy to this choice. Moi described Kenyatta, who had attended Amherst College and spoke American-inflected English, as "a person who can be guided." He was expected to appeal to young voters in a country where half the population was under eighteen, and as a Kikuyu he would leach support from the party's most formidable rival, Mwai Kibaki, a seventy-one-year-old economist and Moi's former vice president. Perhaps more important, having protected the Kenyatta family fortunes for decades, Moi would now expect his anointed successor to guard his fortune and to shield him from possible prosecution.

For Moi, the miscalculation was irremediable. His stalwarts were aggrieved at having been passed over. Six government ministers resigned immediately. The fractured opposition rapidly coalesced behind Kibaki's fifteen-party National Rainbow Coalition, called NARC. Even at KANU rallies where he campaigned for Kenyatta, Moi was booed and heckled. Crowds chanted, *"Yote Yawezekana Bila Moi"*: Everything is possible without Moi.

It remained to be seen whether the president would enlist his security forces, and the estimated one million dead Kenyans he kept on the voter rolls, to tilt the election to his man. He still controlled the Kenya Broadcasting Corporation, the only nationwide radio and TV station, whose viewers could enjoy the scene of Kenyatta handing in his nomination papers, while "technical problems" prevented similar coverage of Kibaki.

Washington ramped up its efforts. "Mr. President, your steadfast application to duty and your efforts to promote peace, to revive the East African Community, to protect the environment, to support free enterprise in Kenya, and to combat past totalitarian and present terrorist threats all have contributed to securing your legacy as a great African statesman," read a draft of a letter from Colin Powell to Moi. "Your capstone achievement will be how you manage Kenya's upcoming critical democratic transition." President George Bush wrote to Moi, saying he valued his counsel and looked forward to a peaceful election.

Gathenji was watching nervously. Three years earlier, his elder son, Leroy, who had worked as his assistant, had left the country to live and work in Atlanta, Georgia. Now, Gathenji was making quiet plans to move the rest of the family to the States, in expectation that Moi's machine would endure. He thought perhaps he'd look into a master's degree there. The lawyer felt as vulnerable as he'd ever been, maybe more so. Not only had he been campaigning for Kibaki, and helping to organize the swearing-in of opposition nominees, but it was no secret that he'd been working with the Kenya Human Rights Commission, plotting legal strategies to bring Moi to justice for his crimes. Just that year, he'd traveled to New York's Columbia University to attend a conference of international human rights lawyers exploring the doctrine of universal jurisdiction—the idea that any given nation had the right to try suspects who committed serious crimes outside that nation's borders, an idea that had gained momentum since it was invoked to arrest Chile's General Pinochet four years earlier in London.

Yes, if Moi's people stayed in office, Gathenji expected there would be a wholesale roundup of dissidents. There would be long lists. He was sure his name would be near the top.

· · ·

WEEKS BEFORE THE election, a pair of shoulder-fired surface-to-air missiles narrowly missed an Israeli-owned charter jet, crowded with tourists, as it lifted off from Mombasa's Moi International Airport en route to Tel Aviv. Nearby, almost simultaneously, killers rammed a vehicle through the gate of the beachfront Paradise Hotel, detonating bombs that killed themselves and thirteen others. Al Qaeda claimed responsibility. Kenyan investigators, despite training from the United States and Israel in the aftermath of the embassy bombing, recklessly opened the bomb site to journalists, even permitting one to pick up a metal shard. Israeli agents sought permission to send evidence back to their own labs; one complained that Kenyan police were "no use except to smile at you."

As chief of internal security, Sunkuli announced that he welcomed technical help, while simultaneously trumpeting the competence of his woefully underequipped, ill-trained, and pervasively corrupt force. "The Kenyan police are running this investigation," Sunkuli boasted. "The police do a lot of investigating every day, and they do have the know-how and resources to be able to unravel the crime." (His confidence was misplaced; the case dragged on and on, without arrests.)

Sunkuli had much besides terrorism on his mind. He was facing his greatest electoral threat in the ten years he'd held the Kilgoris parliamentary seat. This time, opposition voters from the Kikuyu, Kisii, and Luo had refused to flee. His rival, Gideon Konchellah, was a Masai from a rival clan and was running as a National Rainbow Coalition candidate.

Sunkuli evinced no intention of ceding power. He used civil servants (nonpartisan by law) to campaign for him, according to allegations received by Kenyan police. Even more embarrassing were claims of blatant ballot stuffing in the days before the election. "Witnesses said a plane landed in the Masai Mara Game Reserve on Christmas Day and disgorged three large cartons, one of which split open, spilling ballot papers," according to an account in London's *Daily Telegraph*. "The boxes were taken to a tented camp where Mr. Sunkuli's relatives were allegedly seen marking crosses on the ballot papers by his name. . . .

Police confirmed the tent had been rented out to members of the Sunkuli family."

THE LINE OF voters was already long on the morning of December
27, 2002, when Gathenji arrived at his voting station at a marketplace in
Ongata Rongai, a suburb near his home. He put a check near Kibaki's
name. It was a vote less for the man than for the prospect of change.
Then he assumed his post overseeing the Ngong area as a poll observer
for the Law Society. Western governments had financed the training of
thirty thousand poll observers, and the American embassy had its own
one-hundred-person team spread among the provinces.

Gathenji and his colleagues were taking nothing for granted. Even
if rigging could be prevented, what if Uhuru Kenyatta rejected a losing
vote? What if Chief Justice Bernard Chunga refused to swear in Kibaki?
Could they line up a registrar of their own to do it? Fresh in the memory
was the example of Robert Mugabe, Zimbabwe's aging dictator, who had
strong-armed his way to a fourth presidential term earlier that year.

Throughout the election, there had been allegations of widespread
fraud, of vote buying, of destroyed voter cards, of government efforts to
thwart the registration of millions of opposition voters. But the incom-
ing results were unambiguous: Kibaki was ahead, with 62 percent of the
vote, while Kenyatta had just 30 percent, and Moi's ministers, including Sunkuli, were taking a drubbing. In bars where people gathered to
watch the results, one story reported, "cheers resounded . . . when Julius
Sunkuli, the feared internal security minister, lost his seat."

Now the real anxiety took hold: Would Moi's candidate accede to party
hard-liners and reject the results? Would Moi send his security forces into
the streets to crush the inevitable uprising? Raila Odinga, the Luo fire-
brand allied with Kibaki, had warned that if the election were stolen, he
would rally a million people and forcibly take power at State House.

Gathenji could see the fork in the road. In one direction, mass slaughter and civil war; in another, a peaceful transition of power between parties for the first time in the nation's history.

Then a shocking thing happened: Moi announced that he would accept the election results, and Kenyatta conceded. All day, Gathenji watched the trucks rolling through the streets of Nairobi, crowded with ecstatic, yelling celebrators. It was akin to the mood he remembered as a boy in 1963, when the Union Jack had been lowered. Bonfires burned in the streets in Kibaki's hometown near Mount Kenya.

Gathenji himself celebrated quietly over a beer at home with his family. He was as jubilant as anyone, but uncomfortable in mobs. He accepted an invitation to State House for the new president's victory lunch. He was already uneasy with some of the new ruling party's prominent allies, men such as William Ntimama, who had turned against Moi and found himself on the winning side.

The Moi era was over, at least officially. Hundreds of thousands showed up to watch the inauguration on December 30, 2002; millions of others crowded around televisions. "Fellow Kenyans, I am inheriting a country which has been badly ravaged by years of misrule and ineptitude," Kibaki announced as Moi sat expressionless nearby. Promising "zero tolerance" for corruption, the new leader was being hailed in messianic terms.

Once inaugurated, Kibaki would treat Moi like an honored elder statesman and retain many of his people, including Attorney General Amos Wako. Still, there were signs that a page had been turned. To journalists and former detainees, he opened the infamous torture chambers beneath Nyayo House, whose horrors had been hinted at by survivors. And he launched a tribunal to probe the conduct of Chief Justice Chunga, crowning symbol of the judiciary's malignancy, the man who had presided over the torture-fueled nighttime sedition prosecutions of the 1980s, had sanctioned Gathenji's own arrest, and had publicly berated Kaiser at the ethnic clashes tribunal.

Now, the tables turned, Gathenji received a presidential appointment as assisting counsel of the Chunga probe. He went to work devising its logistics, but there was scarcely time for it to get rolling before Chunga resigned. Kibaki suspended twenty-four other justices accused of corruption, and appointed Gathenji as assisting counsel to another tribunal— chaired by none other than Justice Akilano Akiwumi—to investigate the conduct of suspended judges. Restoring the country, Kibaki announced, meant building public confidence in the integrity of the judiciary.

There was also a renewed effort to examine criminal cases, such as the death of John Kaiser, that had been permitted to languish under Moi. Armed with more than 100,000 petition signatures, Catholic bishops met with the new president, himself a Catholic, to urge an inquest into the priest's death. In April 2003, after two years of limbo, Wako announced that the inquest would be allowed to proceed. Gathenji would represent Kaiser's family, the Catholic bishops, and the Mill Hill group. Francis Kaiser gathered donations from his extended family and from the Minnesota church to help finance the undertaking. They had four months to prepare.

17

THE INQUEST

T HE DEEPER THE lawyer probed, the more the case resembled a
hall of mirrors, a maze of ambiguous characters and unknowable
motives. There were hints of conspiracies, trapdoors, scaffoldings of fact
that vaporized into fiction.

Moi was gone, but his loyalists—and those of Sunkuli—remained in
power among the police, park rangers, and other branches of the civil
service. Gathenji needed an investigator who combined skill, discretion, and an instinct for survival—someone who could find information
along the dangerous back roads Kaiser had traveled. He hired a burly,
flint-eyed former Kenyan military intelligence officer, John Wanyeki,
who headed deep into the countryside. He worked at night for his own
protection, and for that of witnesses who refused to meet him in daylight. Many would not go on the record with what they claimed to know.
In Lolgorien, he heard a story that would profoundly shape Gathenji's
view of how Kaiser's death ultimately occurred. The account held that
on August 21, the morning Kaiser left his parish house to answer the
nuncio's summons, he intended to catch a plane to the capital from
the Kichwa Tembo airstrip in the western Masai Mara. Assassins were
aware he'd be making the hour-long drive down into the Mara plain and
to the isolated dirt landing field, and their original plan was to ambush
him en route.

That was how Kaiser was first supposed to die, the investigator was
told. A team of rangers would do it.

Which rangers?

Sunkuli's men. Masais. Joseph Kupasar. Samuel Kortom. Another named Daniel Suya.

What happened?

They were scared off by a witness. A motorcycle happened to be on the road behind Kaiser as he drove up. Kaiser missed his plane.

Where did he get the plane ticket?

Kantai gave it to him. His catechist. A gift meant to lure him.

It was impossible to verify how much was fact and how much invention. Rumor was a profligate currency. Though no one would go on the record with the airstrip-ambush story, to Gathenji's mind, certain things pointed to its plausibility. For one thing, Kaiser's housekeeper, Maria

A marker stands where John Kaiser's body was discovered in August 2000 along the Naivasha-Nakuru road. The FBI believed he died there; Gathenji and others doubted it. *Photograph by Christopher Goffard. Copyright 2009, Los Angeles Times. Reprinted with permission.*

Mokona, confirmed that the priest had driven to the airstrip that day with a ticket, before turning back and opting to travel to Nairobi by road. All of the rangers mentioned were Sunkuli's clansmen. (Two of them, Kortom and Kupasar, had surfaced in the FBI investigation. In addition, Sunkuli was married to Kortom's niece, and Kupasar had been circumcised in the same group as Sunkuli, making them age-mates, a Masai bond so profound that it would have allowed them access, by tribal tradition, to one another's wives.)

Other arresting details came to light when Gathenji, after enduring months of flat refusals and evasions and unveiled hostility from police officials, managed to obtain the investigative files on the case compiled by the Kenyan Criminal Investigation Department. Studying the documents, he came across something that had never made the FBI's report. It was called the Arms Movement Book—a firearms registry kept by rangers at the Mara park. The registry showed that Kortom had checked out a Mark 4 big-game rifle on August 15, 2000—eight days before the priest's death—which was never returned.

To Gathenji, the missing gun assumed sharp importance in connection with the story of the abortive airstrip ambush. It raised the question of whether Kaiser had even been killed with his shotgun. Perhaps it was the high-powered game warden's rifle that had obliterated the back of his head, explaining why no shotgun pellets or wadding had ever been found with the body. Perhaps he'd even been killed elsewhere and dumped at the scene. It struck Gathenji as a plausible theory.

IN AUGUST 2003, as the inquest began in a courthouse in Naivasha, the priest's elder brother left his home in Santa Rosa, California, and boarded a flight to Kenya. Francis Kaiser, seventy-two, a retired quality-control officer for the Carnation Company, would be among the first to testify.

In a way, each brother had led the life the other had imagined for himself. John was the priest Francis thought he might be. Francis had the "good wife and cabinful of kids" John had spoken of wanting. Growing up on a dirt farm in Otter Tail County, Minnesota, the brothers had wandered the woods together and slept in the same bed. Francis remembered his brother as a "totally fearless" boy who did not hesitate to climb a windmill or plunge into a frozen pond to retrieve ducks they'd shot. They got .22 rifles when they were about six years old, and single-barrel shotguns when they were about eight. They'd hunted gophers and woodchucks and carried their rifles on the two-mile walk through the country to school as protection against wildcats. Francis had spent a year in the seminary himself before joining the army and fighting in an artillery division in Korea. Francis thought of his brother as the "John Wayne of priests," a cowboy of the cloth who possessed an absolute certainty of the afterlife: "He didn't have the fear of death that the normal person has."

Now, Francis walked to the witness box to be questioned by Gathenji. He insisted that suicide made little sense. "You don't have to go to the pain of shooting yourself at the back of your head while you can easily do it from the front," he said.

From the start, there was something else that had struck Francis as out of place. His brother's shotgun had two barrels, but when it was found near his body, only the left one contained a spent shell. That was the barrel activated by squeezing the rear trigger. The right barrel, with the easier-to-reach front trigger, was empty, even though the priest had a live twelve-gauge shell in the breast pocket of his jacket.

He knew his brother's habits with firearms. If he'd had two shells, Francis reasoned, he would have loaded both barrels, so he'd have a chance to fire twice. And if by some chance he'd had time to load just one, the shell would have gone in the right. Why load only the left? "This was abnormal not only for John, but for anybody using the shotgun," he told the court.

Francis had brought the last letter he'd received from his brother. It was dated August 17, 2000, six days before his death, and did not seem to bespeak suicidal despair.

"I'm sitting on a veranda watching the world turn green again," the priest had written. "We have had a rather severe drought and the grass gone brown and short and cattle hungry. Then a great blessing and two inches of rain in the past two days so the birds are singing and lots of cows were dancing in the rain."

The letter reflected an aging man soberly confronting his mortality, wondering which of his family members "will be the first to finish it up here below." He wrote, "But at least I hope we can all meet again and have a fishing trip up in the border waters of Northern Minnesota, canoe country. The next time would be late August or September when the mosquitoes and black flies aren't so bad."

Francis Kaiser believed his brother's death was about politics, and politics, he told the court, ensured that it had been covered up. He had been a chess piece in a global game. What did his life mean when compared to America's strategic relationship with Kenya?

Gathenji knew there was no getting around the hospitalizations, but he believed it was important to show that in two of the cases the priest had been confronting what he'd considered injustices. Francis Kaiser was of the same opinion. Of the 1969 hospitalization in New York City, Francis explained that his brother's superior had called police to deflect accusations of sexual impropriety. Of the early-1980s hospitalization in Minnesota, Francis noted that it stemmed from a confrontation between the priest and his brother Joe, who had grown abusive to their mother. He insisted that neither of those episodes amounted to mental illness.

When Gathenji confronted Dr. Frank Njenga, the Kenyan psychiatrist who had prepared the damning Psychological Autopsy Report on Kaiser—apparently the first of its kind in the country—he forced him to acknowledge that he'd never met the priest, had not consulted any of the doctors who had treated him, and had not possessed reports describing treatment for mental illness. A physician who *had* had regular contact with Kaiser—Zulfikar Ali Jaffery, who had treated him for four years for advanced arthritis and neck pain—took the witness box and testified, under questioning from Gathenji, that he'd never seen the priest suffer from mental illness.

. . .

TWO DAYS AFTER Francis Kaiser testified, a surprise witness materialized who appeared to confirm, in the clearest way possible, the murder scenario. His name was Hassan Gollo. He had worked as a night watchman at the Delamere Dairies farm, close to where Kaiser's body had been discovered. He had come forward to tell a story that he'd been keeping to himself.

On the night of Kaiser's death, Gollo testified, he had been walking home from a night shift on the Naivasha-Nakuru road, when he saw the priest's pickup being chased by a sedan. He watched from the roadside bushes, he explained, as the sedan blocked the pickup. Then he heard what sounded like gunfire.

He could give nothing in the way of useful detail, however. In this way, it bore the mark of an invented story. He could not identify the shooter, he could not say what color the sedan had been, and he had never told police his story.

The newspapers gave sensationalized play to Gollo's testimony. Even as the man was leaving the stand, however, Gathenji was skeptical. The story was too convenient. He believed Gollo had made it up, perhaps just hoping for a reward, perhaps with a more sinister motive. Perhaps—the lawyer was willing to consider the possibility—he was a plant intended to divert the investigation. His testimony, if embraced, would establish that Kaiser had been killed where he was found. Maybe that was the point. Maybe his account was meant to mask the possibility that was looming ever larger in Gathenji's mind: that Kaiser had been killed elsewhere. What seemed certain to Gathenji was that no assassin of any competence would stage an execution there on the Naivasha-Nakuru road with its regular traffic. It was not a controlled setting; witnesses could easily stumble upon it; a victim might scramble into the woods and disappear.

Hardly more clarifying than Gollo's account, though reported in the local media with an equally breathless tone, was the testimony of Paul Muite. He told the inquest what he'd told the FBI: that a senior police officer—he would not reveal the name—had confided to him the identities of Kaiser's killers. Reportedly, these were four Kenyan police officers, one of them a brother of Sunkuli, who had enlisted a Catholic priest named Emmanuel Ngugi to lure Kaiser out of the bishop's house into a fatal trap. Nothing came of this allegation, however; Ngugi took the stand to deny it, and the members of the alleged hit team could furnish alibis. Gathenji, who thought the story had a credible ring nonetheless, was frustrated that Muite would not give up his witness to be questioned.

NOTHING EMBODIED THE case's shifting, indecipherable quality more than Francis Kantai, the gaunt, soft-spoken young Masai who had lived with Kaiser. He was ardent in his avowals of love for the priest. Yet over and over, people had told the priest that his catechist was a spy for Sunkuli, a Judas waiting to betray him. Those suspicions were stoked when, according to the testimony of the parish housekeeper, Maria Mokona, Kantai had let Sunkuli's men into the Lolgorien house. She added that on the month Kaiser died, three government men posing as journalists had appeared at the house, trying to gain entry. She said she later saw Kantai in their company at the town market.

Fanning suspicions further: Kantai's admission that he'd led some of Sunkuli's men to the FIDA safe house. Kantai still insisted that the men had held him at gunpoint. Why had Kaiser, who'd been so wary of his enemies, kept Kantai so close, even after he knew Kantai had revealed the location of the safe house? Had the priest feared pushing a man with intimate knowledge of his habits deeper into Sunkuli's arms?

There was a further complication: Kaiser's cousin, Camille Kleinschmit, and Kantai were now married, and had a baby son named after the priest; Kantai had plans to travel to Nebraska to live with her. Gathenji considered Kantai "a very devious character," who had deliberately insinuated himself into the priest's family as a form of protection. He saw the marriage as a gesture of sheer opportunism: Kleinschmit was his ticket to the States.

For months, Gathenji's team had been searching for Kantai, now thirty-two, without success. One day, soon after the inquest began, he appeared in the Nairobi office of Sister Nuala Brangan and declared that he had evidence to give the court.

As Wanyeki, Gathenji's investigator, sped him to the Naivasha court-house, an inexplicable panic appeared to possess Kantai. By the investigator's account, he was driving about sixty miles per hour when Kantai threw open the passenger door, as if to jump out, and had to be calmed down. Was it an act of theater? Or, as Gathenji later thought, did it reflect Kantai's sudden realization that the testimony he was about to give would taint him forever? Did Kantai sense, perhaps, that whoever had encouraged him to testify considered him a sacrificial lamb?

Kantai's claims had always been dramatic. After Kaiser's death, he'd told American investigators that Sunkuli had once urged him to poison the priest. (It was a claim that Charles Ng'ana'a, a Ngong priest, would testify that Kantai had repeated to him.)

Now, taking the stand at the inquest as witness fourteen, Kantai had this to say: "I wish to confess to court that I lied." He had been angry with Sunkuli, he explained. Believing him responsible for Kaiser's death, he'd made up the poisoning story. "I cannot deny having told the FBI about Mr. Sunkuli, since I was totally fed up with him and I could have done anything to remove him from Transmara," he said.

He also denied that he'd met Moi. "I have never been to Mombasa since I was born. It is not true that I met former President Moi in Mombasa. The former President did not promise to give the girls any money to drop the rape allegations against Mr. Sunkuli. Whoever introduced this allegation in my statement wanted to smear the President's name."

And he offered another story, one he claimed he had forgotten in previous interviews. Not long before Kaiser's death, he said, he came upon Kaiser at the Mill Hill compound in Nairobi watching a video of a priest shooting himself. Kaiser seemed fixated by the spectacle, replaying it over and over. When he became aware of Kantai's presence, he stopped the tape.

Kantai did not know the video's title, and no one at Mill Hill could confirm its existence. Gathenji believed it a fabrication, invented by Kantai's handlers in order to portray the priest as a man preoccupied by suicide.

Kantai's tone sounded bitter, persecuted. He knew priests suspected he was involved in Kaiser's death. Kantai maintained that a mysterious Special Branch agent named "Ebu" had hounded him for years over Kaiser's activities. He said Ebu had asked for documents Kaiser would present to the Akiwumi Commission, and that Ebu had been present when Sunkuli's men kidnapped him and forced him to reveal the safe house location. What's more, he said, Ebu had shown a keen interest in whether Kaiser would attempt to take Sunkuli to an international court.

Kantai admitted that in the late 1980s he had done the government's bidding by burning the houses of out-of-favor tribes. Police gave him a match, he said, and he had done it. He had enjoyed their company.

Now, Gathenji confronted Kantai with the anonymous informant's allegation: that he had tried to lure the priest into an ambush in the Masai Mara reserve. Among the alleged assassins in waiting, Gathenji said, were Samuel Kortom, Sunkuli's brother-in-law, and a ranger named Daniel Suya.

To the lawyer, Kantai looked like a man in anguish, about to surrender to tears. To weep would be no small humiliation for a man raised in the stoical Masai codes.

No, Kantai said. He'd loved the priest. "He was like a father. I had not thought of life without him. I felt as if some part of me had left me."

Gathenji demanded Kantai's arrest, on the grounds that he had admitted to lying to authorities and to burning houses. The court had already confiscated his passport so that he couldn't leave the country before he finished testifying. When he left for the United States, Gathenji argued, it would be impossible to arrest him.

The state lawyer, Oriri Onyango, argued that Kantai's admission was irrelevant to the matter at hand. Justin Kaburu, the presiding magistrate, agreed. With the inquest so young, he said, he did not want to do anything that might intimidate witnesses and prevent them from showing up. He ordered the clerk to return Kantai's passport to him. Kantai took it, stepped out of the witness box, and went free. Soon he was on a plane to the United States.

ESTABLISHING THAT SUNKULI possessed motive to kill Kaiser was a crucial plank of Gathenji's strategy, and for that he turned to Anne Sawoyo, whose testimony would prove dramatic but largely uncorroborated. Now twenty-five years old, she spoke in a soft voice. She said she'd loved Kaiser and had regarded him as a father. She said her eight-year-old daughter had been fathered by Sunkuli. She described an aura of menace and control that had surrounded the minister, and testified that he'd entered her life by posing as a benefactor who would pay her school fees. She had been seventeen, a high school student in Kilgoris, when he raped her, she said. "I could not report him because he was above everybody in Transmara," she said. "All the police and chiefs feared him."

When she was eight months pregnant, she said, she went to inform Sunkuli, who told her he would take her to Nairobi for an abortion. "That's how my hatred with him started," she said. She said the minister ignored a promise of financial support after the child's birth. She said Kaiser gave her school fees and sent her to Nairobi to inform FIDA about the case.

She testified that after Sunkuli's men raided the safe house, they took her to the police station, where she refused to sign a statement accusing FIDA of abducting her. Sunkuli's driver took her and Florence Mpayei to a hotel, she said, and the minister entered their room in a solicitous mood, apologizing for not having helped her financially, and pledging that he would open an account for her daughter. She said he left a man there to guard her and Mpayei, and that the guard took no chances, sleeping between them on two pushed-together twin beds, waking to watch them even when they walked to the bathroom. The next day, she said, Sunkuli expressed a certain paternal pride—apparently she had given birth to his only girl—and renewed his vow of financial help.

As Sawoyo told it, eight months later, in May 2000, as Mpayei's suit against Sunkuli was making headlines, three of his underlings visited her at her mother's home to ask whether she, too, planned to sue. To discourage her, they urged her to take a clerical job at the Mara Serena, collecting park fees. She said she agreed, though a month after arriving, she had neither been paid nor been given any work to do. She said the park rangers would not let her leave and that Sunkuli's brother, Charles, kept possession of her identity card. She asked the senior warden why she couldn't leave. Permission came from above, she was told. That meant the minister.

When she talked to Sunkuli, she said, he told her it was a waste of time to pursue a rape case against him, as Mpayei had, because she came from a poor family and he had the backing of the president. "He told me all the money he was using in the suit was given to him by Moi," Sawoyo said.

The last time she saw Kaiser, she testified, was when he attempted to rescue her from the lodge around noon on July 10, 2000. She thought escape too risky: People were monitoring her carefully and would notice if she went missing. After Kaiser left, she said, she was summoned to the game warden's office, where she picked up a phone and heard Sunkuli's voice, demanding to know what the priest had wanted and reminding her that she was being watched. Did she think he was a child?

Later that day, she said, park rangers arrested and beat Levi Marko, with whom she was seen chatting in the lodge cafeteria, apparently because they believed Kaiser had left him behind as a spy.

Around ten o'clock that night, she said, she heard Samuel Kortom comment to Joseph Kupasar on the priest's quick exit: "He is lucky. Today would have been his day." She said the conversation stopped abruptly when they saw her. She said it was an "open secret" in the Mara that rangers planned to kill Kaiser and plant a dead animal next to him to make it look as if he'd been shot as a poacher.

Just days before Kaiser's death, she said, Sunkuli allowed her out of the park to visit him at his government office in Nairobi. She said he seemed to fear that Kaiser would help her file suit against him. She said Sunkuli's people took her to the Shade Hotel in the upscale Karen suburb the following day to wait for the minister, who entered with his bodyguard about 10:00 P.M. in a jovial mood. He walked to a stage, grabbed a microphone, and began singing along in English to a song on the radio. She said she had seen him sing and dance at political rallies, but never like this. (He had good reason for high spirits: Mpayei was preparing to announce that she was dropping her case.) Then, all charm, Sunkuli came to sit between her and another young woman, remarking, "How does a man feel when two beautiful ladies are surrounding him?"

Though Kaiser and the FBI had ultimately harbored doubts about whether she was really a captive of Sunkuli, the testimony she gave now suggested that fear, and close surveillance, had governed her movements even when she was let out of the Mara Serena lodge.

Her testimony grew more chilling as she described what happened when she returned to the lodge after Kaiser's death. She sensed "a lot of enmity" toward her, and said that Sunkuli's brother Charles told her it would be "all over" for her if she implicated the minister in the priest's death. One day, she said, a Sunkuli bodyguard knocked on her door. "He told me that he wanted to give me something to keep under the pillow," she said. He wouldn't tell her what it was, but when she guessed aloud that it was a pistol, he grew agitated and said, "Who said I had a pistol?" He then went outside and vomited. The picture she painted, it seemed, was of a potential assassin sick with what he had been called on to do. "He wanted me to touch the pistol and then kill me with it." It would look like a suicide.

Gathenji continued questioning Sawoyo. She said Sunkuli himself called to threaten her: "You are the one claiming that I killed Kaiser? You will pay for this." She replied that she did not care if she died, as she had lost "the most important person in my life."

Once, she left her keys in her door at the lodge, but returned and found them missing. She bought a new padlock. A stranger called to warn her there was a plot to poison her food, that she shouldn't leave her room unlocked or walk at night, and that she would be killed on a game drive and left for the animals; it would look like she had wandered off and been devoured. She said Kortom asked her to accompany him on a ride to look for rhinos. They would be deep in the grasslands, far from the lodge. She said she refused.

Later, she saw Kortom drinking beers at the canteen. "They didn't go for the rhino search," she said. "Maybe I was the rhino."

Gathenji found himself ambivalent about Sawoyo. "She's an actress," he said later. "She likes to portray herself as a victim. She's an enigma." He could never be certain whether she had really been held captive at the Mara.

Yet some of her story could be corroborated. Under Gathenji's questioning, Douglas Sikawa, a senior warden, confirmed that there were rumors afloat in the Mara that three rangers loyal to Sunkuli—Kortom, Kupasar, and Suya—were plotting to ambush Kaiser. Sikawa testified that it had been Sunkuli's idea to arrest Levi Marko after he was seen chatting with Sawoyo, that Sunkuli had called him directly to give the order.

One by one, the three Masai rangers walked to the witness box and denied everything. Kortom said he had never plotted to kill Kaiser, and, no, he had not held Sawoyo captive at the lodge. There were similar denials from Suya. Kupasar acknowledged he had arrested Marko at the park, but he was ready with an explanation: The man had been drunk and lacked ID. No, of course he hadn't beaten him, and of course he had not plotted to kill the priest.

There was no explanation for the missing rifle.

How did it add up? Kaiser's body had been found more than one hundred miles east of the Mara lodge. To Gathenji, the evidence suggested that multiple murder plots had been in play.

As the inquest progressed, Gathenji tried to find Florence Mpayei, Sunkuli's other main accuser. A women's rights activist, Edith Kirugumi, said Mpayei had called her from Sunkuli's house in Nairobi, not long before the priest's death, to relay that Sunkuli's men were talking about Kaiser and seemed to be planning something. That made Mpayei a potentially explosive witness, perhaps the key to the whole case, but

Gathenji and his investigator could not find her. Was she being held captive? Maybe the words she spoke to Kenyan police about Sunkuli soon after the priest's death—"I love him and he is assisting me"—were all the explanation anyone needed for her absence.

To cement Sunkuli's motive, Gathenji had to establish the centrality, actual or perceived, of the priest's role in the campaign against the minister. Helen Katim, a Transmara women's rights activist, testified that a month before his death, Kaiser had personally urged a group of Kilgoris women to petition the president to sack Sunkuli over claims that he'd raped and impregnated local girls. Some sixty women would travel in three buses to Nairobi for an anti-Sunkuli march the week before Kaiser's death, said Anne Kiruti, chairwoman of the Transmara Catholic Women's Association.

A former Kilgoris priest named James Onyango showed the court a petition from 107 women demanding that Sunkuli be fired. It had been smuggled to him by two women who "came at night for fear of being seen by allies and spies of the then security minister," Onyango testified. "He was feared all over the district and people lived in fear."

THE CRIME SCENE itself yielded little light except on the extent of police incompetence. A policeman named James Muli, possibly the first official on the scene, testified he had found Kaiser's shotgun lying two to three meters from the corpse. Other officers, never having consulted him, had produced a sketch that showed the shotgun about half a meter from the body. The discrepancy could not be reconciled. Humphrey Kariuki, the retired assistant commissioner of police, surmised that an officer or passerby might have moved the shotgun at some point, and he admitted that he'd never thought to ask the on-scene police about its original position. As far as he knew, Kaiser's hands had never been tested for gunpowder traces. He did say that investigators had dusted the gun for fingerprints but had discovered none, a claim for which there was cause for skepticism. There was no reason Kaiser's prints *shouldn't* have been on his own gun. Further, photos showed Kenyan police handling the shotgun bare-fingered at the scene: Why hadn't their prints appeared on it?

HAVING FEATURED JUST twenty-four witnesses—less than a third of those expected to testify—the inquest was temporarily derailed in early 2004 when Justin Kaburu, the presiding magistrate, was named in a report probing judicial corruption. The proceedings would be shifted from Naivasha to the Nairobi Law Courts, floor two, room 62, under a new magistrate, Maureen Odero. Gathenji considered her a good and honest judge. At the conclusion of the inquest, he would have to make his case to her. She would weigh the evidence and decide whether Kaiser had killed himself or been murdered, and, if the latter were true, who should be arrested.

For Gathenji, the years of the inquest were busy ones. Apart from his work as chairman of the Kenya Society for the Blind, he had become what the Kenyan press referred to as a "superlawyer," one of an elite handful who had flourished under the country's new leadership. His name kept coming up in the big cases. Along with his appointments to panels investigating the judiciary, he was hired to represent a man named John Kiragu, who was accused of a role in the brutal armed attack on Ngugi wa Thiong'o and his wife. The attack had occurred during the novelist's triumphant visit to Kenya in the summer of 2004 to celebrate his return from exile and the publication of his masterpiece, *Wizard of the Crow*. Gathenji won an acquittal, arguing that his client possessed no motive and that police, having nabbed the wrong man in a high-profile case, had been forced to fabricate a story. Gathenji suggested that someone was angry about the book, with its thinly veiled savaging of Moi and his people. The novelist himself would never shake the suspicion that the former dictator had somehow had a hand in the attack. He and Gathenji agreed on that much at least, though neither would ever be able to prove this.

. . .

IN GATHENJI'S MIND, there were two credible theories of how Kaiser had met his death. Someone might have lured him into an ambush. Perhaps he'd received a call—someone pleading for help, playing on his gallantry—that drew him from the safety of his bishop's house. Some at the Mill Hill compound reported that he had received a phone call during his stay there, but there was no record of it. If there had been such a call, he'd told no one about it, perhaps because he'd known how it would look. That was Bishop Davies's theory: "He was afraid if he'd spoken to me, I'd say, 'Don't be such a fool. Don't go. It's a trap.'" That might explain the beddings he had stripped from the bedroom and brought to the scene—he'd been planning to give them to somebody in need.

Or what if the priest had been captured or killed at the bishop's house? That would mean the security guard who had claimed he'd seen Kaiser leave in his truck was lying. The guard could not be found to question. He had vanished after Kaiser's death, without even picking up his clothes and other belongings.

Wandering the shadowland the case had become, it was impossible to know what to believe. Gathenji now wondered whether Kaiser had ever really visited the remote homestead in Kiambu where villagers claimed to have seen him standing on a knoll shortly before his death. And maybe it had not been Kaiser who'd appeared that same night at the Moonlight Petrol Station in Naivasha, wrapped in a blanket and hacking off his truck's mudguard. Had that man been a double, a plant meant to conceal the fact that Kaiser had already been killed elsewhere? Gathenji had little trouble believing Moi's security forces would have been able to enlist a white man who resembled Kaiser enough to pass muster. The white settler families were vulnerable to Moi, too: They paid in favors to be left alone.

Serpentine, fantastic and ultimately unprovable as the scenario seemed, it was a testament to Gathenji's cast of mind that he had little trouble envisioning it.

Then there was the witness who placed Kaiser at the gas station, David

Mwania, a warden at the local prison. He said Kaiser had announced where he was from: "Minnesota." Gathenji could not imagine the priest saying this. For one thing, Kaiser had considered himself a Kenyan. For another, a man who'd spent most of his adult life in East Africa would have known that the name of his native state would be as meaningless here as the name Naivasha would be to a denizen of Otter Tail County. To Gathenji, Mwania's claim had the feel of contrivance—of a remark that was meant to establish beyond any doubt that the figure at the gas station had been Kaiser. Fortifying the lawyer's suspicions: a pump attendant who knew Mwania insisted that he had not been at the gas station that night. Why was Mwania lying? Somebody had been eager to put Kaiser in Naivasha, Gathenji thought. That meant the plan had been an elaborate one. Was there significance in Mwania's job as a prison warden? Was it possible that the men who had killed Kaiser had been sprung, at Mwania's engineering, to commit the murder?

Gathenji made preparations to put Mwania in the witness box and eviscerate his story. Maybe this was the loose strand that would unravel the conspiracy. Then he got word: Mwania was dead, reportedly of a heart attack.

Also dead was Aggrey Nyong'o, an eminent Kenyan pathologist, killed in a car wreck on Ngong Road before he could testify on his finding that Kaiser's gunshot wound pointed to murder. Dead, too, under vague circumstances, was "Ebu," the special police agent said to have been following Kaiser. Gathered with other church volunteers, Sister Nuala Brangan, who was helping Gathenji prepare his case, tried to tally up the deaths and disappearances associated with the case: "We counted about nine of them one night."

FINALLY, IN LATE February 2007, Sunkuli entered the courtroom, his stout frame filling out a sharp suit. He was witness 109. As a lawyer and a former magistrate, he was practiced in a courtroom setting. He insisted he had hardly known the priest and that he'd had no motive to kill him. He had not even had a grudge against him. The priest's accusations against him at the Akiwumi Commission had long been public. So why would he have wanted to kill him?

Sunkuli surrendered what Gathenji considered a key admission: that he had been worried enough about the priest's role in the rape accusations to complain to Kaiser's bishop about it, confirming the bishop's own account. "I believe the sexual abuse allegations were heaped up on me by Father Kaiser and FIDA with a view to extort me," Sunkuli said. And, he added, he believed his political enemies had used the claims in an attempt to thwart his rise. "There was a lot of information that President Moi wanted to appoint me to the position of the vice-president then. I think my political opponents wanted to use the allegations to tarnish my name and ruin my chance."

In one breath, Gathenji's chief suspect was denying he'd had a grudge against the priest; in another, he was describing solid grounds for holding one. Sunkuli seemed untroubled by the contradiction. As the questioning continued, Gathenji asked Sunkuli when he had learned of Kaiser's death. Sunkuli said it was at about the time everyone else had.

Sunkuli: "It was at 10 a.m. just as I was about to board a plane for a tour of Taita with the former president."

Gathenji: "You knew of the death at 6 a.m. because you were involved in the arrangement."

Sunkuli: "That is ridiculous."

MORE THAN THREE years had passed since the inquest began, and in early 2007, Gathenji wanted to put the FBI on the stand. He would ask the agents about the leads they had failed to pursue or had dismissed as irrelevant, the ones that led to the secret police, to the Mara rangers, to Kantai and Sunkuli.

He would ask them to acknowledge a conflict between their avowed aim to discover the truth and their wish to stay on friendly terms with the Kenyan authorities collaborating on the embassy bombing investigation.

He would ask why they ignored an unexplained thumbprint of Kaiser's blood on the door of his truck. He would demand to know why there was no ballistics report. He would confront the pathologist, Vincent DiMaio—who had not attended the autopsy or viewed clear, close-up photos of the body—and demand to know how he'd concluded that Kaiser had died where his body had been found.

That January, at Gathenji's prompting, the Kenyan attorney general asked the U.S. embassy to request the FBI's testimony. The response was auspicious. In a letter, the embassy said the government "fully supports" the FBI's presence at the inquest, promising that Agents William Corbett and Thomas Neer, along with DiMaio, would be available in Nairobi on March 5.

At one point, Agent Tom Graney was planning to fly back to Kenya to testify. He was under contract with the FBI, though retired from active service, and his supervisor forbade him from working on the Kaiser matter on company time. To bone up on the case, Graney stayed after hours for three weeks, reading. He wanted to testify, even if it meant going on his own time and on his own dime. He was proud of the work he'd done on the case, had suffered shingles and dengue fever as a result of it. "The case meant a lot to me," he'd say. "I worked my ass off on it. I had health problems as a result of it." His wife didn't want him to go—she made "stern protestations"—but he wanted an end to the unease the case had left with him.

The FBI missed the appointed date, citing the difficulty of getting its scattered agents to Kenya at the same time. Later, Corbett offered another explanation, one the court said it never received. He said the FBI planned to attend until it became clear that Kaiser's family would not release his psychiatric records. Without them, the FBI "would be handcuffed and not be able to tell the whole story," Corbett said. "There was some thought, you know—'We did do good work here and we stand behind the facts that we found. There's value in helping people to understand what we learned. Let's assist in being as transparent as possible.' " But without all the facts, Corbett said, "you're going into this thing with less than a full armory of ammunition." The FBI's public affairs branch and the criminal investigations branch supported sending agents to the inquest, he said, but the Bureau's lawyers decided to pull the plug. The unavailability of medical records was "a showstopper for them."

The magistrate, apparently in the dark about the FBI's misgivings, set a new date for the agents to appear; they did not show. Another date was set; still the agents did not materialize. Appearances were against the Americans: Given the opportunity to defend its much-assailed report in open court, the FBI seemed simply to be ignoring the request. Once so conscious of its image, the agency was inexplicably indifferent to it now. To magistrate Odero, the FBI's absence sent a clear message, one that would loom large in her ultimate conclusion.

AFTER FOUR YEARS of testimony and 111 witnesses, had Gathenji made a strong-enough case for murder? As he gave his summation, he knew his job was to tell a better story than the FBI's. The evidence, he argued, pointed to a scenario dramatically at odds with the one painted by the Americans. Kaiser had not died at the side of the Naivasha-Nakuru road, he said. He had been shot elsewhere and dumped there, with the bedding tidily arranged on the spurious assumption that the priest would have laid it out that way.

There was no explanation, Gathenji reminded the court, for the absence of shotgun pellets or wadding at the scene. Nor was there an explanation for a small smear of blood found on Kaiser's truck; nor for the green paint found on the left front tire, which might have come from another vehicle ramming it.

Gathenji turned to the forensic evidence. Dr. Alex Olumbe, the government pathologist who performed the autopsy, had damaged Gathenji's case by testifying that the wound was consistent with suicide. Still, Gathenji pointed out that other experts who attended the autopsy had emphasized that there was no sign of blackened soot, or singed hair and skin, suggesting that this was not a contact wound. Dr. Ling Kituyi, an independent pathologist, had put the distance at two or three feet away, and had noted bruises on the priest's knees and shin, suggesting he had fallen—or been pushed—before his death. Moreover, Kituyi noted that the FBI had ignored a trail of blood running down the back of Kaiser's right hand, and bloody fingerprints above his right pants pocket. By her analysis, these signs indicated that before the fatal shot, Kaiser had suffered a blow to his head, which he clutched with his right hand.

Gathenji argued that the priest's activity in his final days—his erratic movements, his request for prayers, his preoccupation with death—reflected not the behavior of a sick man, but that of a scared man who knew he was being followed.

Sunkuli had had a clear motive to kill Kaiser, Gathenji argued, since the priest's crusade had threatened his political fortunes. The summer of his death, the priest had encouraged the group of women to petition the president to sack Sunkuli. Further, the beating of Levi Marko at the Mara lodge showed how intensely threatened the minister felt by the priest's presence. Yes, Gathenji argued, Sunkuli had been concerned enough about Kaiser to approach Bishop Davies about his removal, and the raid on the safe house had shown Sunkuli's willingness to use state security forces for his personal ends.

The evidence "irresistibly points" to a conspiracy to kill Kaiser, the lawyer argued—a conspiracy that encompassed Sunkuli, the secret police, the Criminal Investigation Department, game rangers, and any number of political functionaries.

Arrest Sunkuli for murder, Gathenji said.

The lawyer representing the state, James Mungai Warui, countered that the evidence didn't establish murder at all. He blamed the Catholic Church for refusing to turn over the letter Kaiser had written to the papal nuncio in his final days. The nuncio had insisted the letter was a privileged communication concerning private church business. But Warui was suspicious. He thought Kaiser's letter might hold "crucial leads" that would resolve the death. Was it in fact a suicide note? Had the nuncio asked Kaiser to leave the country, plunging him into despair? Had the nuncio asked him to compile some hand-over notes for the next priest of Lolgorien, bringing him up-to-date on affairs in the parish?

Kaiser was no ordinary priest, Warui said. He was a former soldier who carried an ax and a shotgun. He would have defended himself against attackers. As many people had before, he asked one of the case's abiding imponderables: Where were John Kaiser's defensive wounds?

SEVEN YEARS TO the month after the priest's death, on August 1, 2007, Gathenji sat in the crowded courtroom with Kenya's bishops to hear Magistrate Maureen Odero read her findings. She was adamant: It was murder.

Pointing to the absence of shotgun pellets or gunpowder residue on his hands, and to the oddly neat position of his body, she determined that Kaiser had been killed elsewhere and placed beside the dark road. If he had died there, she reasoned, there would have been more blood at the scene, and the recovered brain matter would have been embedded with more dirt, grass, and twigs. She found the supposed position of Kaiser's body—supine, one hand atop the other—contrived.

Given that Kaiser's shotgun was three feet long, she found it a "physical impossibility" that an arthritic sixty-seven-year-old man could have performed the "contortionist acrobatics" necessary to reach the trigger with the muzzle placed behind his ear. It struck her as more plausible that he was forced to his knees—she pointed to the bruises on his knees—and shot from behind. As for the FBI report, she declared it "superficial" and "seriously flawed." Noting that the agency had failed to appear for the inquest without explanation, she said, "This court can only conclude the FBI did not consider their report one worth defending."

Neither the FBI nor the Kenyan police had supplied a ballistics report, which she described as "a crucial missing link." Without it, there was no proof that the priest's shotgun had killed him, nor even the "pretense at any serious or meaningful investigations." She was critical of the Catholic Church, however, for withholding Kaiser's letter to the nuncio, which she believed might contain valuable evidence. She noted there was no explanation for the smear of green paint on Kaiser's truck wheel, nor for the fact that the driver's side window had been smashed in, apparently from the outside, as suggested by pieces of glass found inside the cab. The fact that glass had been found on his clothing suggested he had been sitting in the front seat when the window was broken. Of Muite's testimony about the hit squad, the magistrate was skeptical, going so far as to doubt that his unnamed source "actually existed."

Given that no psychiatric evidence had been presented to show Kaiser suffered from mental illness, the magistrate deemed the claim "pure fiction." She eviscerated Dr. Njenga's Psychological Autopsy Report as "shallow, biased, contradictory and non-conclusive," "an unfortunate attempt to justify the conclusion made by the FBI," and said the doctor owed an apology to Kaiser's family and Mill Hill. Kaiser's attempt to give away his shotgun showed "he feared that he may have been tempted to use it against a fellow human being in case of attack." She noted that witnesses had been adamant that Kaiser would never have taken his own life. She concluded that given the threats he had endured, his fears for his life "were not a figment of his imagination."

She was troubled by the "evasive and contradictory" testimony of Kantai. She characterized him as someone who "pretended to be a friend to Fr. Kaiser" but had betrayed him by leading police to the Nairobi safe house. "He is one person who in court's view needs to be interrogated further to establish what role if any he may have played in the death of Fr. Kaiser," the magistrate wrote. She was also troubled by the missing rifle, and called for deeper investigation of the Mara rangers, Kortom and Kupasar, whose testimony she had found "evasive," and Suya.

She directed the police to "institute fresh and comprehensive investigations" into the case. That Kaiser had been murdered, she concluded, was not a mystery. "The only mystery is why the police failed to investigate this matter with the seriousness and diligence that it deserved."

But it was hardly the only mystery, as her own ruling—puzzling and bittersweet—implicitly acknowledged. She recommend no one's arrest for the crime. She said there was no evidence implicating Sunkuli. She cited his "airtight alibi"—a bizarre gesture, given that nobody had ever claimed he'd killed Kaiser with his own hands. She appeared to have gone out of her way to accommodate Sunkuli. He was "quite under-standably" angered by the rape allegations. "If Hon. Sunkuli wanted to eliminate any person because of these allegations, then in court's view he would have targeted the girls themselves or his named political detrac-tors and not Fr. Kaiser who was not the source of the allegations," she said, describing Kaiser's role in the cases as "peripheral," and essentially ignoring the fact that Kaiser had been working doggedly to assemble other cases against Sunkuli.

Back at his office, Gathenji fired an e-mail to Francis Kaiser in the States: We won. But it was an uneasy and qualified victory. The exonera-tion of Sunkuli made little sense in light of the recommendation that his underlings be investigated. "These people are so connected to Sunkuli that there's no reason that his name doesn't appear," Gathenji would say. "The master is left, and the servants are to be investigated."

One possible explanation for Odero's charitableness toward Sunkuli: he'd once been a judge himself, a member of an exclusive and clubby community. Another theory: the magistrate was afraid to target such a well-connected player in the KANU hierarchy, a man who retained close ties to the former dictator and his abidingly large and ominous network, and who was making efforts at a political comeback. A resurgent Sunkuli would be a dangerous foe indeed. It would be imprudent to humiliate him with arrest unless his conviction could be guaranteed.

What the inquest had failed to do was put anyone who had threatened Kaiser close to him when he died. The Mara, where the rangers had sup-posedly plotted, was located hours from the road where the body had been discovered. Yet Moi was gone, and with it much of the fear that had impeded the original search; Gathenji had not abandoned hope of bring-ing someone to justice.

18

THE LABYRINTH WITH NO CENTER

I F GATHENJI HAD grown rich as a "superlawyer" in the Kibaki years, his tiny office off Ngong Road did not reflect it. His window overlooked a courtyard covered with browning grass and a clothesline strung with clothes; to deter thieves, glass shards had been embedded in the top of the surrounding wall. His office contained little beyond his own small wooden desk and chair, a couch, plain fabric chairs for visitors, a filing cabinet, and shelves containing statute books, tomes on forensics, and case files. At work, he dressed immaculately in cuff links, pinstriped shirts, and patterned ties. On Fridays, he tried to kick off work a little early to spend time with his wife, and on weekends he enjoyed playing with his grandson and working on his small farm in the shade of the white jacaranda and other trees he'd planted. It was a serene setting away from the hurly-burly of the city center, though invaded now and then by monkey packs from the Nairobi National Park.

"If I was a high-profile person, I would have gone years ago. That is certain," he said not long after the inquest was completed. "Even now, there are some people who'd be very happy to put a bullet in my head." Though he conveyed stolidity itself, his emotions rarely showing, now and then passion made him raise his voice. "The FBI document was a lie," he said. "A lie! A very bad lie!" His suspicions about the case were wide-ranging. He wondered if everyone in the Catholic Church had told the whole truth about what they'd seen and heard. "Go back to the time this was happening," Gathenji said. "There were very few people in the country who had reason to tell the truth. Father Kaiser stood alone."

At one point, as he talked, Gathenji unlocked his cabinet safe and took out some clippings. Here was the newspaper from October 1969 showing his father's coffin being carried to its grave, and here was a photo of a young, bespectacled, terrified-looking Charles Mbuthi Gathenji, captured in the immediate aftermath of the trauma, and here was the hospital photo, his father's bloody body. It had been a senseless killing, the product of mob frenzy. And yet his father had been a genuine martyr, he explained; his death had touched Kenyatta's conscience and compelled him to stop the coerced oathing. For decades, Gathenji had been forced to live and work alongside the orchestrators of his father's death, compelled to confront in microcosm the crucible that had marked Kenyan history since the Mau Mau years: the choice between vengeance, however legitimate, and its difficult, if not impossible, sublimation. Across the continent, in countries like Rwanda, people had been forced to coexist among the unpunished killers of their friends and family; in South Africa, reconciliation with apartheid-era atrocities meant the guilty walked free. Over and over, Africans had been asked to surrender claims to justice as the price of moving forward.

In the streets now and then, Gathenji said with a little amusement, he spotted Sunkuli, whose law office was just a few miles away. The former minister remained an active member of the Catholic Church, a Christian in good standing. Yet history had leveled him, stripping him of his entourage and his aura of power. He had been close to the throne once, in line to be East Africa's most powerful man. Now, he was another lawyer trying to make a living, another Kenyan walking to the grocery store.

Gathenji had not abandoned his hope of seeing Moi brought to the Hague on war crimes; even if he was acquitted, he believed, there should be some reckoning. But it did not seem likely that Moi would be called to account, either for Kaiser's death or for the carnage that had attended his twenty-four years as president. He had retired to his vast estates as one of Africa's richest men, and had launched the Moi Africa Institute, dedicated to "conflict prevention and resolution" in Africa.

Gathenji scarcely had time to savor the inquest victory in the Kaiser case—and the investigation demanded by the magistrate had had little time to progress—when ethnic carnage convulsed Kenya again.

In the years after Kibaki took office, Kenya had given the appearance of a place reborn: a growing economy, a new respect for freedom of speech and of the press, an end to the nightmare of casual torture and arbitrary imprisonment. But portents of trouble had been evident as the 2007 election approached—notably, Kibaki's sacking and replacement of members of the Electoral Commission. Far from the savior who had promised to cleanse the state machinery of corruption, he seemed determined to cling to power and to protect the fortunes of the Kikuyus who surrounded him, known as the "Mount Kenya Mafia." Reinforcing this perception was his apparent indifference to massive graft among his top men. The plunderers kept their jobs, and his own antigraft czar was forced to flee the country.

Luos and other ethnic groups remained fearful of Kikuyu dominance, while Kikuyus dreaded the prospect of Luo control. As polling day approached, machetes disappeared from the supermarket stands; in the countryside, elders mobilized young men for war. Luo challenger Raila Odinga at one point appeared to have a million-vote lead. Its sudden evaporation—and Kibaki's hasty swearing-in—seemed to confirm fears of a stolen election. Odinga supporters attacked Kikuyus indiscriminately, burning and looting their shops and hacking them with pangas. In the Rift Valley, Kalenjin raiders, whipped into a rage by renewed calls from tribal elders to expel "non-indigenous" Kikuyu "thieves" from the region, disguised their faces with mud and advanced in great packs, chanting war songs, wielding machetes, bows and arrows, and jerrycans of fuel, setting fire to farm after farm.

In a crowning symbol of the horror, a mob swarmed the Kenya Assemblies of God church in the village of Kiambaa on New Year's Day, where dozens of Kikuyu villagers had sought safety from the surrounding fighting. The attackers barricaded the door, piled mattresses and cornhusks against the church, doused them with gasoline, and set the church ablaze.

Dozens were incinerated alive, mostly women and children; those who tried to escape were hacked to death. There was ferocious retaliation from the Mungiki, a Kikuyu slum gang, with reports they were forcibly circumcising their victims with broken bottles before killing them. At roadblocks, bus riders were hauled from their seats and massacred for possessing the wrong ethnic surname. Government security forces gunned down protesters. Nobody was sure who was in charge. Having helped to ruin the courts for so long, Attorney General Amos Wako, a Moi-era relic, now called feebly for them to resolve the election dispute. Ultimately, more than 1,000 were killed and some 350,000 displaced in the fighting. The killing abated with a power-sharing arrangement—Kibaki would remain president, while Odinga became prime minister—but the sense of menace lingered well into 2008.

Gathenji viewed the postelection carnage as the direct lineal consequence of Moi's long epoch, with its calculated mobilization of ethnic animosities, often over the question of land, and a judicial system in which no top politician had ever been prosecuted for corruption.

Moi supplied tinder for the conflagration in these and other ways, as scholar Susanne Mueller has argued. He cemented a winner-takes-all system in which political parties had little to do with ideology but were seen instead as collectors of spoils. The winners got their turn "to eat"; the losers were banished from the table; compromise was impossible. During his long power grab, Moi had systematically gutted counterbalancing institutions like the courts, which might have resolved a tight election without bloodshed if anyone had considered them legitimate.

For years, Moi had relied on packs of young thugs to kill and oust rivals, the scholar noted, and had presided over a proliferation of goon squads, militias, and gangs that served the state's Big Men. Though Kenyatta had used brute force and imprisonment, Moi had spread the violence far beyond the state's control. Chaos, once unleashed, could not be reined in.

Moi had made himself kingpin of a gangster state, and the convulsions of late 2007 and early 2008 could be seen as its logical manifestation.

In *The Graves Are Not Yet Full,* Bill Berkeley described inflamed ethnic rancor in Africa as the consequence, rather than the catalyst, of political strife; prejudice became murder in the charged vacuum of a "lawless environment." Describing the continent's ethnic fighting as "a form of organized crime," he argued, "The 'culture' driving Africa's conflicts is akin to that of the Sicilian Mafia, or of the Crips and Bloods in Los Angeles, with the same imperatives of blood and family that bind such gangs together. Africa's warring factions are best understood not as 'tribes' but as racketeering enterprises, their leaders calculating strategy after the time-honored logic of Don Vito Corleone."

The postelection mayhem would consume Gathenji's attentions for years. He would file suit against the attorney general for failing to stop the violence. He would help to arrange a series of specialized surgeries in California for four children who had been burned in the Rift Valley church fire. He would appear before the so-called Waki Commission, a panel meant to probe the causes of the postelection violence and to hold its sponsors accountable, and would watch in dismay as the Kenyan government ignored its recommendations. He would help indigent clash victims document their experiences and seek reparations with the International Criminal Court at the Hague. And he would be named as one of the handful of Kenyan lawyers to participate in the ICC's case against those accused in the election mayhem. The court's chief prosecutor had initiated an investigation under the 1998 Rome Statute, which made the ICC the first permanent court with authority to try individuals for human rights abuses.

Gathenji knew only a fraction of the guilty would ever face charges, in the best-case scenario. He believed it important work nonetheless, even as critics derided the ICC as "the white man's court" and Kenya's leaders, while making promises of cooperation, demonstrated their contempt for the court by inviting Sudanese president Omar al-Bashir to an event celebrating Kenya's long-awaited new constitution. Under the Rome Statute, Kenya had been obligated to arrest Bashir, who faced an ICC warrant for large-scale atrocities in Darfur. Yet there he was at the Uhuru Park

ceremony in August 2010, flanked by other African leaders, releasing a
white dove into the air.

Gathenji saw promise in the new constitution, however. It curbed
the president's power, created a bicameral parliament, and provided for
the return of stolen land. Its passage was, satisfyingly, a rebuke to Moi,
who had campaigned aggressively against it. How closely Kenya's leaders
would follow the constitution remained an open question. Gathenji saw
little cause for optimism in the courts. Bribes were still changing hands,
but it seemed to be happening with less brazenness now, on golf courses,
in back rooms, through proxies. Maybe that was a kind of progress.

Sunkuli, for his part, had found a comfortable place in the new order.
Apparently to deter his bid for his old parliamentary seat, the government gave him an ambassadorship to China. He boarded a plane to Bei-
jing, where he was received with all the honor due a diplomat from East
Africa's most important country. He would be the face of Kenya to more
than a billion Chinese.

G. K. CHESTERTON, Kaiser's intellectual hero, wrote of a labyrinth
without a center—a serviceable image for a case in which every train
of promising evidence leads to yet another corridor, another turn into
darkness and ambiguity. One could wander forever in the devious maze
of the death of John Kaiser. Who and what killed the priest represents a
singular thought experiment about human nature, each assessment casting light as much on the observer as the case itself. Shot through subjec-
tive prisms, the evidence yields fierce and opposite conclusions.

Magistrate Odero's ruling of murder, for all its symbolic value, and for
all she might be right, is, of course, just the opinion of one person who
spent some time in that maze and offered a guess, however shaded by
politics, about its center. But it takes little effort to perceive the cracks in
her lens. She never got Kaiser's psychiatric records and the full details of
his hospitalizations; one cannot wish them away.

Certainly every sinew of the priest's moral and philosophical makeup militated against suicide; it would be hard to find someone in whom the moral revulsion would have been stronger. And yet the black derangement of clinical depression is not easily imagined by those who haven't lived in its coils. Because plain language is inadequate, survivors of the experience grope for metaphors to convey its essence. They speak of feeling trapped under a lake of thick ice; of being stuck at the bottom of a well with unscalable walls; of wandering in an infinite fog bank or mapless wilderness; of smothering, drowning, and suffocation. They describe a closed landscape of monochromatic horror, a sense of living entombment, in which one's own body becomes evil-smelling and hope is literally inconceivable. They are seized by inexplicable dreads. Voices reach the ear as if through miles of sea. The effort required to button one's collar is excruciating. In such a psychic landscape, by the report of those who have wandered there, death can become a seductive prospect, the focus of daily fantasy and longing.

Certain factors did put Kaiser at increased suicide risk—he was a white, older man, a demographically vulnerable category. And yet he had no known prior suicide attempts, was not suffering from a terminal illness, and "did not appear to have active psychiatric symptoms" in his last days, according to Dr. Steven Altchuler, a psychiatrist at the Mayo Clinic in Minnesota, who reviewed the case for the Kaiser family. He concluded the priest had been at no greater risk for suicide than the average person and would have been unlikely to make the attempt; he'd had no diagnosed symptoms of bipolar disorder since the early 1980s.

Is it possible that Kaiser just got better? Studies show that 25 percent of those who suffer manic depression recover fully, while from 55 to 65 percent recover only partially; from 10 to 20 percent suffer continually. It has been estimated that one of every four attempts suicide; one of ten succeeds. What renders such figures flawed as probabilistic assessments is that Kaiser's circumstances were sui generis. The studies do not involve manic-depressive priests. They do not involve this *type* of manic-depressive priest.

Did Kaiser's decision to discontinue lithium indicate that he didn't need it anymore? People who quit the drug give many of the same explanations.

Particularly if the dose is wrong, it can make the hands shake, impair concentration, and deaden the mind, so that even reading becomes impossible. It can produce the sense of one's core leaching out. There are other reasons one quits. One might be in denial about having a disease. One might be a proud farm boy and ex-soldier, schooled in rugged self-reliance, who shuns a perceived psychopharmacological crutch and thinks, *A man hacks it.* One might be reluctant to forfeit the ecstasies of the manic phase, the vaulting thoughts, the sharpened senses, the feeling of deep kinship with the universe. It's possible Kaiser stopped taking lithium not because he got better but because it blunted his experience of God.

Kaiser's condition was not obvious to everyone. His exuberance, his bursts of life and energy, his herculean building efforts, his earthy good humor—that was the side of himself he showed. The darkness he contended with remained largely hidden, and the bush seems to have been an ideal hiding place: far from any psychiatric hospital or any doctor qualified to diagnose mental illness, a place where tumultuous mood swings might easily be written off as the eccentricities of a foreigner whose lifestyle was unusual at the best of times.

In his confrontation with Moi's Gorgon-state, he risked condemnation and estrangement from the Church he loved, and he risked his life. But the man who had lived so close to death for so long—hardly a week passed in thirty-six years without sending someone he knew into the soil—seemed to have reconciled himself, clear-eyed, to the possibility of a violent end. By all accounts, his certainty in the afterlife was firm. *We are only here,* he liked to say, *to get out of here.* This life was preparation for the one to come, a transient prelude, a blink, "a minor preview of the main attraction in the next." Heaven, Hell, God, Satan—these weren't metaphors, but the governing, indisputable realities.

The danger to his soul would have been the graver one, by his thinking, and a man who carried a shotgun—and who thrust himself again and again into circumstances of extreme peril—could not be oblivious to the risks. Sooner or later, such a man might be tempted to shoot, to save his life or someone else's life. Whether Kaiser was capable of taking another life was one of the mysteries of his character. Some who knew him said yes; others, no. He might have known, at his core, that the shotgun was a bluff, a prop—that he couldn't use it, and would have to rely on his enemies' misunderstanding of his nature to keep them away. He was akin to a soldier rushing the cannon's mouth with a toy weapon, naked and defenseless save for his faith. But he also must have understood that in the face of enough terror and heat and fatigue and pain and injustice, even someone attuned to the eternal stakes might pull the trigger. And it is worth asking whether his repeated warnings not to call his death a suicide reflected a certain lingering dread that in exactly the right circumstances, his mind unspooling in some dark place of consuming and unendurable horror, he might be tempted not just to homicide but to what he believed a greater, inexpiable sin.

DURING HIS STAY with Kaiser in Lolgorien, Father Tom Keane got perhaps the closest sustained glimpse of his behavior under conditions of extreme stress. He saw him sleep by day and keep vigil with his shotgun at night, double-checking the locks, expecting killers. He saw him buoyant with energy one day, dejected and drawn into himself the next. "He suffered from depression," he said. Some of Kaiser's admirers seemed to be in denial about it, and had accused Keane of inflating his account and thereby bolstering the FBI's suicide finding.

When he took over the Lolgorien parish after Kaiser's death, Keane found himself unpopular with the local people. He broke with Kaiser's habit of freely distributing food and money. He didn't like the idea of Africans lining up for handouts from a white man. He thought it trespassed on their dignity. But he loved Kaiser and was proud of his association with him. Sometimes, in a jam, he let it be known that they had been close. That was currency; even the police respected it. "There's nobody, even little kids, who don't know Father Kaiser," Keane said. "He's known everywhere, in every corner of Kenya."

Keane sometimes wondered whether the young women who approached Kaiser for protection against Sunkuli were really part of a plot to destroy the priest. Keane did not elaborate on this thought, except to say that he considered Africans to be capable of no end of scheming and devious convolutions.

He described an episode that seemed to encapsulate the loneliness of a Western missionary's existence in Africa. Though Keane had lived among the Kisii for years, had baptized their children and buried their relatives, he found it impossible to persuade his own church elders to testify against a fellow Kisii who'd nearly killed him in a car wreck. Instead, they simply vanished. The underlying message seemed to be that the white priests, in the end, were just passing through, fleeting presences on an old landscape governed by adamantine obligations of blood and clan. It was painful knowledge for a man who had given much of his life to the country.

Had Kaiser, in the end, felt something of the same thing? Had he come to believe that Anne and Florence had been playing him as a dupe, as a pawn in some elaborate game? Had this—the realization that he was an outsider tilting at windmills—pulled the final thread that unraveled him?

Keane didn't think *martyr* was quite the right word for his friend.

"I always got the sense that John Kaiser was looking for martyrdom at a deep unconscious level," Keane said. A genuine martyr tries to avoid trouble, he explained, "but when he can't avoid it, he says, 'I'll give my life for God.'" Yet Kaiser courted danger, and "kind of wanted to go with a bang." Keane thought of him departing the safety of the bishop's house, heading off into the darkness, into an ambush. "That was somebody kind of in a sense looking for death."

In cases of what psychologists call "subintentional" suicide, victims play an unconscious role in engineering their deaths. They do it by consuming excessive quantities of drugs and alcohol; they do it by deep-sea diving or rock climbing without the full array of safety gear; they do it by driving too fast on bad roads; they do it in a thousand ways. By now, the "suicide by cop" phenomenon, in which people looking to die force police to gun them down, is well known. More obscure is what might be called "suicide by murder." In Samantha Power's *A Problem from Hell,* Canadian major General Roméo Dallaire, commander of the UN peace-keeping forces in Rwanda during the 1994 genocide, confessed to having harbored a death wish after failing to stop the slaughter. "At the end of my command, I drove around in my vehicle with no escort practically looking for ambushes," he said. "I was trying to get myself destroyed and looking to get released from the guilt."

"I AM A suspect in Father John Kaiser's death. They say I am not reliable. I am already labeled," Francis Kantai said. "I am in a very tight situation." He had been in the States since 2003, and was working as a certified nursing assistant at a hospital in Omaha, Nebraska. His tone was harassed and self-pitying. "I'm victimized very much." On a brief return to Kenya some years back, he said, the reception had been chilly. "I went to my own parish, and they wouldn't open the door for me," he said. "That's one [reason] I'm glad to leave Kenya." He said he had a three-year-old son named Kaiser, and added, "I am what I am because of him."

He blamed the Catholic Church for trying to isolate Kaiser in the years before his death. "They never supported him. If Father was killed, I think the Church contributed for leaving him alone. He was very careful not to be seen by the bishop doing these things. If somebody wanted to silence him, they knew nobody else would follow."

He spoke of the video he insisted had seen Kaiser studying at the Mill Hill house, the one supposedly depicting a priest shooting himself. He said he walked in upon Kaiser in the act. "Father rewinded [*sic*] it four times. This I wish I hadn't seen. I just sat behind Father. I just said, 'Father.' He turned and said, 'Let's go.' He seemed angry about it."

As seemed common with Kantai, his story got better as he continued speaking, with increasingly colorful details. Not long before his death, Kantai now alleged, the priest had uttered ominous words. "He told me, 'This is the time I should do what I have been planning to do for a long time.' I said, 'Father, tell me what it is.' He said, 'You will not like it, my friend.' "

He denied any role in Kaiser's death, denied even knowing that the priest was leaving for Nairobi in his final week. "In the name of God, in the name of Father Kaiser, I am innocent. I am very innocent. God knows that. Kaiser knows that. My wife and her family accepts me, and that's all that matters."

Asked to clarify what accounts he had given to whom, and what parts of those accounts he was now disavowing, he showed no appetite for the exercise. "Sir," he said, "don't put me on a cross."

His wife, Camille, for her part, knew some in the Kaiser family resented her for marrying Kantai, and that they remained deeply suspicious of him. This was painful for her, but she loved her husband. She said the suspicions stemmed from a basic misunderstanding about the special role that Kaiser had created for his catechist. By maintaining contact with Kaiser's enemies, she said, "Francis was able to get information from both sides of the fence. That information was used to help Father, so he could better help the people. . . . He was basically a spy. 'You come and get information and you tell me what's going on.' But that created a sense of distrust with the people."

PAUL BOYLE HAD been one of the last priests to see Kaiser alive. Like Keane, he had supplied the FBI with an account that bolstered its suicide verdict—"Tomorrow I'll be dead," he'd reported Kaiser as saying—and had suffered the same cold reception among some of Kaiser's admirers. Boyle was in his mid-forties and Scottish. He had left Mill Hill and married a Muslim woman. They had a young son. He worked as a stress counselor.

He sat in a Nairobi coffee shop, trying to stress the point that a Roman collar was no surefire amulet against despair. Looking into Kaiser's eyes, he said, he had seen the torment of a man hunted beyond endurance. He had seen a version of himself. Though some pointed out that Boyle had not worked closely with Kaiser for years, Boyle believed he grasped Kaiser's state in a way few others could. "I know what darkness is," he said. "I understand maybe more than anyone his mental health. His stress. How many people have written me off?"

Boyle said he spent thirteen years as a missionary in Sudan, and ran a camp for displaced people in Khartoum. He was chased through the desert, shot at, kidnapped, jailed. He found himself courting extreme danger, daring fate, ready to kill or die. Once he was driving a sickly four-month-old boy toward medical help, when the child died in his arms. He put the child on the seat beside him. His phone rang. It was a friend. He explained about the dead child, and then made plans to get a beer. The friend said, "What?" Boyle replied, "What's the big deal?"

Later, he would think of that moment and realize how numb he had become.

Sitting in the café, telling his story, he tapped his finger against a cup of sugar to illustrate what had happened to him. He had felt nothing. Insensate as this glass. Nothing.

Once, he continued, Sudanese soldiers took him at gunpoint into the desert, and he felt a great happiness at the prospect that they would execute him; his torment would be over. "If those guys had put me before a firing squad, you would have seen a smile. People would have said, 'That's a saint.' I was a sick man."

Like Kaiser, he said, he'd felt a compulsion to keep raising the stakes, playing out what might be described as a death wish. He believed that Kaiser, after the misery he'd seen, after being chased and hunted and threatened, might have felt a sense of peace at the end. "The man had had enough," he said.

Describing his last encounter with Kaiser, he recalled Kaiser approaching him at the Mill Hill house to shake his hand, with the words "I'm going now. Tell Brother Martin I'm taking this bottle of water." Boyle asked, "Why are you shaking my hand?" Kaiser had said, "Tomorrow I'll be dead."

Boyle remembered his own response: "Okay, then." He wasn't sure what Kaiser meant—whether he was planning to kill himself or surrender to his pursuers—but there was a sense of finality in his voice. "Do you call it grace? Do you call it self-knowledge? Do you call it it's your time?" he said. "He knew what was coming, one way or the other." Boyle wanted it understood that priests, like soldiers, can have enough. "The question is, did he give up all he believed in and commit suicide?" Boyle said. "Is it possible? Is it plausible? I don't know."

Boyle believed Kaiser's struggles with his own mind may have gone hand in hand with his outsize courage, his willingness to pick fights and stand his ground, to defy everyone. "Kaiser didn't take shit from nobody, not even the bishop," Boyle said. He remembered Kaiser as "an American from the movies." Remembered a night rolling through the Masai Mara, when Kaiser leaned out of the door of his moving truck and, with a spot of distant brush illuminated by the headlights, took aim with his rifle and fired at an impala. When Boyle said, "John, you've missed," Kaiser replied with a touch of braggadocio, "I've never missed in my life."

They ate the animal's liver and the heart that night, out under the stars.

At first, Boyle had considered suicide a real possibility. With the magistrate's ruling, he had to reconsider. But there were riddles that taunted, such as: In an ambush, why hadn't Kaiser, the former paratrooper, used his shotgun to defend himself?

Boyle thought about his final moments. He considered the scenarios.

"He's faced with the murderers, and he's got a choice. Kaiser has the gun. No one can shoot like Kaiser."

But ending the life of another man—or several of them—might have broken him. "Killing himself, he'll end up in hell. Kill others, he may end up in hell. Did he say, 'They've come to do what they've come to do?' Is that suicide? I don't know. It could be martyrdom."

He could see him handing over his shotgun and sinking to his knees in the darkness.

FOR ALL THE ambiguities, the murder verdict seems to have settled over the country with the weight of fact. The writers of history have embraced the assessment. In her 2009 book, *It's Our Turn to Eat*, Michela Wrong, among the most clear-eyed observers of the Kenyan scene, puts Kaiser's death unequivocally on the roll call of political murders: "Did Kenya have a history of ruthless political assassination? Absolutely—I could reel off the names: Pio Pinto, Tom Mboya, J. M. Kariuki, Robert Ouko, Father Kaiser—and those were only the most notorious cases. Kenya had always been a venue for the well-timed car crash, the fatal robbery in which both gangster and high-profile victim conveniently lose their lives, the inquiry that drags on for decades and then sputters out without shedding any light on what had really happened."

Many who championed the inquest didn't anticipate any arrests. "I expect the actual killers are probably dead," said Carolita Mahoney. For the Kaiser family, the removal of the suicide verdict would have to be enough. Said Mary Mahoney Weaver, the priest's niece: "We feel vindicated. John's name is no longer marred. If they ever name somebody, we'd be surprised."

The ruling did nothing to budge the FBI agents who handled the case. William Corbett called the magistrate's reasoning "fanciful" and maintained that untreated manic depression, not an assassin, was the culprit. "Ultimately, he died of a disease," the FBI agent said. "It's not something that everyone is comfortable talking about."

After his retirement from the FBI, Thomas Graney found himself driving his son to a wrestling tournament in Fargo, North Dakota, and realized he was very close to the Kaiser family home in Minnesota. The case had left him with a lingering disquiet, and he was tempted to pay a visit. He wanted to express his sympathy for the loss of a genuinely good man. He wanted them to see his face, and to understand that he'd attacked the investigation with a sense of dedication and duty, attacked it as thoroughly as any case he'd worked during his twenty-two years as a special agent. It had bothered him to hear the Kaisers malign his investigation. He told people he didn't mind being second-guessed—that was part of the job—but in this case he felt his competence and integrity were under assault. The suggestion that he'd tailored his report to suit the Kenyan government, well, he resented the hell out of that. Be real, he wanted to say. Kaiser had a serious mental illness, and the big mistake in the case had been the FBI brass's decision not to wait for psychiatric records to prove that beyond any doubt.

As he neared the turnoff that would lead to Kaiser's family, Graney thought about how the conversation with them might go. He would tell them, maybe, that his conclusion about Kaiser's death did not subtract anything from the priest's heroism, and that the last page of a man's life didn't cancel out the rest. And maybe he'd remind the family that the FBI had worked in Kenya as guests of its government and could only do so much.

He hoped it would be a positive meeting, and that seeing his face might give the Kaisers a little peace. He couldn't be sure. It might just as easily break bad.

He explained his thinking to his wife, who was riding beside him. She asked whether he planned to do this for the Kaisers or for himself. The turnoff approached. He drove on past.

EVEN TO THOSE he baptized, to those who understood the nature of his vows, there remained something bewildering about the life he chose. In the far-flung Kenyan parishes he had served over thirty-six years, big families were a given, childlessness a calamity, and here was a man who would leave no offspring, no link to the earth walking upright when he left it. His legacy would be measured in other ways.

Wangari Maathai, the first African woman to be awarded the Nobel Peace Prize and a pioneer of Kenya's pro-democracy movement, said that Kaiser represented "the people's voice in an era when ordinary people did not have a voice." His importance grew after his death, she said, when he became a byword for the Moi regime's ruthlessness. The ditch where Kaiser's body was found became not just a memorial site but a place where the opposition mobilized. In the long campaign to oust Moi's government, she said, "he became a very powerful symbol."

His battle on behalf of Sunkuli's accusers was another element of his legacy. In a country where rape went widely unpunished and the rights of poor women were scant, the fact that a powerful minister was summoned to court to answer the charges represented a crack in a culture of impunity, even if Sunkuli ultimately avoided prosecution.

There were other measures, and one could be found in a story Francis Kaiser told.

When he and his wife went to Kenya in September 2003 for the inquest, they attended a Mass in his brother's honor in Nyangusu, a western town where the priest had spent many years. Francis was asked to bless the crowd.

Afterward, a family brought their baby for him to hold, and the child was named John Kaiser. Francis learned that the church was full of young boys—infants and toddlers and kids already running—who had been named after his brother.

It was the same, he found, in village after village. There were hundreds across the countryside, maybe more.

His brother had disappeared into the red soil, perhaps along with the truth about his death, but you could travel anywhere now and find John Kaiser.

ACKNOWLEDGMENTS

The author is in debt to the editors the *Los Angeles Times,* with special gratitude owed to Marc Duvoisin, who edited the original newspaper series; Rick Meyer, who first championed the story; and Davan Maharaj, Steve Marble, David Lauter, and Russ Stanton, who gave me the time to research it and write it. Others, at the paper and elsewhere, provided useful advice, technical information, encouragement, or friendship during the writing of the series or the book, including Jesse Wilson, Danny Wein, Gary Bortolus, Matt Snyder, Dana Parsons, Mike Anton, Tom Lake, Tom Curwen, Tom French, Josh and Lesley Nippell, Mark & Anne Albracht, Mike and Kate Brassfield, Stuart Pfeifer, Ashley Powers, Mike Wilson, Chuck Natanson, Andy Conn, Jamal Thalji, Brady Dennis, Sue Horton, Shelby Grad, Scott Kraft, Roger Smith, Kurt Streeter, Steve Padilla, Alistair and Maria Nicklin, Jon Lundberg, Francine Orr, John Canalis, Will Fischbach, Susanne Mueller, Eddie Sanders, Bill Varian, Bill Lobdell, Sean Keefe, and Josh Marks. Special thanks to Seth Jaret, Norton editor Alane Salierno Mason, and agents Lydia Wills, Philip Patterson, and Luke Speed. Finally, with love and thanks too deep to express in words, to Jennifer.

SOURCES AND NOTES

This narrative is based on nearly one hundred interviews I conducted in the United States and in Kenya; on several hundred of Kaiser's letters and on his other writings; on books, media accounts, and human rights reports; on Kenyan police reports and on transcripts of legal proceedings; and on documents obtained through the Freedom of Information Act, including U.S. State Department memos, FBI reports, and internal memos. I am grateful for the assistance of David T. Schultz, a Minneapolis attorney enlisted by the Kaiser family, who shared the fruit of his own FOIA requests with me; for that of Charles Mbuthi Gathenji, who helped me get ahold of the Kenyan records; and for that of Sister Nuala Brangan, who had collected scores of Kaiser's letters and shared them with me. Kaiser's letters—which he sometimes dashed off in his truck during rainstorms, or on the hood while he was stuck behind a car mired in the dirt—provided an invaluable source of information.

1. The House at the Edge of the Dark

2 **late summer:** Kenyans do not typically speak of the seasons as winter, spring, summer, and fall. Instead, periods of rain and dryness define their seasons. The four-season model is used throughout the book for chronological convenience and clarity.

3 **a lifetime without physical love:** Africans in general regard the practice of celibacy as even more unnatural than Americans do—it's not much of a secret that some of the continent's bishops had sired children who sat undisguised in the front row during Mass, a fact related to the author by more than one former missionary.

4 **"He is a baptized Catholic":** letter from John Kaiser to Barbara and Francis Kaiser, August 17, 2000.

4   **"biggest worry":** letter from John Kaiser to Carolita and Joe Mahoney, January 12, 1998.

5   **He found that a Coke bottle was a serviceable receptacle:** Details about improvising Mass with a Coke bottle and chapati are from the author's interviews with Tom Keane.

6   **Though he hated seeing the doctor:** from declassified portions of the FBI's FD-302 report of its interview on December 8, 2000, with a Nairobi doctor (name redacted) who treated Kaiser twenty-eight times from 1994 to 1998.

6   **he bowed his head and listened to their confessions:** Kaiser once estimated that he received ten thousand confessions a year (a letter from John Kaiser, addressed "Dear Friends," February 6, 1990). When I interviewed him at his Nairobi office, Paul Muite recalled that Kaiser had told him that he'd received the confessions of people who admitted to burning houses at the government's behest. Francis Kantai, Kaiser's catechist, admitted such acts of arson first to Kaiser and later openly.

7   **one writer compared the experience to having a sack pulled over your head:** Ryzard Kapuscinski, *The Shadow of the Sun* (New York: Knopf, 2001), p. 49.

8   **"When the missionaries arrived, the Africans had the land":** David Lamb, *The Africans* (New York: Vintage, 1987), p. 59.

11   *A decision has been made to eliminate you:* Mechizedek Ondieki, a carpenter in the Transmara who had known Kaiser since the 1970s, told me when I interviewed him in Lolgorien that he was present when a game warden told Kaiser there was a plan afoot to shoot him as a poacher; Kaiser also related a similar warning to Paul Muite, who reported it to the FBI (FD-302 report of the FBI's interview with Muite on February 26, 2001).

12   *Utaona moto:* No physical copy of this note has been found. Its existence became publicly known during the September 2003 inquest testimony of Francis Kantai. There is corroboration from Romulus Ochieng, one of Kaiser's catechists in the priest's final months, who affirmed without hesitation when I met him in Lolgorien that he remembered the note. James Juma, then the parish priest of Kilgoris, told me he recalled Kaiser talking about it. Further, a man as informed and skeptical as Charles Mbuthi Gathenji does not doubt this note existed. Nevertheless, like so much else in this story, the evidence cannot be held in the hand. To my mind, the note illustrates, in a small way, the maddening epistemological slipperiness, the mist-and-shifting-sand nature, of the entire Kaiser case; it's no accident that I have chosen this phrase

for the title. "You will see fire" is one possible translation; it could also be read as "You will feel the heat" or "It's going to get hot for you." It should be remembered that Bishop Alexander Muge was threatened with this phrase not long before a milk truck plowed into him and killed him.

12 *Kikulacho kimo nguoni mwako*: The friend was Stephen Naiguta, who worked with Kaiser as the parish coordinator of the Catholic Church's Justice and Peace Commission; he told me of the encounter when I met him at his home in the hills above Kilgoris.

2. The Lawyer

14 **Charles Mbuthi Gathenji:** Portrayals of Gathenji's experiences and thought processes in this chapter, and elsewhere in the book, are based on the author's interviews with Gathenji, with corroboration, where possible, from the available historical record.

3. The Collar and the Gun

22 **Along the narrow dirt roads:** For this and other details about the landscape, lifestyle, and practices of the Kisii, I have drawn on the following sources. Robert and Barbara LeVine, *Nyansongo: A Gusii Community in Kenya* (New York: Wiley, 1966); Sarah LeVine, with Robert LeVine, *Mothers and Wives: Gusii Women of East Africa* (Chicago: University of Chicago Press, 1979); John Kaiser, *If I Die* (Nairobi: Cana Publishing, 2003); interviews with Tom Keane, who ministered to the Kisii for years; and personal observations.

23 **"a great sign of Divine favour":** Kaiser, *If I Die*, p. 17.

23 **he installed a drain under an old woman's hut:** ibid., p. 18.

24 **"clever rogues":** ibid., p. 19.

24 **"organized cosmology":** LeVine, *Nyansongo*, p. 56.

25 **"fear and fatalism":** Kaiser, *If I Die*, p. 18.

25 **"distinctively paranoid":** LeVine, *Nyansongo*, p. 190.

26 **"a few boys achieve a hurried and fearful act of coitus":** ibid., p. 42.

26 **mass clitoridectomies:** To demonstrate the euphemistic inadequacy of the oft-used term *female circumcision*, it is worth quoting a description of the procedure, from *Nyansongo* (p. 169): "A crowd of women surrounded a stone on which the girl to be operated on was seated. A woman squatting behind the girl supported her back on her knees and, with her arms thrust under

the girl's arms, firmly held the girl's hands over her eyes. This grip served to prevent the girl from seeing what was going on and from moving her arms or the upper part of her body during the operation. The operator spread the girl's legs, put white flour on the genital area, and cut off the head of the clitoris with a sawing motion of her small knife. As soon as the piece of flesh had dropped to the ground, the crowd of women began trilling loudly, gaily screaming and shouting and, in some cases, dancing individually. The girl was then led over to the side of the house to squat, shivering under the eaves at the sides of the girls who had gone before her." By the 1970s, though clitoridectomies were vanishing in some parts of the country, the practice remained nearly universal in Kisiiland. (It remains common today, and when I asked a Kisii man the point of the procedure, he put it this way: "To turn the temperature down." To diminish female sexual appetite, it was assumed, thwarted marital straying.)

27　**"tenacious and stubborn":** Kaiser, *If I Die*, p. 17.

27　**He was born in November 1932:** Information on Kaiser's early years is based on interviews with his sister, Carolita Mahoney, and his brother, Francis Kaiser.

29　**He served from April 29, 1954:** Information on Kaiser's army years is based on interviews with William Meek and Francis Kaiser, and on surviving military records.

31　**Kaiser faithfully attended the Latin Mass:** A place in the bosom of large, tradition-bound institutions seems to have held some comfort for Kaiser, for all he came to chafe against them. In some ways, soldiering for country and soldiering for God are pursuits less paradoxical than they might seem: The army and the priesthood are enclosed systems, set apart from the ordinary world and governed by special laws and rituals that remind adherents of membership in something greater than themselves. Such systems can harness a scattered will, mitigate the tyranny of mood, and narrow the daily choices to a manageable number.

32　**his sister Carolita's account:** the FBI's FD-302 report of its interview with Carolita Mahoney in Underwood, Minnesota, on November 7, 2000; author's interview with Mahoney.

32　**That account was echoed by Kaiser's brother Francis:** author's interview with Francis Kaiser.

33　**Mill Hill:** Information on Kaiser's seminary years at Mill Hill and St. Joseph's College is based on the author's interviews with Tony Barnicle and Harrie van Onna.

35 **He stood on a hill:** Kaiser, *If I Die*, p. 22.

36 **the spectacle profoundly affected him:** ibid., pp. 15–17.

36 **He returned to Kenya:** letter from John Kaiser to Tony Barnicle, November 20, 1969.

4. Oaths

38 **Kenya's . . . preindependence history:** The colonial adventure had begun in earnest around the turn of the century, with the building of the railway from Mombasa westward to what is now Uganda. The British had mercantile motives in what would be called Kenya—to tap Africa's bounty of cotton and coffee, ivory and gum, and to secure the headwaters of the Nile—as well as avowed idealistic ones, such as facilitating the advance of Christian missionaries and eradicating the Arab slave trade. The land itself, though populated by three million people, was perceived as tabula rasa. A popular image portrays aristocratic white settlers enjoying a lordly life of cheaply bought land, enormous estates tended by domestic servants, polo, and pink-gin breakfasts. The hedonism of White Man's Country reached its apogee in the highlands outside Nairobi, where free-flowing cocaine and partner-swapping enlivened weekend bacchanals in the so-called Happy Valley. It's a canard to conceive of precolonial Kenya as an idyll of racial harmony—tribes had been skirmishing for centuries, as well as trading and intermarrying. One of the British Empire's bequests, however, was an amplified sensitivity to ethnic origins. By the late 1930s, colonists had seized prime lands, scrambled traditional territories, and carved Kenya into twenty-four increasingly crowded "native reserves," forbidding African men from straying beyond their ethnically defined borders without a *kipande*. To divide the tribes, rendering them atomized nations vying for land and privileges, ensured they would not coalesce into a rebel force. The promulgation of ethnic cleavages was also a useful way of managing a vast country with a relative handful of soldiers and administrators. This was the dynamic of "indirect rule": find willing Africans, lavish them with wealth, autonomy, and the title of chief, and rely on them to collect taxes and recruit wage laborers for the big European farms.

39 **Mau Mau:** No one knows the origin of the term *Mau Mau*. Some believe it a Kikuyu riddle. The novelist Ngugi wa Thiong'o told me he believes it an invention of the British, a linguistic weapon meant to cast the Crown's ostensibly demonic enemy as utterly apart and incomprehensible: To call the movement

the Land and Freedom Army would be to grant it legitimate motives, while the phrase Mau Mau, instead, reinforced the movement's shudder-inducing opacity.

39 **The British had responded to the rebellion:** For information on the history of the Mau Mau war and the Kikuyu gulag system, see Caroline Elkins, *Imperial Reckoning: The Untold Story of Britain's Gulag in Kenya* (New York: Henry Holt, 2005); David Anderson, *Histories of the Hanged* (New York: W. W. Norton, 2005). Elkins writes (p. 172), "Many detainees had already recognized the insidious partnership between Christianity and Britain's civilizing mission, but in the camps it became utterly transparent." Gun-bearing Catholic priests, she adds, sometimes accompanied British soldiers on nighttime patrols.

41 **loyalty oath:** Elkins and Anderson both provide good accounts of oathing.

41 **"the most bestial, filthy and nauseating incantation":** Colonial Secretary Oliver Lyttleton quoted in Elkins, *Imperial Reckoning*, p. 50.

43 **"African leader to darkness and death":** Kenya's governor Sir Patrick Renison quoted in ibid., p. 357.

44 **"My people have the milk in the morning":** Andrew Morton, *The Making of an African Statesman* (London: Michael O'Mara Books, 1998), p. 96.

44 **"Mau Mau was a disease which had been eradicated":** Elkins, *Imperial Reckoning*, p. 361.

47 **Samuel Gathenji lay on his back:** Information on Samuel Gathenji's slaying is based on the author's interviews with Charles Mbuthi Gathenji. The killing is cited in chapter 2 of Joseph Karimi and Philip Ochieng, *The Kenyatta Succession* (Nairobi: Transafrica Books, 1980). Though Gathenji is unnamed, the slaying is also cited in chapter 8 of Waithaka Waihenya and Ndikaru wa Teresia, *A Voice Unstilled: Archbishop Ndingi Mwana 'a Nzeki* (Nairobi: Longhorn Publishers, 2009), along with a description of the subsequent visit of church leaders to Kenyatta.

52 **a group of elephant poachers:** John Kaiser, *If I Die* (Nairobi: Cana Publishing, 2003), p. 29.

52 **"Indeed, we regarded him as a great Christian prince":** ibid., p. 30.

53 **"cancer that threatens to eat out the very fabric":** David Lamb, *The Africans* (New York: Vintage, 1987), p. 9.

55 **"The coup attempt was a terrible shock":** letter from John Kaiser to Douglas Beumer, August 23, 1982.

55 **"Things are quiet":** letter from John Kaiser to Don and Jackie Beumer, August 26, 1982.

5. The Dictator

56 **Moi:** In the pantheon of great kleptocrats, Moi would secure himself a solid perch, presiding over the looting of a country he managed to pauperize. Kroll, a risk consultancy group, issued a 110-page report in 2004 concluding that Moi, his sons, and his associates had looted more than two billion dollars from the government, with a portfolio of properties in New York, London, Australia, and South Africa. The Kibaki government, which commissioned the report, ignored it. (See "Leaked Report Says Moi Clique Moved $2bn out of Kenya," *Guardian Weekly*, September 7, 2007.) The major financial scandal of the Moi years was the Goldenberg affair, in which hundreds of millions in public money were bilked in the export of phantom gold, diamonds, and jewelry. See Michela Wrong, *It's Our Turn to Eat: The Story of a Kenyan Whistle-Blower* (New York: HarperCollins, 2009) for a good overview.

57 **Public Order Act:** see George Ayittey, *Africa in Chaos* (New York: St. Martin's Press, 1999), p. 70.

57 **torture squads:** Blaine Harden, "Police Torture Is Charged in Kenya; After Detention, 66 Have Confessed to Sedition in Past Year," *Washington Post*, March 12, 1987. Amnesty International estimated that more than seventy-five people were tortured into giving false confessions.

57 **large-scale bribery and intimidation:** See Smith Hempstone, *Rogue Ambassador: An African Memoir* (Sewanee, Tennessee: University of the South Press, 1997), and Blaine Harden, *Africa: Dispatches from a Fragile Continent* (New York: Houghton Mifflin, 1991).

58 **"I would like ministers, assistant ministers, and others to sing":** Harden, *Africa*, p. 260.

58 **even the fish of the sea:** Minister of Livestock Development Elijah Mwangale quoted in Hempstone, *Rogue Ambassador*, p. 91.

58 **"Kenya is a one-man state":** ibid., p. 39.

58 **"You know, a balloon is a very small thing":** Davan Maharaj, "Kenya's Big Man Is Belittled," *Los Angeles Times*, August 18, 2002; see also Harden, *Africa*, p. 260.

58 **a vast network of chiefs and subchiefs:** By the year 2000, there were six thousand subchiefs alone, and Moi thwarted attempts to trim them. (See George Mwangi, "Economic Reform in Kenya Bogged Down by Political Interest," Associated Press Worldstream, March 16, 2000.)

58   **"a pro-Western, free-market island":** Smith Hempstone, "Confessions of a Boat-Rocker," *Los Angeles Times*, June 1, 1993.

58   **Timothy Njoya:** See "Church is Consistently Opposed to Change, Says Njoya," *All Africa*, April 30, 2010, and Tanya Ho, "No Price Tag on Democracy," *Toronto Star*, September 12, 1997. The sermon that got Njoya defrocked was in October 1986.

59   **"Moi's Christianity is our protection":** Timothy Njoya quoted in Scott Kraft, "President Moi Sees Threat to Rule," *Los Angeles Times*, February 2, 1987.

60   **"peasants in Central Kenya were talking about a man":** Ngugi wa Thiong'o, *Moving the Centre* (Oxford: Heinemann, 1993), p. 157.

60   **the abolition of secret balloting:** For the 1988 general election, despite the objections of some churches and the country's outspoken lawyers, Moi imposed "queue voting," further eroding what little democratic choice Kenyans actually possessed. Rather than casting secret ballots, voters were made to stand in line behind posters of their candidates. Election officials pretended to count the people and told them to go home; when the winner was declared, there was no awkward record to contradict the result. In parliament, only Moi's most sedulous stooges kept their jobs. See David Throup and Charles Hornsby, *Multi-Party Politics in Kenya* (Athens, Ohio: Ohio University Press, 1998), p. 42.

60   **Moi accused an Oregon-based missionary group:** Scott Kraft, "President Moi Sees Threat to Rule," *Los Angeles Times*, February 2, 1987.

60   **deported seven American missionaries:** Scott Kraft, "Klan-Missionary Plot in Africa? 'Absurd,' U.S. Says," *Los Angeles Times*, November 18, 1987.

60   **Moi sent police to seize a package of school textbooks:** Michael Hiltzik, "U.S. Envoy Back in Kenya Regime's Doghouse," *Los Angeles Times*, March 19, 1991.

61   **"pull back from the darkness of torture":** Edward Kennedy quoted in Chege Mbitiru, "Kenya Marks Big Date," Associated Press, December 15, 1988.

61   **Why should Kenyans expect democracy? he asked:** Ayittey, *Africa in Chaos*, p. 262.

61   **His authorized biography:** The publication of Andrew Morton's *Moi: The Making of an African Statesman* (London: Michael O'Mara Books, 1998), drew the curiosity of Kenyans, who knew almost nothing about their president. Unabashedly hagiographic, the book proved useful mostly for its insights into how Moi himself rationalized his behavior and preferred to present himself. It's a good look at his disguise. By Morton's account (p. 3),

the decor of the president's three-thousand-acre estate near Nakuru reflected "an owner who eschews fussy and ostentatious display . . . a man who has little time either for self-aggrandisement or for the materialism of modern living." The shelves teemed with "well-thumbed bibles," their owner a Christian pacifist "not much given to the fripperies and diversions of life . . . a country-lover of simple tastes and demands who enjoys nothing more than to sit under the trees on his estate." Impatient with praise, Moi possessed "a guileless, almost other-worldly quality, akin to the lifestyle of a studious man of the cloth." Morton attributes to him (p. 9) "qualities of fortitude, composure and self-control, which have now become reflexive," adding, "Perhaps because serving his nation is now second nature, he rarely, if ever, thinks of himself before his country." If massive looting and electoral fraud attended his rule, well, it was because he trusted the people around him too much. Morton states (p. 113) that Moi had endured "endless petty personal humiliations" and "political provocations" at the hands of Kenyatta's Kikuyu circle. His face was slapped, his seat usurped at social functions, his estate raided, his motorcade searched. Kikuyu elites had never embraced his rule, and when they called for democracy, Morton's argument went, their interest was tribal, rather than the good of the nation.

61 **only fantasy can capture:** Years earlier, Ngugi wrote (in *Moving the Centre*, p. 157) what might serve as the novel's credo, arguing that "in a neocolonial situation, fiction seems to be more real than the absurdity of the factual world of a dictator. The world of a dictator has an element of pure fantasy. He will kill, jail, and drive hundreds into exile and imagine that he is actually loved for it."

61 **"on the throne so long":** Ngugi wa Thiong'o, *Wizard of the Crow* (New York: Anchor, 2007), p. 5.

61 **tower that stretches to heaven:** ibid., p. 16.

61 **"insatiable desire for humiliating the already fallen":** ibid., p. 10.

61 **"a Solomonic prince of peace":** ibid., p. 231.

Ngugi wrote from personal experience. The novelist, widely regarded as Kenya's greatest, is now in his seventies. Slightly built, stooped, and cheerful, he is a professor at the University of California at Irvine and a regular contender for the Nobel Prize in literature. Under Moi, one developed a kind of sixth sense that one ignored at mortal risk, he explained to me one day at his office. He compared it to the tingling one felt amid animals hidden in the bush. He had such a premonition just before Moi's police came for him one night in December 1977. Settling onto his bed to sleep, he had inexplicably left his clothes on, as if he were waiting for something. "I'll never understand why," he said. In minutes, police were swarming his house, rifling his shelves for Marx and Lenin. He had a reputation as a radical. He was imprisoned without trial in a maximum-security cell. His writings had angered the government, but he never learned which passages were to blame, or why. During his incarceration, which lasted a year and engendered a global campaign to free him, he wrote a book on rough prison-issue toilet paper.

Across his desk, Ngugi passed me a copy of his detention order, signed by Moi himself, then Kenya's vice president and minister for home affairs. When Moi became president and freed Ngugi and other political detainees, it was meant not to inaugurate a new era of liberalization, as it was portrayed, but "to clear the jails for his own prisoners," Ngugi said.

Pervading those years was a sense of threat, of a vaporous yet all-pervasive state hand. Once, the writer found himself unable to get a license to put on a play at the National Theatre in Nairobi. Government bureaucrats refused to give explanations; questions were simply referred to other bureaucrats in a maddening loop. "In the end, we would never know who had done what, and nobody would take responsibility, and yet the National Theatre was locked. It was very Kafkaesque," Ngugi said. "Even today, we can't say, 'So-and-so stopped the play.' All we can say is we were locked out."

That year marked the beginning of Ngugi's twenty-year forced exile. He was in London promoting a book, preparing to return to Kenya, when he received word that assassins were awaiting him at Jomo Kenyatta Airport. "The Cold War phrase was 'They will give you the red carpet,' " he said. It would be another fifteen years before he began writing *Wizard of the Crow,* the opening lines materializing in his head while he was riding in the car beside his wife in Orange, New Jersey. The early pages offer various popular (and fantastical) rumors about why the fictional ruler has been sick, a fitting start to a book in which the pervasiveness of rumor is a key theme. The ruler, like Moi, would exist in a kind of half-fabulous ontological realm, and into the void of reliable facts people would pour their imaginings; rumor became a function of dictatorship and a weapon against it. "Rumor takes wings when you no longer rely on official statements," Ngugi told me. "Rumor becomes a way of humanizing or demystifying a dictator." But its ubiquity also reflected the endless uncertainty of existence under Moi. Instructions would be passed from someone to someone, assassinations and atrocities would follow, and the links running back to their orchestrator were carefully effaced. "The word of mouth is very important," he said. "Moi would order the elimination of someone and it wasn't written anywhere."

62 **"more as recreation than a serious war":** John Kaiser, *If I Die* (Nairobi: Cana Publishing, 2003), p. 35.

62 **But what he witnessed now:** ibid., pp. 26–29.

62 **"the usual fights over cattle rustling":** ibid., p. 28.

62 **"Impossible!":** ibid., p. 29.

62 **"the best informed Christian"** and **"I did none of these things":** ibid., pp. 33–34.

63 **"the grumbling of what I was sure were giant forest hogs in the bush":** letter from John Kaiser to Don and Jackie Beumer, September 2, 1980.

64 **"lovely little gun"** and **Kaiser's tally of kills:** letter from John Kaiser to Don Beumer, Paul Sneva, and Peter Peterson, April 13, 1986.

64 **"I have just come back from a sick-call":** letter from John Kaiser to Don and Jackie Beumer, April 10, 1985.

65 **"nourish democratic institutions":** Hempstone, *Rogue Ambassador*, p. 91.

65 **the latest thrust of white domination:** Moi's biographer and amanuensis, Morton, argued that "just as the missionaries who came to Kenya never once considered the existing culture of the tribes they tried to 'civilize,' so the West has embarked on another bout of colonialism, imposing its governmental structures on people and leaders about whom they know little and care even less." See Morton, *Moi*, p. 165.

65 **the murder of Robert Ouko:** Chapter 5 of Hempstone's *Rogue Ambassador* contains an account. Moi and Biwott filed a suit against Hempstone in the Kenyan courts, alleging he had libeled them by linking them to the Ouko murder; they won a court injunction preventing the local newspaper from publishing excerpts. See Marc Lacey, "In Libel Case, Kenyan Wins Late Round Over Envoy," *New York Times*, August 23, 2001. See also Michael Hiltzik, "Who Killed Kenya's Foreign Minister?" *Los Angeles Times*, September 21, 1990.

66 **"what did appear obvious was that the murderer was too highly placed":** Hempstone, *Rogue Ambassador*, p. 69.

66 **issued a pastoral letter:** Jane Perlez, "Rising Political Discontent in Kenya Is Tarnishing Its Progressive Image," *New York Times*, July 29, 1990.

66 **Anglican bishop named Alexander Muge:** For information on the Muge case, see Throup and Hornsby, *Multi-Party Politics in Kenya*, pp. 200–211;

Hempstone, *Rogue Ambassador*, pp. 117–119; and Paul Gifford, *Christianity, Politics and Public Life in Kenya* (New York: Columbia University Press, 2009), p. 36.

67 **"the chap who never got malaria for 20 years":** letter from John Kaiser to Don and Jackie Beumer, January 17, 1990.

68 **James Ongera:** Kaiser, *If I Die*, pp. 37–39.

68 **"There are almost daily murders":** letter from John Kaiser to Carolita and Joe Mahoney, August 30, 1991. ·

68 **"I have quite a bit of building to do"** and **"I got a haircut":** letter from John Kaiser to Carolita and Joe Mahoney, February 23, 1992.

69 **"Tribal roots go much deeper than the shallow flower of democracy":** Morton, *Moi*, p. 23.

Self-serving and hypocritical as Moi's remarks obviously were, they reflected sentiments that had been expressed by some disinterested Western observers. "The splintered, struggling Africa of today cannot afford the luxury of multiparties and independent presses and honest debate," wrote David Lamb, a longtime *Los Angeles Times* correspondent, in the mid-1980s. "National institutions are not strong enough to withstand these pressures.... At this stage most African countries are best served by benign dictators." (See David Lamb, *The Africans* [New York: Vintage, 1987], pp. 57–58.)

69 **ethnically fractured nation:** An account of the so-called *Majimbo* movement can be found in Throup and Hornsby, *Multi-Party Politics in Kenya*, pp. 173–179. Should multiparty elections force Moi from power, *Majimbo* advocates warned, the dreaded Kikuyu would dominate. The solution: an ethnically pure Rift Valley populated by pastoralist inhabitants loyal to Moi.

69 **militias descended on opposition strongholds:** See ibid. To win the presidency, by law, a candidate required at least 25 percent of the vote in five of Kenya's eight provinces.

69 **By early 1992, even Kenya's cautious Catholic bishops were uniting:** In March 1992, the Catholic Church published a pastoral letter, signed by all eighteen Kenyan bishops, entitled "A Call to Justice, Love and Peace," which accused the government of abetting the rampant violence. A pastoral letter carried enormous moral authority in a country where an estimated one in four people was Catholic. But pastoral letters were typically swaddled in generalities. As historian Paul Gifford noted, Kenyan churchmen "were particularly prominent in challenging abuses of the one-party state. However, the actors were individual churchmen rather than the churches themselves. And this role was not played by many, for a large number supported Moi either

from ethnic or patrimonial-clientist considerations or out of a theological conviction that political involvement was not the role of churches." See Gifford, *Christianity, Politics and Public Life in Kenya*, p. 41.

6. The Clashes

70 **his rift with his elderly bishop:** Information regarding Kaiser's clash with Mugendi is based on various Kaiser letters and the author's interviews with Tom Keane.

70 **attacked the bishop's judgment in appointing a headmistress:** letter from John Kaiser to Bishop Mugendi, June 6, 1990.

72 **"Here in Africa you never discuss the Father":** letter from John Kaiser to Don and Jackie Beumer, June 28, 1993.

72 **"the Catholic failure as regards Human Rights":** letter from John Kaiser to Dick Quinn, June 12, 1992.

72 **"I can hardly be appointed away":** letter from John Kaiser to Maurice McGill, May 29, 1992.

72 **"I told him not to write the letter":** author's interview with Tom Keane.

73 **"My conscience is clear":** letter from John Kaiser to Dick Quinn, June 12, 1992.

73 **Violence was not Moi's only tactic:** See chapter 18 in Smith Hempstone, *Rogue Ambassador: An African Memoir* (Sewanee, Tennessee: University of the South Press, 1997) for an account of widespread electoral fraud in 1992.

73 **"having put our imprimatur on a flawed electoral process":** ibid., p. 267.

73 **After riots and protests:** Violence extended to polling day itself, December 29, 1992. At the Enoosupukia Trading Center in the Rift Valley, armed Masai warriors attacked and killed three Kikuyus who were waiting in line to vote, apparently because the Kikuyu flashed the two-finger salute of a party seeking to unseat Ntimama, the local incumbent. The result was the flight of many Kikuyu, who comprised the area's majority and favored Ntimama's defeat. See Government of Kenya, *Report of the Judicial Commission Appointed to Inquire into Tribal Clashes in Kenya* (informally called the Akiwumi Report, Nairobi, July 31, 1999).

74 **"Exile":** letter from John Kaiser to Carolita and Joe Mahoney, June 18, 1993.

74 **"These days it's mighty hard":** ibid.

74 **lowered himself to his knees before the bishop's car:** author's interview with Tom Keane.

75 **"People say I hate the Kikuyu":** William Ntimama quoted in Ethnic Clashes

Network, "Deception, Dispersal and Abandonment: A Narrative Account of the Displacement of Kenyans from Enoosupukia and Maela Based upon Witness, Church/NGO and Media Accounts," January 1995.

75 **"The British suppressed us":** Ntimama's remarks were delivered in a speech to parliament days after the raid. In this speech, he cast himself as a defender of Masai land rights against rapacious Kikuyu. He also said, "Mr. Deputy Speaker, how come everybody else and all the publications here were supporting the right of the Kikuyu to stay there and making sure that we all die, downstream? That is a situation that we definitely cannot tolerate, and if necessary we have to defend our rights and we will continue to defend them! We were provoked beyond any reasonable doubt. And our cattle were mutilated. . . . I am saying that we have lived with these people but we can no longer be suppressed! We can no longer be looted! We can no longer be milked!" See the Akiwumi Report, pp. 168–169.

75 **In October 1993, five hundred Masai warriors:** Details of the Enoosupukia attack are from the Akiwumi Report, pp. 165–170; "Deception, Dispersal and Abandonment"; and Keith B. Richburg, "Kenya's Ethnic Conflict Drives Farmers Off Land; Ruling Politicians Blamed for Masai Raids," *Washington Post*, March 17, 1994. Even as he stoked hatreds, Ntimama would claim the Enoosupukia clash was a spontaneous uprising against the Kikuyu sparked by the beheading of a Masai elder, an incident that almost certainly never happened—the alleged victim's son, who was supposed to be present, did not report it to the police. Moreover, even before the phantom decapitation, some three thousand men dressed as Masai warriors—believed to be Ntimama's private army—were seen assembling near the Enoosupukia Trading Center. That number exceeded the area's entire Masai population. It was clear they had been ferried in for war.

76 **"No way":** Ntimama quoted in Richburg, "Kenya's Ethnic Conflict Drives Farmers Off Land."

76 **Attorney General Amos Wako:** Wako's and Ntimama's comments are taken from Bill Berkeley, "An Encore for Chaos?" *The Atlantic Monthly* 277, no. 2 (1996): 30–36.

7. The Terrible Place

77 **Of Maela, people remembered the dust:** The most detailed account of conditions at Maela can be found in chapters 4–7 of John Kaiser's *If I Die* (Nairobi:

Cana Publishing, 2003). I have also drawn from Kaiser's letters; from Ethnic Clashes Network, "Deception, Dispersal and Abandonment: A Narrative Account of the Displacement of Kenyans from Enoosupukia and Maela Based upon Witness, Church/NGO and Media Accounts"; and from interviews with eyewitnesses Nuala Brangan, Sarah Wamboi, Colin Davies, and Francis Mwangi.

77   **"This terrible place"**: letter from John Kaiser to Tony Barnicle, August 12, 1994.

77   **a two-year-old girl sitting in the dust**: Kaiser, *If I Die*, p. 43.

78   **Julius Chege**: ibid., p. 64; author's interview with Chege's widow, Sarah Wamboi, who said she ultimately spent a year and a half in the camp.

78   **"but he refused without giving a reason"**: letter from John Kaiser to Tony Barnicle, August 12, 1994.

78   **"I pray that those who are responsible"**: ibid.

78   **"a bunch of bureaucrats"**: Kaiser, *If I Die*, p. 45.

79   **"Compared with these big camps"**: letter from John Kaiser to Tony Barnicle, August 12, 1994.

79   **It reminded Kaiser of Longfellow's *Evangeline***: ibid.

80   **He told them he loved them**: Kaiser, *If I Die*, p. 49; the BBC Monitoring Service, "President Moi Visits Rift Valley, Calls on Kikuyus to Join KANU," October 3, 1994.

80   **Maela needed to be erased**: Details on the razing of Maela and Kaiser's arrest and removal are from *If I Die*, pp. 57–73; author's interview with Francis Mwangi.

81   **They had twenty minutes to evacuate**: "Police Seal off Clash Victims' Compound," Agence France-Presse, January 2, 1995; "Police Move Displaced Kikuyus out of Sports Stadium," Agence France-Presse, January 5, 1995.

81   **Kilian Kleinschmit**: Manoah Esipisu, "Kenya's Displaced People in Desolate Conditions," Reuters News, December 27, 1994.

83   **Kenyan Roman Catholic bishops issued a statement**: "Roman Catholic Bishops Accuse Government of Atrocities," Agence France-Presse, January 13, 1995; Nicholas Kotch, "Kenyan Bishops Attack 'Inhuman' Administration," Reuters News, January 13, 1995.

83   **Kaiser showed signs**: ibid. See also Robert M. Press, "Nomads and Farmers in Kenya War Over Increasingly Scarce Land," *Christian Science Monitor*, January 18, 1995.

84   **"No doubt to protect me"**: Kaiser, *If I Die*, p. 93.

84 **"Some people aren't talking who are supposed to be talking":** author's interview with Francis Mwangi.

84 **Months earlier, another had been murdered:** This was Father Martin Boyle, killed on a highway near Nairobi in September 1994 during an alleged robbery.

8. The Raid

85 **Charles Mbuthi Gathenji:** Information in this chapter is drawn primarily from interviews with Gathenji.

9. Lolgorien

94 **Kaiser's new home:** The description of Lolgorien is based on the author's personal observations, interviews with inhabitants, and Kaiser's letters.

94 **"the most beautiful in the world":** John Kaiser, *If I Die* (Nairobi: Cana Publishing, 2003), p. 93.

94 **Mohammed Yusuf Haji had ordered the eviction:** Akiwumi Report, *Government of Kenya: Report of the Judicial Commission Appointed to Inquire into Tribal Clashes in Kenya* (Nairobi: July 31, 1999), pp. 181–182.

95 **They ate it "for breakfast, lunch, and tea":** author's interview with Nuala Brangan.

95 **Maria Mokona:** Details regarding Mokona's background and interactions with Kaiser are from the author's interviews with Mokona in Lolgorien, translated from the Swahili by Alan Selempo.

95 **Kaiser took to the building:** author's interviews with Sophia Gucho, Winnie Joseph, and Leah Agan.

96 **"I should be studying Masai":** letter from John Kaiser to Joe and Carolita Mahoney, June 23, 1995.

96 **a twelve-year-old Kuria girl:** author's interview with Leah Agan.

96 **"Lolgorien is quite a town":** letter from John Kaiser to Carolita and Joe Mahoney, December 16, 1995.

97 **"major falsehoods":** Kaiser, *If I Die*, p. 71.

97 *Res clamat domino*: ibid., p. 90.

97 **"a serious mistake":** ibid., p. 89.

97 **"Is the exaggerated adulation given to President Moi":** ibid., p. 90.

98 **"paramount evil":** ibid., p. 85.

98   **"Why then do we so easily accept the admonition"**: ibid., p. 88.

98   **"I have no intention of leaving this parish voluntarily"**: ibid., p. 94.

98   **"There is nothing in it against faith or morals"**: letter from John Kaiser to Carolita and Joe Mahoney, December 16, 1995.

99   **"the need for our society to do something in a unified and organized way"**: letter from John Kaiser, addressed "Dear Mill Hill Brothers and Sisters," undated.

99   **the Rwandan genocide:** Moi's stance on the genocide was hardly reassuring. As the UN War Crimes Tribunal moved to bring the *genocidaires* to justice, some found sanctuary in His Excellency's bosom. Moi threatened to jail agents of the tribunal if they pursued Hutu Power extremists into Nairobi, where a least a dozen were believed to reside. Moi had counted as a friend the former Rwandan president Juvénal Habyarimana, whose mysterious death had provided a catalyst for the mass killings. See John Balzar, "Kenya President Offers Shelter to Rwanda Suspects Sought by War Tribunal," *Los Angeles Times*, October 6, 1995.

100 **By Kantai's account:** Details regarding Kantai's story are taken from a transcript of his testimony before the Akiwumi Commission.

101 **"to reach these backward Masai herdspeople"** and **"a group of pretty young Masai girls"**: letter from John Kaiser to "Lou & Al," March 12, 1996.

102 **"run down"**: letter from John Kaiser to Carolita and Joe Mahoney, April 12, 1996.

102 **"We should not go mad"**: letter from John Kaiser to Carolita and Joe Mahoney, April 27, 1996.

102 **build a house for the widow and children of Julius Chege:** letter from John Kaiser to Carolita and Joe Mahoney, January 12, 1997.

103 **"He could easily slap you"**: author's interview with Melchizedek Ondieki.

103 **"The cat woke up & looked at me"**: letter from John Kaiser to Carolita and Joe Mahoney, January 12, 1997.

104 **"I'm perfectly safe"**: author's interview with Carolita Mahoney.

104 **monk named Larry Timmons:** The policeman in question was named Francis Kimanzi Mbaya; it wasn't until July 2004 that the High Court in Nakuru sentenced him to ten years in prison. See "Police Officer Charged with Murder of Irish Priest," Associated Press, January 28, 1997; Paul Cullen, "Shadowy Death of an Irish Idealist Under African Skies," *Irish Times*, February 1, 1997; "Andrews to Query Inquest Delays on Mission Killing," *Irish Times*, November 22, 1999; Francis Ngige, "3 Assessors Find Policeman Guilty," *East*

African Standard, May 6, 2004; "AP Jailed for Shooting Monk," *East African Standard*, July 26, 2004.

105 **1997 elections:** Along with terror, Moi could rely on an arsenal of other tactics, such as the gerrymandering of parliamentary districts. In his Rift Valley stronghold, he ensured that more than two million voters were registered (twice as many as in the more populous Kikuyu central highlands). He waited until November, a month before the election, to legalize the opposition Safina party (founded by Muite and paleontologist Richard Leakey), too late for it to field a presidential candidate. Week after week, while essentially ignoring his rivals, the state media highlighted Moi's campaigning as he flew between rallies in a fifty-million-dollar jet. See the Akiwumi Report; Human Rights Watch, "Playing with Fire: Weapons Proliferation, Political Violence and Human Rights in Kenya," issued May 2002; and Stephen Buckley's coverage in the *Washington Post*: "Tribal Tensions Explode in Carnage in Kenyan City; Government Is Accused of Inciting Violence in Which Coastal Clans Attack Interlopers," August 21, 1997; "Tribal Fears Play Powerful Role in Today's Kenyan Presidential Vote," December 29, 1997; "Election Chaos Brings Accusations in Kenya," December 31, 1997; "Kenya Electoral Panel Names Moi Winner in Flawed Presidential Vote," January 5, 1998; "Kenyan Leader Vows Reforms; Sworn In for 5th Term, Moi Targets Economy, Graft," January 6, 1998.

106 **"Here in Africa Kenya has always been called a stooge":** from an October 1997 interview in Alec Russell, *Big Men, Little People* (New York: New York University Press, 2000), pp. 79–80.

107 **the regime found gangs of unemployed young men:** Davan Maharaj, "Rights Group Blames Ruling Party for 1997 Kenyan Violence," *Los Angeles Times*, June 1, 2002. The story details findings by the Human Rights Watch, which cited witnesses who said the ruling party had instigated the violence and aimed it at "non-indigenous" groups in places where the opposition had prevailed at the last election.

107 **"a lot of chaos":** letter from John Kaiser to Carolita and Joe Mahoney, November 15, 1997.

108 **"Moi needed and wanted Masai political support":** author's interview with an unnamed American diplomat. As one of Moi's enforcers, and—later— a man accused of sex crimes, Sunkuli was "unsavory enough that a lot of people didn't want to deal with him in the embassy," another American diplomat told me. These diplomats served at the U.S. embassy in Nairobi in the

last years of Kaiser's life; they were serving elsewhere in the State Department when I spoke to them, and they granted interviews only on the condition that I would not use their names.

108   **"bully-boy"**: letter from John Kaiser to Paul Muite, September 6, 1996.

108   **"Nobody here wants him . . ."**: letter from John Kaiser to Carolita and Joe Mahoney, December 10, 1997.

108   **Sunkuli allegedly urged the Masai:** Akiwumi Report, p. 188, where it is also noted that Sunkuli held authority over the impassive local police and that "the concerned officers in Trans Mara must have feared taking a position in the clashes which would have displeased him."

108   **"escape route" and "But everything is beautifully green"**: letter from John Kaiser to Carolita and Joe Mahoney, December 10, 1997.

109   **"Because of the murder & mayhem"**: letter from John Kaiser to Carolita and Joe Mahoney, November 28, 1997.

109   **He expected that a Moi-Sunkuli victory was preordained:** letter from John Kaiser to Carolita and Joe Mahoney, December 10, 1997; letter from John Kaiser to Paul Muite, December 19, 1997.

109   **"almost no one"**: letter from John Kaiser to Paul Muite, December 19, 1997.

109   **"He is my biggest worry"**: letter from John Kaiser to Carolita and Joe Mahoney, January 12, 1998.

110   **Moi won reelection:** James C. McKinley Jr., "Kenya's Leader Wins a 5th Term, but Opposition Candidates Gain," *New York Times*, January 5, 1998. Kikuyu runner-up Mwai Kibaki, a former vice president, took 1.8 million (31 percent); the remaining 27 percent of voters were split between three other candidates. Kibaki drew the Kikuyus, Raila Odinga the Luos, Charity Ngilu the Akambas, Michael Wamalwa the Luhyias.

110   **"The Catholic Bishops know all this"**: letter from John Kaiser to Carolita and Joe Mahoney, January 12, 1998.

110   **"We are determined to eliminate corruption"**: Daniel arap Moi quoted in Stephen Buckley, "Kenyan Leader Vows Reforms," *Washington Post*, January 6, 1998.

110   **Kaiser's physical afflictions:** from declassified portions of the FBI's FD-302 report of its interview on December 8, 2000, with a Nairobi doctor (name redacted) who treated Kaiser twenty-eight times from 1994 to 1998.

110   **"I'm wearing down, no doubt"**: letter from John Kaiser to Carolita and Joe Mahoney, April 3, 1998.

111   **"Africans have their own way"**: author's interview with Colin Davies.

111 **"Was my voice going to make a difference?"**: Colin Davies, *Mission to the Masai (1959–2003)* (apparently church-published in 2006; the book cites no publisher).

111 **"Most of our priests are now African"**: letter from John Kaiser, addressed "Dear Bill" (apparently Bill Vos), July 14, 1998.

111 **"I went & hid my motorcycle in the bush"**: letter from John Kaiser to Carolita and Joe Mahoney, May 6, 1998.

111 **A pride of "bad lions"**: letter from John Kaiser addressed "Dear Bill" (apparently Bill Vos), July 14, 1998; author's interview with Melchizedek Ondieki.

112 **On the morning of August 7, 1998:** An account of the U.S. embassy bombings can be found in Lawrence Wright, *The Looming Tower: Al-Qaeda and the Road to 9-11* (New York: Random House, 2006), pp. 306–316.

113 **"That bombing had nothing to do with Kenya, I believe"**: letter from John Kaiser to Carolita and Joe Mahoney, August 10, 1998.

10. The Tribunal

115 **he convened a commission:** The Moi-appointed commissions are innumerable. My favorite was constituted to investigate reports of flesh-eating devil worshipers said to be at large in the land. In August 1999, the Presidential Commission of Inquiry revealed—relying on anecdotal evidence, and citing witnesses who claimed to have passed ghostlike through walls and metamorphosed into snakes—that this cannibalistic, blood-drinking cabal had infiltrated schools and churches, abetted by the Latter-day Saints, the Freemasons, the Seventh-Day Adventists, and something called the "Lucifer Golfing Society." An internal U.S. embassy memo dryly observed: "Most members of the commission are senior clergymen of traditional churches. Some observers suspect their dislike of more recent competitors, such as the Mormons, colored their report."

115 **Three judges:** The chairman was a Cambridge-educated court of appeals justice named Akilano Akiwumi, who had served on the Ouko Commission earlier in the decade (Moi had it dissolved when it became inconvenient). Also on the panel was a High Court judge, Sarah Ondeyo. The vice chair was another court of appeals justice, Samuel Bosire, famous for having presided, twelve years earlier, over the Otieno burial case, which had become a national obsession. (This case involved a Kikuyu widow's fight for burial rights to her dead husband. S. M. Otieno, who happened to be one of Gathenji's legal

mentors, had been a renowned and urbane criminal defense attorney. His estranged Luo clan insisted his corpse was theirs to bury, in keeping with their tribal customs. In an evolving Kenya, the clash provided a window on the enduring Kikuyu-Luo rift and on the tension between modern mores and traditional practices. Discounting myriad witnesses who said the lawyer had wished to be buried in Nairobi, rather than in Luoland, the good justice Bosire sided with the Luo clan members. It was likely a decision dictated by Moi, intended as a sop to the Luo and a humiliation to the Kikuyu. Blaine Harden devotes chapter 3 of *Africa: Dispatches from a Fragile Continent* [New York: Houghton Mifflin, 1991] to the Otieno case. He describes witnessing a Special Branch officer—clumsily masquerading as a reporter for the *Daily Nation*—grilling the widow's lawyer about whether he thought the verdict was fair, thereby tempting criticism of Moi. This convinced Harden that the president had had a hand in the verdict.)

115 **"the charade of the decade":** Andrew Ngwiri, *Daily Nation*, July 26, 1998.

115 **"a waste of time":** author's interview with Colin Davies.

115 **"John, we have to sort this out":** author's interview with Tom Keane.

116 **Keane quickly sensed the depth of Kaiser's fear:** Details regarding Kaiser's behavior during this period are taken from the author's interviews with Tom Keane.

116 **"My child"** and **" . . . *Since gold is tested in the fire*":** These quotations are from chapter 2 of the Book of Sirach (Ecclesiasticus) in the Catholic Bible, by all accounts a Scripture that Kaiser returned to repeatedly in his last years. The quote on the memorial plaque that hung in Kaiser's Lolgorien church came from the same chapter.

117 **But his testimony was cloaked in generalities:** Maguta Kimemia, "Ndingi Says Top Leaders Implicated," *Daily Nation*, July 23, 1998. (Ndingi, long one of the Catholic Church's human rights lodestars, had been in the news for years for daring to speak out. In 1988, when Moi's assistant minister of national guidance, Shariff Nassir, announced that public queueing would proceed "whether people liked it or not," Ndingi denounced the remarks as "totalitarian." See Blaine Harden, "Kenya's Democracy du Jour," *Washington Post*, August 14, 1988.)

117 **a former state lawyer named David Maari:** Gichuru Njihia, "Witness Blames Moi, AG for Molo Violence," *Daily Nation*, July 24, 1998.

118 **John Keen:** *Daily Nation*, November 6, 1998.

118 **an investigation into the slayings of thirteen Kikuyus:** The official was

Joseph Chumo, quoted in Michael Njuguna and Mark Agutu, "Ethnic Violence Claimed 36 Lives in Two Years, Inquiry Told," *Daily Nation*, March 22,
1999.

118   **When Ntimama appeared before the commission:** Michael Njuguna and
Mark Agutu, "Ntimama States His Stand on 'Majimbo,' " *Daily Nation*, April
14, 1999. For further details on *Majimboism*, see David Throup and Charles
Hornsby, *Multi-Party Politics in Kenya*, pp. 173–199.

119   **"I know far too much":** letter from John Kaiser to Carolita and Joe Mahoney,
undated but likely December 1998.

119   **"I am old":** author's interview with Melchizedek Ondieki.

119   **he paid a surprise visit to Julius Sunkuli's home:** from declassified portions
of the FBI's FD-302 report of its interview with Sunkuli on December 6, 2000;
from the Rift Valley CID's report of its interview with Sunkuli, dated December 6, 2000; and from the Kaiser inquest testimony of Father John O'Brien,
who accompanied Kaiser on the visit.

120   **"very out on a limb":** letter from John Kaiser to Alfonse Borgman, December
6, 1998.

120   **"easy to break":** letter from John Kaiser, addressed "Dear Maurice" (possibly
Maurice Crean), March 9, 1999.

121   **Bernard Chunga:** Even U.S. ambassador Johnnie Carson, whose public criticism of the Moi regime tended to be mild or nonexistent, would single out
Chunga as symptomatic of the regime's corruption. From an internal State
Department memo of April 2000 bearing Carson's name: "In a less-than-
surprising (or sterling) defense of the GOK [government of Kenya], Chief
Justice Bernard Chunga declined to admit that corruption could be found
in the judiciary. At the official launch of the high courts criminal division in
early March, Chunga told the assembly with a straight face that no one had
condemned the judiciary for corrupt practices. Apparently the new CJ has
quickly forgotten the unimplemented Kwach Commission report, which, in
1999 drew up a laundry list of ills, including corruption, from which the judiciary suffers." In September 2003, soon after leaving Kenya, Carson gave a
speech in the States in which he lauded Kikabi, the new president, for ousting
Chunga as chief justice. As Carson said in his mild way, Chunga was "widely
regarded as ineffective, corrupt and easily influenced by officials in President
Moi's former government."

121   **Kaiser faced the room:** Kaiser's testimony is taken from a transcript of the
proceedings. Kaiser wanted to testify. In an interview, Francis Mwangi told

me, "He wanted to be there. Very few people could. I'd be afraid to say what we knew."

123 **"a white Catholic priest"** and **"The mere fact that a man is wearing a collar":** Oanga Oyugi, "Sunkuli, DC Turn Preachers at Rally," *People*, February 9, 1999.

124 **"I think they are really playing with me":** letter from John Kaiser to Carolita and Joe Mahoney, February 8, 1999.

125 **"We could be killed":** author's interview with Nuala Brangan.

125 **Stephen Mwita:** After Kaiser stepped down, the tribunal agreed to hear from two witnesses he had brought. The first was Stephen Mwita, the subsistence farmer, who recounted how the provincial commissioner, Haji, had come to Lolgorien in early 1989 and demanded that non-Masais like himself, who had been growing maize and millet on a fifteen-acre plot for nearly a quarter of a century, abandon their properties. Police arrived soon after to torch the houses.

Bosire: "Did you see them do it?"

Mwita: "My Lords, I witnessed this. They even burnt my house. They were merciless because they also burnt the stores."

Then came Francis Kantai, twenty-eight years old, Kaiser's catechist. He explained that he was studying to be a Catholic brother.

"And you will become the assistant to the Father?" Bosire asked.

"Not really."

Bosire's words were barbed: "Carrying his bibles?"

Kantai told his story of being coerced by police into burning Kisii houses in 1989. There was little Kantai could give in the way of useful detail. He could not recall the month this happened. He did not know the names of the police who had put him up to it. It had happened in broad daylight, he said, but he could not identify their vehicles.

126 **"It was exhausting but worth it":** letter from John Kaiser, addressed "Dear Maurice" (likely Maurice Crean), March 9, 1999.

126 **"Don't worry, I'm a good shot":** author's interview with Nuala Brangan.

127 **he'd prevented the beating of a friend:** author's interview with William Meek.

127 **he'd grabbed a lug wrench:** author's interview with Joseph Okemwa.

128 **Noah arap Too:** The exchange between Too and Akiwumi is taken from Benson Wambugu, "Ex-CID Boss Testifies on Why Ministers Were Not Charged," *People*, June 3, 1999.

129   **The report described the raid on Gathenji's home:** Akiwumi Report, pp. 43–45.

129   **He refused to release the report:** The report would not be released until October 2002, as Moi's era was ending. Named as a suspect warranting further investigation, Biwott promptly sued to have his name removed, his argument being that he had not been called to testify and hadn't had a chance to defend himself; in December 2002, the courts acquiesced.

129   **the following exchange occurred:** author's interview with Tom Keane. Sunkuli gave an account of the meeting, saying Kaiser "boasted" of having won the job for him, in a statement to the Rift Valley CID, dated December 6, 2000.

11. The Girls

130   **they set out from Kilgoris:** Details regarding the ensuing chase are taken from the author's interviews with Tom Keane. The description of the road is based on the author's observations while traveling it.

132   **Keane perceived a hint of pride:** Keane's observations about Kaiser during this period and the details regarding the confrontation with the game wardens are taken from the author's interviews with Tom Keane.

134   **Kaiser came down with typhoid:** Records of St. Joseph's Hospital in Kilgoris indicate that Kaiser was admitted for treatment of typhoid and malaria on May 31, 1999, and was discharged three days later.

134   **Her account of what happened next:** Anne Sawoyo told the story at the Kaiser inquest in October 2003, the transcript of which provides the quotes here. She also gave an account to the Kenyan police, the FBI, and to the BBC, which aired her remarks in its documentary *Death of a Priest*.

135   **Florence Mpayei:** Details of Mpayei's story are taken from accounts she gave pursuant to her criminal case against Sunkuli, to the BBC, and to the UN forum on women's justice.

136   **Sunkuli arranged a meeting with her:** author's interview with Martha Koome.

136   **Sunkuli admitted to an affair with Mpayei but characterized her as a spurned lover:** Philo Ikonya, "Envied or Pitied—Girl Who Accused Minister of Rape Excited Jealousy at Home," *Daily Nation*, November 29, 2000.

136   **FIDA hid both of Sunkuli's accusers in a house:** Sawoyo's account of the raid on the safe house and its aftermath are taken from her testimony at the Kaiser inquest.

137 **Kantai admitted to giving it up:** Kantai's account is taken from the BBC's *Death of a Priest*.

137 **Sunkuli portrayed the raid:** Sunkuli's account is taken from the Rift Valley CID's report of its interview with Sunkuli, dated December 6, 2000.

137 **one story has him shimmying down a pipe:** author's interview with Francis Kaiser.

137 **Those closest to Kaiser believed he feared deportation more than death:** author's interview with Carolita Mahoney.

137 **Kaiser appeared in Gathenji's lobby:** author's interview with Charles Mbuthi Gathenji.

138 MYSTERY DEEPENS OVER MISSING AMERICAN PRIEST: *Sunday Standard*, October 31, 1999.

138 **"a defender of clash victims":** "Fr. Kaiser: A Defender of Clash Victims," *Daily Nation*, November 1, 1999.

138 **"a mockery of the law":** from an editorial in *Daily Nation*, October 31, 1999.

138 **the intervention of the then U.S. ambassador:** author's interview with Johnnie Carson; declassified State Department memo of November 1999.

139 **"a beacon of hope":** Gakiha Weru, "A Beacon of Hope in a Sea of Misery," *East African Standard*, November 7, 1999.

139 **"designed and executed a plan":** press conference, November 8, 1999.

139 **a flattering profile:** Stephen Mburu, "Sunkuli's Tough Climb," *Daily Nation*, December 12, 1999.

139 **A *Daily Nation* reporter trekked to Lolgorien:** *Daily Nation*, November 17, 1999.

140 **"Here in Kenya I still get some press coverage"** and **"I think the President feels like a man on a small island":** letter from John Kaiser to Carolita and Joe Mahoney, November 25, 1999.

140 **"I think a *real* professional killer":** letter from John Kaiser, addressed "Dear Peter" (likely Peter Housman), November 29, 1999.

140 **"rather weak and tired"** and **"If the police come with a trumped up reason":** letter from John Kaiser to Don and Jackie Beumer, December 8, 1999.

140 **"before we all hang up our boots":** letter from John Kaiser to Don and Jackie Beumer, December 23, 1999.

12. We Will All Be Sorted Out

141 **"I hope we aren't all rounded up":** letter from John Kaiser to Carolita and Joe Mahoney, March 11, 2000. In a letter to them on April 16, 2000, he wrote:

"We all went to the best hotel in Nairobi and ate expensive food and wondered what the poor people were doing."

141 **Reading the citation aloud:** The text is reproduced in the *Congressional Record*, 106th Cong. 2d sess., 2000, 146, pt. 15: 21281. October 6, 2000.

142 **"That's one of those thugs":** This and Kaiser's other remarks and experiences in the company of Beumer are from the author's interview with Don Beumer.

143 **Kaiser told Vos they were from CID:** author's interview with Bill Vos.

143 **"You know if you go, you won't get away with it":** author's interview with Nuala Brangan.

143 **"I very much wish to support you":** letter from John Kaiser to Paul Muite, April 5, 2000.

143 SUNKULI ACCUSED OF SEX ATTACK: *Daily Nation*, May 26, 2000.

144 **a major achievement:** author's interview with Judith Thongori.

144 **Kaiser had a guest that summer:** Kleinschmit's account of her summer in Lolgorien is from the author's interview with Camille Kleinschmit.

144 **"I would like to grow old gracefully":** letter from John Kaiser to Carolita and Joe Mahoney, July 1, 2000.

145 **He decided to rescue her:** Details regarding Kaiser's attempt to rescue Sawoyo are taken from the author's interview with Camille Kleinschmit and from Sawoyo's inquest testimony.

145 **"depressed and fearful":** letter from John Kaiser to Paul Muite, undated.

145 **Kaiser was having tea in the Kilgoris parish house:** This scene is drawn from the author's interview with James Juma.

146 **"I am considered enemy no. one by the Kenyan government":** letter from John Kaiser addressed to "Richard & Ann," July 19, 2000.

146 **Father Cornelius Schilder:** Details regarding Schilder's visit are taken from the author's interview with Cornelius Schilder and from his testimony at the inquest, as recounted in "Kaiser Named Moi and Sunkuli," *Daily Nation*, May 21, 2005.

147 **Along came Bernard Phelan:** Details regarding Phelan's visit are taken from the author's interview with Bernard Phelan.

147 **Kaiser gave two thousand shillings to Helen Katim:** author's interview with Helen Katim at her farm.

148 **Kaiser got a personal warning:** author's interview with Melchizedek Ondieki, who identified the visitor as a game ranger, and the account of Paul Muite, who said Kaiser relayed word that he'd been warned by a security officer. Muite repeated the claim in a September 16, 2000, letter to U.S. senator Paul Wellstone.

148   **Kaiser complained to one of his catechists:** author's interview with Romulus
      Ochieng.

148   *Utaona moto:* author's interview with Francis Kantai.

148   **"At present our Honorable Minister is a minor obstacle":** Letter from John
      Kaiser to Martin van Leeuwen, August 15, 2000.

149   **The letter that would summon him from Lolgorien:** Details on Kaiser's
      mood and movements from August 19–23 are taken from the FBI's final
      report into the death of Father John Kaiser, April 19, 2001, and from the
      author's interviews with Lucas Agan, Melchizedek Ondieki, Colin Davies,
      Marten van Leeuwen, Francis Mwangi, and Paul Boyle.

150   **Someone gave Kaiser a newspaper that said Florence Mpayei was firing her
      lawyers:** author's interview with Francis Mwangi.

150   **Kaiser called the nuncio:** Details regarding this conversation and subsequent
      visits with Tonucci are taken from the nuncio's written account in "Consider-
      ations on the FBI Report on the Death of Fr. John Kaiser," May 3, 2001. That
      the visit concerned the nuncio's request for Kaiser's views on a successor to
      Bishop Davies comes from the CID's account of its interview with Tonucci.

150   **Bishop Davies:** Davies's first account of Kaiser's state of mind is from the
      BBC's *Death of a Priest*; his later account is from a conversation with this
      author.

150   **"but if it's urgent then it must be Politics":** letter from John Kaiser to Helen
      and Peter Housman, August 21, 2000.

153   **The watchman noticed a truck:** The watchman's account is taken from
      declassified portions of the FBI's FD-302 reports of interviews with the
      watchmen (names redacted) on August 30, 2000.

154   **The butchers, too, noticed the truck:** The butchers' account is taken from
      declassified portions of the FBI's FD-302 reports of interviews with the
      butchers (names redacted) on August 31, 2000.

154   **police found a stack of Kenyan shillings:** "Moi Welcomes FBI in Kaiser
      Murder Probe," *Standard*, August 27, 2000.

154   **Dr. Alex Olumbe:** The pathologist's assessment is from Olumbe's autopsy
      report, dated August 28, 2000.

155   **Dr. Ling Kituyi:** author's interview with Kituyi.

13. The Bureau

156   **the priest's death was a tinderbox:** The ambassador's reaction to Kaiser's
      death is from the author's interview with Johnnie Carson.

156   **"anchor state"**: from declassified State Department memos, which also describe Kenya's significance as the region's undisputed economic powerhouse. Kenya had the best port between Suez and South Africa; its transportation routes were the veins and arteries of commerce for great parts of eastern and central Africa; it gave sanctuary to hundreds of thousands of refugees from war- and famine-racked neighbors; and it served as a staging ground for humanitarian relief efforts in Sudan, Somalia, Burundi, Congo, and Rwanda.

156   **"an unguided missile"**: author's interview with American diplomat who wished to remain anonymous.

157   **Carson marched into the stately Nairobi offices of Kenya's attorney general:** Details of Carson's visit to Amos Wako are taken from the author's interviews with Johnnie Carson and William Corbett.

158   **"Those who killed him"**: from David Mugonyi, "Kaiser Killed to 'Silence Church,' " *Daily Nation*, August 31, 2000.

158   **"this terrible crime"**: from Andrew England, "Thousands Attend Mass for Slain American Priest," Associated Press, August 30, 2000.

158   **Some five thousand people waited along the roads:** "Thousands Go to Mass for U.S. Priest," Associated Press, August 30, 2000.

158   **Vos was struck by the incredible damage to Kaiser's head:** author's interview with Bill Vos.

159   **Florence Mpayei appeared in a Nairobi courtroom:** Pamela Chepkemei, "Drop My Sunkuli Rape Case," *Daily Nation*, September 1, 2000. Nearly three months later, a *Daily Nation* reporter found Mpayei with Sunkuli at the Fairview Hotel. Though she had dropped the case against Sunkuli, nevertheless "she insists she was raped" on the red carpet of his government office. This, the newspaper noted with what seemed inconceivable coarseness, had "excited jealousy" in her hometown of Kilgoris, where—according to an anonymous source—other girls had been "laid on grass." The reporter assessed her character as comprising "coyness, shyness and spurts of boldness," and quoted her uncle, a Masai chief, as saying that a circumcised fourteen-year-old girl like Mpayei was considered a woman and could have sex, the implication being that there had been no crime. Sunkuli cast Mpayei's complaint as the fabrication of a spurned woman. "The minister does not deny having an intimate relationship with Florence, but he says that was all. Florence had wanted to be his wife, but he refused. He is already married to Lucy," the story read. (See Philo Ikonya, "Envied or Pitied—Girl Who Accused Minister of Rape Excited Jealousy at Home," *Daily Nation*, November 29, 2000.)

159 **Speaking to Rift Valley police, Mpayei would give an explanation:** Mpayei, then attending the Afro Dite Beauty School in Nairobi, gave this account to the Rift Valley Criminal Investigation Department on December 7, 2000, according to the report.

159 **"My conscience is clear":** "I Have Nothing to Hide: Sunkuli," *Daily Nation*, September 2, 2000.

160 **In an exchange with reporter Andrew Harding:** from *Death of a Priest*.

160 **"It simply looks too perfect a murder to fit that bill":** This and subsequent *Newsline* quotes are from Mwenda Njoka, "The Sinister Motive in Father Kaiser's Killing," *Newsline*, September 4–17, 2000.

160 **"cannot be excluded" and "No one has any moral right":** from a declassified State Department report, September 2000.

161 **"When deaths occur, people say many things":** "Moi Condemns Rumors on Priest's Death," *Daily Nation*, August 27, 2000.

161 **The FBI team:** Graney's and Corbett's accounts of the investigation are taken from the author's interviews with Thomas Graney and William Corbett.

162 **"You are already compromised":** author's interview with Melchizedek Ondieki.

162 **the slayings of five other Catholic clerics:** The unsolved slayings involved Brother Larry Timmons, a politically active Catholic monk shot to death near Nakuru in January 1997 by a policeman who called it an accident; Father Luigi Andeni, a priest who had tried to settle local ethnic conflicts and was killed in his Samburu sitting room in September 1998 in what was deemed a robbery; Father Martin Boyle, killed on a highway near Nairobi in September 1994 in another apparent robbery; Father Luigi Graiff, killed by raiders in Samburu in January 1981 for unexplained reasons; and Father Michael Stallone, killed by bandits in November 1965.

162 **"Those who knew Kaiser recall him as humble":** *Congressional Record*, 106th Cong., 2d sess., 2000, 146, pt. 15: 21281.

163 **"Clearly, there are questions":** *Daily Nation*, September 28, 2000.

163 **"With the Embassy bombing trial commencing":** from an internal FBI memo dated November 22, 2000.

164 **"Father Kaiser was just a footnote":** author's interview with Tom Neer.

165 **Villagers told a strange story:** This account is from a declassified portion of the FBI's FD-302 report of its interviews in Kiambu on September 21, 2000, and from the author's interviews with Thomas Graney and William Corbett.

166 **David Mwania:** Mwania's account is from declassified portions of the FBI's FD-302 report of its interview with Mwania on September 7, 2000.

167   **One guard recalled having heard the rattling, thumping sound:** The guard is identified as Paul Omunga in a report entitled "Psychological Autopsy on Fr. John Anthony Kaiser (deceased)," by Dr. F. G. Njenga, December 2000.

167   **a different account to a BBC reporter:** The guard is identified as Paul Omouga in the documentary *Death of a Priest*, where he gives this account.

169   **"He seems to be sort of walking into death":** Colin Davies quoted in *Death of a Priest*.

170   **"provided no provable evidence that any high-ranking GOK official had committed a crime":** from an internal FBI memo to Deputy Director Thomas Pickard, dated October 22, 2001.

171   **the agents interviewed the men on Muite's list:** from an internal FBI memo to Deputy Director Thomas Pickard, dated October 22, 2001. It should be noted that these reports, in the form I received them, were heavily redacted. The Freedom of Information Act affords the FBI broad discretion to white out what it doesn't want publicized. Even in a closed case, the basis for withholding information can range from shielding informants to the supposed need to protect an uncharged suspect's privacy. Since you don't see what you're not given, it's often impossible to determine the Bureau's logic in any particular case.

171   **He explained that three strangers pulled up:** The account of the three men is from declassified portions of the FBI's FD-302 report of its interview with a man named "Kihara" on September 4, 2000.

172   **"In European cases there are words one believes":** Graham Greene, *The Heart of the Matter* (New York: Penguin, 1991), p. 140.

172   **"During our time in Gusiiland":** Sarah LeVine, with Robert LeVine, from *Mothers and Wives: Gusii Women of East Africa* (Chicago: University of Chicago Press, 1979), p. 315.

173   **The FBI sat down with him:** The details of the meeting with Francis Kantai are taken from declassified portions of the FBI's FD-302 report of its interview with Kantai on September 20, 2000, and from the author's interviews with Thomas Graney and William Corbett.

175   **Tonucci refused to release the letter:** In a press release issued on April 23, 2001, Giovanni Tonucci emphasized that the letter Kaiser had handed to him on the morning of August 23, 2000, "has nothing to do with the priest's death." In May 2001, Tonucci would also criticize the FBI's report on the grounds that "the investigators have presented every detail that could hint at some kind of abnormal or at least strange behavior on his part, but have left

aside those episodes that, being totally normal and reasonable, could have changed the entire interpretation of the facts." The nuncio criticized the FBI's suggestion that Kaiser had violated church protocol by refusing to stay and talk when he dropped off his letter. The nuncio called this claim "baseless and evidently aiming at finding signs of errant behavior even when there was none."

177 **He was beaten with one stick until it broke:** from Levi Marko's interview with the Rift Valley CID on September 4, 2000.

14. Manic Depression

178 **the episodes started with sleep deprivation:** the FBI's paraphrase of Carolita Mahoney's remarks to agents, from the FBI's FD-302 report of its interview with her on November 7, 2000.

178 **The first time was in New York:** Details regarding Kaiser's experience in Albany and his institutionalization in New York are taken from the following sources: letter from John Kaiser, addressed "To whom this concerns," dated November 2, 1969, from Freeport, Long Island; he gave a copy to Barnicle and, it is presumed, others. Records of Kaiser's 1969 hospitalization, and of Riordan's assessment, are described in a February 15, 2005, report by Steven Altchuler, a Minnesota psychiatrist who was enlisted by the Kaiser family to review the case, and who examined the records and interviewed Riordan. In 1969, Riordan thought Kaiser might be "a schizophrenic paranoid," though some thirty-five years later he would acknowledge that bipolar disorder would likely be the current diagnosis; schizophrenia and manic depression were not regarded as clearly distinct conditions until the proliferation of lithium in the 1970s. The "paranoia" Kaiser apparently evinced would be consistent with manic psychosis, and so would the "somewhat grandiose" aspect that medical records described in Kaiser's manner.

178 **"he had resisted the NYPD officers":** the FBI's paraphrase of Carolita Mahoney's remarks to agents, from the FBI's FD-302 report of its interview with her on November 7, 2000.

180 **a young Albany nun:** The woman in question left her vocation as a nun, married, had a child, worked for years as a social worker, and had retired in Oldham, England, where I tracked her down. She was living under her late husband's surname. She had been twenty-four years old when she was in Albany, but she remembered Kaiser vividly. "Just the most incredible man,"

she told me. "John Kaiser was incorruptible. I mean that in more ways than one." Kaiser had been strapping, broad-shouldered, ruggedly handsome, and they had grown close to each other at the Mill Hill house, she said, "too close to keep in contact." After parting ways, they had deliberately decided not to maintain a correspondence. "It would have been very easy to be fond of John." He wouldn't do anything to compromise the cloth, she said, but still. "You don't put temptation in the way." She recalled that she and other nuns were "absolutely livid" at Kaiser's arrest and had visited him at Bellevue.

About Father Heymans, she was less eager to talk. There was good in him, she said, but also "an awful lot beyond my comprehension."

What did happen under Heymans? What had Kaiser confronted?

Her uneasiness grew. She did not want to talk about it. She explained that she had been very young and naïve, and raised in a pre–Vatican II English church, which lacked the modern-mindedness of its American counterpart. She said Heymans spent a lot of time at the novitiate house with the young nuns.

"We weren't sophisticated," she said. "He had ideas about discipline. In those days I believed very strongly in discipline. I was in favor of sacrifice and discipline."

Her point was elusive. Had Heymans make sexual passes at her?

"He did make sexual passes," she said. "I thought he was disciplining himself for his sins."

Could she explain?

"I believed what he was doing was to punish himself for his sins. He admitted a lot of things to me. I thought he was being very humble. If you read the life of Saint Francis . . ."

She couldn't quite say it. She was supplying the clues and hoping that was enough. The image she seemed to be hinting at was that of Saint Francis casting off his clothes as a sign of devotion to God.

"He disrobed and asked you to whip him?"

"Yes. He had an instrument like a whip."

"How often?"

"It was numerous times."

Her voice was trembling. She said she wanted to hang up the phone. She was still a devout Catholic. She didn't want to seem uncharitable. She continued.

"I thought he was being very holy," she said. "It was purely, purely spiritual. I was a very young woman. I was a nobody. It was not earthly love." It was a different time, she kept saying. "Think of Saint Francis standing there naked. We were reared on this. Perhaps it's hard to understand." She was much older now, able to see the truth. "I think he took advantage of me. I didn't see anything wrong about it at the time."

Had Heymans done this with other nuns?

"I don't think I was special at all."

180 **"an absolute nut"**: This and subsequent remarks are from the author's interview with Tony Barnicle.

181 **At least two other times in his life**: According to Steven Altchuler's report, medical records indicate that Kaiser was hospitalized at Fergus Falls State Hospital in 1981 and then was transferred to St. Joseph's Hospital in St. Paul, Minnesota. His report also indicates that Kaiser had been hospitalized at St. Joseph's in early 1972.

181 **Father Bill Vos**: Vos's account is from the author's interview with him.

182 **he grew furious with his younger brother, Joe**: Details regarding this confrontation are taken from the author's interviews with Carolita Mahoney, Joe Kaiser, George Hess, and Mary Mahoney Weaver.

183 **"Within the Catholic church"**: from declassified portions of the FBI's FD-302 report of its interview with Francis Kaiser in Santa Rosa, California, on December 14, 2000.

184 **"one for every 2 million persons"**: David Lamb, *The Africans* (New York: Vintage, 1987), p. 267.

184 **He concluded that the priest had been suffering from "acute adjustment disorder"**: Njenga's analysis is from "Psychological Autopsy Report on Fr. John Anthony Kaiser (Deceased)," prepared by Frank Njenga, December 2000, and from declassified portions of the FBI's FD-302 report of its interview with Njenga on February 22, 2001.

185 **"Most affective disorders that would warrant institutionalization"; "highly unique social structures of Father Kaiser's cultural and religious existence"; and "any attempted application of common psychological assessment"**: from declassified portions of an internal FBI report, dated November 8, 2000 (author's name redacted).

185 **Carolita Mahoney had been ill at ease**: author's interview with Carolita Mahoney.

186 **"manic cycling from high to low"**: author's interview with William Corbett.

187   **"end game and exit strategies"**: from declassified portions of an internal FBI memo, dated November 22, 2000 (author's name redacted).

188   **FBI agents and their Kenyan counterparts interrogated Sunkuli**: Details regarding this interrogation are taken from declassified portions of the FBI's FD-302 report of its interview with Sunkuli on December 6, 2000, and from the author's interviews with Thomas Graney.

188   **That didn't necessarily make him a murderer**: According to a declassified report from the American embassy in Nairobi to the secretary of state in Washington, D.C., dated December 2000: "Evidence emerged that individuals purporting to act on behalf of Sunkuli engaged in a concerted effort to co-opt or silence those making allegations against the cabinet minister, and were willing to violate the law in specific instances. No credible evidence has yet emerged, however, that links any of these individuals directly or indirectly to Fr. Kaiser's death."

191   **"unreadable for all practical purposes"**: This and subsequent remarks by Vincent DiMaio are from the author's interview with him.

15. The Verdict

194   **"We're going to Kenya next Monday"**: In an interview, Carey told me he does not recall this exchange but did not dispute its essence. "I'm sure it was, 'Tom, you've done everything you can on this case; it's time to wrap it up.' " The Bureau had scarce resources, the Kaiser matter was one of many cases, and "Tom had been tied up in it for quite a while," Carey added. He acknowledged meeting with Cardinal Bernard Law, archbishop of Boston, over lunch at FBI headquarters in D.C. a month or two before the Bureau closed its case. By Carey's account, FBI brass hoped that Law, considered "a traveling diplomat of the Church," might listen to the FBI's findings about the Kaiser case and present them to church leaders in Kenya in a way that underscored the investigation's integrity: "He could make it clear to the papal nuncio that we weren't lap dogs to the Kenyan government." Law's trip to Kenya was canceled, apparently because of health.

195   **"a significant life stressor"**: this and other quotations are from the FBI's final report into the death of Father John Kaiser, April 19, 2001.

196   **"drove the final nail"**: Martin Masai, "Kaiser's Death and Judging Others," *Kenya Times*, April 20, 2001.

197   **"You're bought off"**: author's interview with Thomas Graney.

197 **"terribly old-fashioned"**: the phrase is Cornelius Schilder's, from the author's interview with Schilder.

197 **"Not only is suicide a sin"**: This and subsequent quotes from the book are in G. K. Chesterton, *Orthodoxy* (Garden City, New York: Image, 1959), pp. 72–73. The trouble with Chesterton's sharp line between the suicide and the martyr is that human motivation is infinitely tangled and mysterious. It's difficult enough to trace the intertwined threads of one's own motives to their psychic source, much less attempt to do so for someone else. A man might believe he's sacrificing his life for the glory of God, but on some unacknowledged level he has come to detest the weary torment of earthly existence and aches to shuffle it off. Against the vast unknowability of the human soul, rigid divisions between the damned and the saved tend to wither. The ambiguities are ancient. Even the Spartans, for whom war zeal was a cardinal virtue, knew it was possible for courage to mask deeper motivations. There was the case of Aristodemus, whose outsized valor in the Battle of Plataea resembled nothing so much as a death wish to atone for past shame; he won not honor, but rebuke. Sneering in the teeth of death was the height of glory; climbing into its maw was an embarrassment.

198 **"suicide, thinly disguised as martyrdom"**: A. Alvarez, *The Savage God: A Study of Suicide* (New York: W. W. Norton, 1990), p. 90.

199 **When a member of Pope John Paul II's Swiss Guard**: Daniela Petroff, "Funeral for Swiss Guard Who Killed Commander Held at Vatican Church," Associated Press, May 7, 1998.

199 **"There's something about"**: author's interview with David Durenberger.

199 **"It's just completely alien to his constitution"**: author's interview with Don Montgomery.

199 **"It would be the unforgivable sin"**: author's interview with Carolita Mahoney.

200 **a week after the FBI released its report**: Something else happened that week: FBI director Louis Freeh paid a visit to Kenya. According to a declassified memo from the American embassy in Nairobi to the secretary of state in Washington, D.C., dated May 2001, Freeh visited embassy staff and "reviewed the mission's engagement in counter-terrorism cooperation with the GOK [government of Kenya]." He praised the "diplomatic skill" of FBI agents in handling the Kaiser case. He thanked Attorney General Amos Wako and top Kenyan police officials for their "outstanding support" in building a case against the embassy bombers and in "dozens of other sensitive cases." To

underscore America's gratitude, he presented Wako and Kenya's top cops with "individual certificates of appreciation."

200   **Paul Wellstone . . . summoned some of the FBI agents:** author's interview with Colin McGinnis; Charles Laszewski, "Wellstone Grills FBI Agents, Insists Priest Was Murdered," *St. Paul Pioneer Press*, April 27, 2001; Greg Gordon, "Wellstone Considers Taking Slain Priest's Case to U.S. Attorney General," *Minneapolis Star Tribune*, April 27, 2001.

200   **"It requires physical gymnastics":** author's interview with Colin McGinnis.

200   **"deeply skeptical":** letter from Paul Wellstone to Attorney General John Ashcroft, June 19, 2001. In October 2002, as Wellstone was running for a third term in office, his charter plane plunged into the thick woods of northern Minnesota, killing him, his wife, his daughter, and four others. The official account blamed incompetent piloting.

201   **During their research, the *60 Minutes* crew:** Letter from *60 Minutes* correspondent and producer (names redacted from document) to FBI acting director Thomas Pickard, June 25, 2001.

201   **In a letter to the show's producer:** Letter from Thomas Pickard (then FBI Deputy Director) to *60 Minutes,* May 25, 2001.

16. The End of the Time of Moi

202   **Charles Mbuthi Gathenji worked his way:** The portrayal of Gathenji's thoughts and actions in this chapter—and the use of his quotations—are based on author's interviews with him.

203   **other shells found in Kaiser's desk:** from an FBI lab report dated April 18, 2001.

206   **guilty verdicts against the four bin Laden followers:** They were Khalfan Mohamed, a Tanzanian; Mohamed al-'Owhali, a Saudi; Wadih el-Hage, a Lebanese-born American; and Mohamed Odeh, a Jordanian. To some Kenyans, the embassy bombing and its aftermath left deep and abiding resentment toward the United States government. Congress had approved compensation for the bombing's U.S. victims but had proved ungenerous to the vastly more numerous Kenyan survivors, many of them maimed or blinded by exploding glass. In comparison to the one to two million dollars received by surviving victims of the 9/11 attacks, the amount collected by the Kenyan embassy survivors—which ranged from four hundred to nine thousand dollars—seemed bitterly small. In March 2003, as he approached the tag

end of his ambassadorship, Johnnie Carson presided over the unveiling of the new American embassy in a suburb north of Nairobi. A 125,000-square-foot four-story structure set back one hundred feet from the street, with three-inch-thick blast-resistant glass, reinforced fortresslike walls, and a thirty-foot-wide moat ringed by marines, it reflected the realities of the age of terror. Al Qaeda was considered an abiding threat.

206 **"No one at the embassy or in CID wants a public inquest":** memo from the FBI's Office of the Legal Attaché in Nairobi to the FBI's Washington Field Office (names redacted), August 27, 2001.

207 **pauperization:** In a country of 30 million people, more than half lived on less than one dollar a day, some 40 percent were unemployed, and some 2.2 million were afflicted with HIV. There were at least 1.5 million AIDS orphans. Over the last twenty years, roughly, life expectancy had dropped from fifty-four to forty-nine years.

208 **"positive reinforcement":** from declassified State Department documents obtained through the Freedom of Information Act. The flattery of Moi did not stop with his party's defeat, as evidenced by a letter Colin Powell wrote him afterward: "There is much to do, and we will always need your help and wise counsel."

208 **"the most important year in Kenya's post-independence history":** The U.S. assessment of Moi and the upcoming election is taken from declassified internal embassy and State Department documents.

208 **"I cannot just jump ship because my term is about to end":** from Moi's remarks to a party conference in 1999, as reported in a State Department memo.

209 **a symbolic twenty-five years in power:** His nearly quarter-century rule made him a champion among the continent's Big Men. Save for three men who'd held power since the late 1960s—Libya's Qaddafi, Gabon's Omar Bongo, and Togo's Gnassingbé Eyadéma—Moi had survived longer than any other African ruler.

209 **"a person who can be guided":** from Davan Maharaj, "Kenya's Big Man Is Being Belittled," *Los Angeles Times*, August 18, 2002.

210 **"Mr. President, your steadfast application to duty":** a draft of a letter from Colin Powell to President Moi, obtained through the Freedom of Information Act

211 **Weeks before the election:** Details on the Mombasa attacks are from Marc Lacey and Dexter Filkins, "Terror in Africa: The Investigation; Witnesses

Describe Their Glimpse of Suspects in Attacks in Kenya," *New York Times*, December 2, 2002.

211 **the case dragged on and on:** In June 2003, Ambassador Carson expressed alarm that Kenya had not arrested anyone for the Mombasa attacks. "In the last 2 1/2 to 3 years, we have had a number of terrorist activities around the world," Carson said. "In every case, save in Kenya, the individuals have been arrested by their governments, put on trial, and in most cases, convicted and punished. . . . The problem, as we see here, quite honestly, is that we believe there are Al Qaeda terrorists in Kenya, and that some of them are Kenyan citizens." (See Davan Maharaj, "Kenya to Charge 4 Suspects in Mombasa Bombing," *Los Angeles Times*, June 24, 2003.) Intense Western pressure ultimately led to arrests, but in June 2005, a Kenyan judge dropped murder charges against four men accused of the hotel bombing, saying evidence against them was nonexistent; one was quickly rearrested. (See "3 Suspects Cleared in 2002 Kenya Bombing," Associated Press, June 10, 2005.)

211 **claims of blatant ballot stuffing:** Adrian Blomfield, "Minister 'Forged Thousands of Ballot Papers,' " *Daily Telegraph*, December 27, 2002.

212 **"cheers resounded":** Adrian Blomfield, "Kenyans Rejoice as Moi's Party Loses Power," *Daily Telegraph*, December 29, 2002.

213 **the conduct of Chief Justice Chunga:** In November 2002, Carson had written letters to the top presidential contenders urging them, if elected, to combat the "pernicious cancer" of corruption by establishing a new anticorruption authority, passing ethics legislation, and privatizing the economy. Noting that "Kenya has one of the most corrupt and politically influenced judiciaries in Africa and its poor record has tarnished the country's legal system," he said the new president should oust Chief Justice Bernard Chunga and review the performance of Attorney General Amos Wako, who had failed to secure the conviction of a single top official for corruption. From a declassified State Department memo dated November 2002, obtained through the Freedom of Information Act.

17. The Inquest

215 **John Wanyeki, who headed deep into the countryside:** Details on Wanyeki's trip and what informants told him are from the author's interviews with John Wanyeki and Charles Mbuthi Gathenji.

217 **Francis Kaiser:** Kaiser's recollections of his brother are from the author's interviews with Francis Kaiser.

218   **Francis walked to the witness box:** Francis Kaiser's inquest testimony is taken from a transcript of the proceedings.

220   **Gollo testified:** "Fresh Claims at Priest Kaiser's Death Inquest," *Daily Nation*, September 8, 2003.

220   **the testimony of Paul Muite:** Joseph Murimi, "4 CID Men Executed Kaiser, MP Alleges," *East African Standard*, August 15, 2005.

222   **Kantai had this to say:** Watoro Kamau and Maore Ithula, "FBI Death Inquiry Notes Cited Sunkuli," *Daily Nation*, September 12, 2003; Kamau and Ithula, "Lawyer Accuses Catechist of Taking Part in Conspiracy to Murder Kaiser," *Daily Nation*, September 13, 2003.

224   **Anne Sawoyo:** Sawoyo's testimony is taken from a transcript of the proceedings; see also Watoro Kamau and Francis Mureithi, "Ex-Minister Sunkuli Raped Me, Woman Tells Court," *Daily Nation*, October 14, 2003; "Sunkuli Raped Me, Witness Tells Kaiser Inquest," *East African Standard*, October 14, 2003; "Sunkuli Implicated in Kaiser's Murder," *East African Standard*, October 15, 2003.

227   **"She's an actress":** author interview with Gathenji.

227   **Edith Kirugumi:** testimony from a transcript of the proceedings.

228   **Helen Katim:** "Slain Missionary Told Aggrieved Women to See Moi," *Daily Nation*, July 8, 2006.

228   **Anne Kiruti:** Francis Thoya, "Ministers Named In Kaiser Inquiry," *Daily Nation*, December 5, 2005.

228   **James Onyango:** Onyango's testimony from Francis Ngige and Karanja Njoroge, "Kaiser Died After Memo, Inquest Told," *East African Standard*, February 11, 2004.

228   **James Muli:** Muli's testimony from Cyrus Kinyungu, "Kaiser Murder Scene Sketch Is Contested," *Daily Nation*, February 8, 2005.

228   **Humphrey Kariuki:** testimony from "Ex-Police Chief Grilled Over Kaiser Murder Scene," *Daily Nation*, August 11, 2005.

229   **Justin Kaburu . . . named in a report probing judicial corruption:** Kaburu was one of eighty-two magistrates named in a report by High Court justice Aaron Ringera. He subsequently retired. See Tom Maliti, "Inquest into Death of U.S. Roman Catholic Priest Resumes, Then Adjourns, in Kenya," Associated Press, February 10, 2004; "Court to Rule on Kaiser Probe's Fate," *East African Standard*, November 21, 2003; and "Fr. Kaiser Inquest Deferred," *Daily Nation*, October 22, 2003.

229   **"superlawyer":** Mwangi Githahu, "How Lawyers' Fortunes Changed with Kanu's Exit from Power," *Daily Nation*, February 22, 2004.

230   **"He was afraid if he'd spoken to me":** author's interview with Colin Davies.

231   **"We counted about nine of them":** author's interview with Nuala Brangan.

231   **Sunkuli entered the courtroom:** The account of Sunluki's appearance is taken from a transcript of the proceedings; from interviews with Gathenji; from "Kaiser Inquiry—Sunkuli Laments," *Daily Nation*, February 22, 2007; and "Chief Suspect in Kaiser Murder Pleads Innocence," Catholic Information Service for Africa, February 26, 2007. Sunkuli continued making headlines, many of them unflattering, in his years out of power. He had retained sway as a KANU party leader, though at one function he was allegedly punched by a fellow party member, Anthony Kimetto, who blamed him for rigging him out of nominations in 2002. As Moi-era malfeasance continued coming to light, Sunkuli was accused of having signed off on questionable contracts during his stint in the cabinet. On top of that, Gideon Konchellah, the man who beat him out of his parliamentary seat, had accused him of operating a "terror gang," a charge Sunkuli indignantly denied. See "Former Minister Denies Operating Terror Gang," *Daily Nation*, March 6, 2003. Sunkuli's links to Moi remained tight; he had served as the former president's lawyer in a dispute with a man who claimed Moi had stolen his family's one-hundred-acre farm.

233   **the government "fully supports" the FBI's presence:** diplomatic letter from the U.S. embassy in Nairobi to the Kenyan attorney general, January 24, 2007.

233   **"The case meant a lot to me":** author's interview with Thomas Graney.

233   **"would be handcuffed":** author's interview with William Corbett.

236   **"physical impossibility":** This and subsequent statements by Odero are from a transcript of her ruling on August 1, 2007.

238   **"These people are so connected to Sunkuli":** author's interview with Gathenji.

18. The Labyrinth with No Center

239   **"If I was a high-profile person":** author's interview with Charles Mbuthi Gathenji.

241   **ethnic carnage convulsed Kenya again:** Chapter 17 of Michela Wrong's *It's Our Turn to Eat: The Story of a Kenyan Whistle-Blower* (New York: HarperCollins, 2009) contains a good overview.

241   **In the years after Kibaki took office:** See *It's Our Turn to Eat*, which focuses on anticorruption crusader John Githongo's quixotic attempt to expose

government graft. Expose it he did, irrefutably, with secretly recorded con-
versations of highly placed ministers in the Kibaki regime who implicated
themselves in the Anglo Leasing scandal. The scheme involved a fictitious
company, created under Moi, that received millions in public money for
inflated security contracts, including one for tamperproof passports. Kibaki,
who had hired Githongo as his anticorruption czar, essentially ignored the
findings and reinstalled the guilty; Githongo fled to England.

241   **a mob swarmed the Kenya Assemblies of God church:** Robyn Dixon,
       "Screams of Dying Arose from Kenyan Church," Tribune Newspapers, Janu-
       ary 3, 2008; Mike Pflanz, "11-Year-Old Boy Relives Horror of Church Mas-
       sacre," *Daily Telegraph*, January 3, 2008; Stephanie McCrummen, "In Kenya,
       Distrust Deep as the Scars," *Washington Post*, December 22, 2009.

242   **Susanne Mueller has argued:** Susanne D. Mueller, "The Political Economy of
       Kenya's Crisis," *Journal of Eastern African Studies* 2, no. 2 (2008): 185–210.

243   **Bill Berkeley described inflamed ethnic rancor:** Bill Berkeley, *The Graves
       Are Not Yet Full* (New York: Basic Books, 2001), pp. 15–16.

244   **the devious maze:** I have borrowed this phrase from Frank Stockton's classic
       short story, "The Lady or the Tiger?"—an insoluble psychological riddle. A
       semibarbaric king throws his daughter's low-born paramour into an arena
       and forces him to choose between two identical doors. Behind one is a tiger
       waiting to devour him. Behind the other is a lovely maiden—a hated rival of
       the hot-blooded princess—he will marry on the spot. The princess learns the
       secret of the doors and clandestinely directs her lover to one of them. The
       story never reveals whether the lady or the tiger emerges from that door, and
       we are left by our own lights to navigate the human heart and its "devious
       mazes of passion." Would she rather see him mauled than in the arms of her
       rival? To guess at an answer, and to defend that answer, is to reveal something
       about yourself: your beliefs about certain types of people and what moti-
       vates them, your prejudices about human nature. As your frame of reference
       changes, your answer changes; it becomes a different story when read at age
       sixteen than it is when read at age forty.

245   **Studies show:** E. Fuller Torrey and Michael B. Knable, *Surviving Manic
       Depression* (New York: Basic Books, 2005), pp. 101–104.

246   **"a minor preview of the main attraction in the next":** letter from John Kai-
       ser to Don and Jackie Beumer, September 2, 1980.

247   **Father Tom Keane got perhaps the closest sustained glimpse:** Keane's
       remarks are taken from the author's interview with him.

249   **"At the end of my command"**: Samantha Power, *A Problem From Hell* (New York: Harper Perennial, 2007), p. 385.

249   **"I am a suspect"**: This and subsequent remarks by Francis Kantai and those of his wife, Camille, are taken from the author's interviews with them.

250   **Paul Boyle had been one of the last priests**: Boyle's remarks are taken from the author's interviews with him.

253   **roll call of political murders**: Wrong, *It's Our Turn to Eat*, p. 26.

253   **"I expect the actual killers"**: author's interview with Carolita Mahoney.

253   **"We feel vindicated"**: author's interview with Mary Mahoney Weaver.

253   **"Ultimately, he died of a disease"**: author's interview with William Corbett.

254   **"the people's voice"**: author's interview with Wangari Maathai.

255   **a story Francis Kaiser told:** author's interview with Francis Kaiser.

SELECTED READING

Alvarez, A. *The Savage God: A Study of Suicide*. New York: W. W. Norton, 1990.

Anderson, David. *Histories of the Hanged*. New York: W. W. Norton, 2005.

Ayittey, George. *Africa in Chaos*. New York: St. Martin's Press, 1999.

Berkeley, Bill. *The Graves Are Not Yet Full*. New York: Basic Books, 2001.

Chesterton, G. K. *Orthodoxy*. Garden City, New York: Image, 1959.

Elkins, Caroline. *Imperial Reckoning: The Untold Story of Britain's Gulag in Kenya*. New York: Henry Holt, 2005.

Gifford, Paul. *Christianity, Politics and Public Life in Kenya*. New York: Columbia University Press, 2009.

Harden, Blaine. *Africa: Dispatches from a Fragile Continent*. New York: Houghton Mifflin, 1991.

Hempstone, Smith. *Rogue Ambassador: An African Memoir*. Sewanee, Tennessee: University of the South Press, 1997.

Kaiser, John. *If I Die*. Nairobi: Cana Publishing, 2003.

Kapuscinski, Ryzard. *The Shadow of the Sun*. New York: Knopf, 2001.

Karimi, Joseph, and Philip Ochieng. *The Kenyatta Succession*. Nairobi: Transafrica Books, 1980.

Lamb, David. *The Africans*. New York: Vintage, 1987.

LeVine, Robert, and Barbara LeVine. *Nyansongo: A Gusii Community in Kenya*. New York: Wiley, 1966.

LeVine, Sarah, with Robert LeVine. *Mothers and Wives: Gusii Women of East Africa*. Chicago: University of Chicago Press, 1979.

Maathai, Wangari. *Unbowed*. New York: Anchor, 2007.

Meredith, Martin. *The State of Africa: A History of Fifty Years of Independence*. New York: Simon & Schuster, 2005.

Morton, Andrew. *Moi: The Making of an African Statesman*. London: Michael O'Mara Books, 1998.

Ngugi wa Thiong'o. *Moving the Centre*. Oxford: Heinemann, 1993.

——. *Wizard of the Crow*. New York: Anchor, 2007.

Russell, Alec. *Big Men, Little People*. New York: New York University Press, 2000.

Throup, David, and Charles Hornsby. *Multi-Party Politics in Kenya*. Athens: Ohio University Press, 1998.

Waihenya, Waithaka, and Ndikaru wa Teresia. *A Voice Unstilled: Archbishop Ndingi Mwana 'a Nzeki*. Nairobi: Longhorn Publishers, 2009.

Wright, Lawrence. *The Looming Tower: Al-Qaeda and the Road to 9-11*. New York: Random House, 2006.

Wrong, Michela. *It's Our Turn to Eat: The Story of a Kenyan Whistle-Blower*. New York: HarperCollins, 2009.

INDEX

Page numbers in *italics* refer to illustrations.